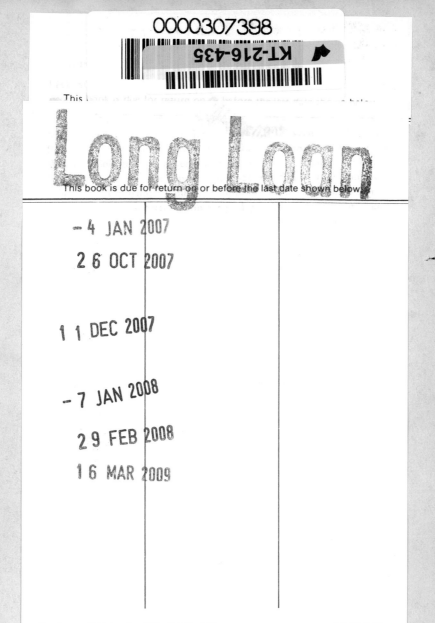

Michael Argyle, D.Sc., D.Litt., F.B.Ps.S., F.B.Psych., is Emeritus Reader in Social Psychology at Oxford University, a Fellow of Wolfson College, and Emeritus Professor of Psychology of Oxford Brookes University. He was born in 1925, went to Nottingham High School and Emmanuel College, Cambridge, and was a navigator in the RAF. He has been teaching social psychology at Oxford since 1952. He has been engaged in research in various aspects of social psychology and is particularly interested in the experimental study of social interaction and its application to wider social problems. He has been a visiting professor at a number of universities in the USA, Canada and Australia, and has lectured in thirty-four countries. He established the Oxford Social Psychology group, which has so far produced seventy D.Phils, some of them now professors elsewhere.

His recent books have been *Psychology and Social Class*, *The Social Psychology of Everyday Life*, *The Psychology of Happiness*, *The Anatomy of Relationships* (with Monika Henderson) and new editions of *Bodily Communication*, *The Social Psychology of Work* and *The Psychology of Interpersonal Behaviour*. He has written numerous articles in British, American and European journals. He helped to found the *British Journal of Social and Clinical Psychology* and was social psychology editor (1961–7). He was editor of the Pergamon Press *International Studies in Experimental Social Psychology* and Chairman of the Social Psychology Section of the British Psychological Society (1964–7 and 1972–4).

He is married and has four children; his hobbies are travel, interpersonal behaviour, Scottish country dancing, Utopian speculation, theological disputation and playing the goat.

CONTENTS

MICHAEL ARGYLE

THE SOCIAL PSYCHOLOGY OF LEISURE

PENGUIN BOOKS

PENGUIN BOOKS

Published by the Penguin Group
Penguin Books Ltd, 27 Wrights Lane, London w8 5tz, England
Penguin Books USA Inc., 375 Hudson Street, New York, New York 10014, USA
Penguin Books Australia Ltd, Ringwood, Victoria, Australia
Penguin Books Canada Ltd, 10 Alcorn Avenue, Toronto, Ontario, Canada m4v 3b2
Penguin Books (NZ) Ltd, 182–190 Wairau Road, Auckland 10, New Zealand

Penguin Books Ltd, Registered Offices: Harmondsworth, Middlesex, England

Published in Penguin Books 1996
10 9 8 7 6 5 4 3 2 1

Filmset in 10/12pt Monophoto Bembo by Datix International Limited, Bungay, Suffolk
Printed in England by Clays Ltd, St Ives plc

CONTENTS

MICHAEL ARGYLE

THE SOCIAL PSYCHOLOGY
OF LEISURE

PENGUIN BOOKS

PENGUIN BOOKS

Published by the Penguin Group
Penguin Books Ltd, 27 Wrights Lane, London w8 5TZ, England
Penguin Books USA Inc., 375 Hudson Street, New York, New York 10014, USA
Penguin Books Australia Ltd, Ringwood, Victoria, Australia
Penguin Books Canada Ltd, 10 Alcorn Avenue, Toronto, Ontario, Canada M4V 3B2
Penguin Books (NZ) Ltd, 182–190 Wairau Road, Auckland 10, New Zealand

Penguin Books Ltd, Registered Offices: Harmondsworth, Middlesex, England

Published in Penguin Books 1996
10 9 8 7 6 5 4 3 2 1

Filmset in 10/12pt Monophoto Bembo by Datix International Limited, Bungay, Suffolk
Printed in England by Clays Ltd, St Ives plc

CONTENTS

CONTENTS

LIST OF TABLES

LIST OF FIGURES

I have long had a secret list of topics which psychology has not done much about yet, where it might be possible to make some contribution. Leisure is one of these topics. Although it doesn't appear in psychology books, there is a lot of scattered research into particular kinds of leisure carried out by psychologists and others. It has been enormous fun tracking it down, and adding some of my own. Leisure is a topic of great interest; it is of theoretical importance to psychology since a lot of the findings don't fit those from better-known areas; it is of great practical importance, because among the several causes of happiness it is the only one that can easily be modified; and it is going to be even more important in the future as work shrinks, and unemployment and other sources of free time increase.

I am grateful to several colleagues for help with parts of the book: John and Margaret Ackrill, Olivia Byard, Peter Collett, Luo Lu, Sonia Livingstone and Noraini Noor. I should also mention my companions in several kinds of leisure, both for their company, and for their observations about these activities. I am indebted to the Leverhulme Trust for financial support, and to the librarians of the Bodleian Library, the Radcliffe Science Library and Oxford Brookes University Library.

This is the first book which I have typed myself, on WP 5.1, and Papyrus, with help as usual from Ann McKendry, and from Jim Casey, and a lot of help from CD-ROM databases, Psychlit and Sociofile.

MICHAEL ARGYLE
Oxford

Christmas 1994

CHAPTER ONE

Introduction

Leisure is a very important topic, for several reasons. Many people spend more time at their leisure than at work; many find their leisure more satisfying than their work; leisure can be a major source of happiness and of mental and physical health; however, many who have a lot of spare time fail to make good use of this opportunity to find satisfying forms of leisure.

Another reason that leisure is very important is that there is going to be a lot more of it. There is a lot more already, compared with the last century, as a result of shorter hours of work, longer holidays, high rates of unemployment and earlier retirement. This should create a tremendous opportunity for more leisure and therefore more well-being, but this is not what has happened. The unemployed often don't know how to use their new free time and become demoralized. The retired often miss their work and they too may be at a loose end. Most economists think that work will decline much further, as it is taken over by computers and automation; so there is a pressing problem here, of how to spend our growing free time. Many observers of the social scene have been concerned with this issue, have been worried about the distress of those with too little to do, the prevalence of 'Sunday neurosis' – symptoms which occur on days off – and the need for leisure to replace work as a means of giving fulfilment to what may otherwise become empty lives (Neulinger, 1981).

Leisure has not really been accepted by psychologists as a recognized field of research, though there has been work on certain kinds of leisure, such as sport, listening to music and watching TV. Leisure raises some interesting issues for psychology. For example, how is voluntary work motivated, and how are people socialized into it?

The contrasts between the way voluntary workers and paid employees work lead to other questions about how work might be done in a more enjoyable way. TV watching produces various questions, such as why do people watch so much, are they really awake when they are watching, and how far do they believe they know the characters? Sport makes us wonder why people make such colossal efforts, for no material reward, at marathons, for example, put up with pain and discomfort, or expose themselves to considerable danger, in bungee-jumping, or white-water rafting. One leisure activity which has been extensively studied already is religion, and here there is a lot of new research to report, and some new questions to ask. Why is religion good for people? What is going on in charismatic churches and fanatical cults? Why do people join them? It is very interesting and rather surprising that psychology has no ready answers to most of these questions; so the good news is that looking at leisure may be a way of opening up psychology to a range of new issues, which may force us to revise our model of human nature.

I have long been concerned about the removal of much psychological research from reality. In order to test abstract theories about social behaviour, subjects in psychological experiments have been made to sit in 'booths', to press buttons, led to believe that they are giving other people shocks, to dress up in Ku-Klux-Klan outfits, or paid to eat fried grasshoppers. Instead of studying any real group or type of group – a tennis club, a family, a church house group, for example – 'groups' of three to four students meet in the lab to discuss 'human relations' problems (Argyle, 1992). Leisure is very much part of the real, every-day world, and raises issues which may not be apparent in the lab.

If I tell an academic colleague that I am studying leisure, this is likely to be regarded as a laughably frivolous activity. If I were to admit that I am interested in actual, specific kinds of leisure, such as collecting stamps or engine numbers, reading detective stories, or doing Scottish country dancing, this would be seen as even more frivolous. It will appear later that, whether they are regarded as frivolous or not, such activities can have powerful positive consequences. If I mentioned some other kinds of leisure, it might be regarded as less laughable, such as voluntary work with the old, sick or delinquent, serious political or religious activities, or saving the environment, with pick and shovel.

THE MEANING OF LEISURE

There has been a lot of learned discussion about the definition of leisure. I propose to start with an easy definition – it is those activities which people do in their free time, because they want to, for their own sake, for fun, entertainment, self-improvement, or for goals of their own choosing, but not for material gain.

There are some important distinctions which can be made here. Leisure is obviously not the same as free time. Neulinger (1981) found that a sample of mainly middle-class adults regarded about one-third of their free time as leisure. We shall see later that many of the unemployed don't know what to do with their free time; much of this time is not experienced as leisure, but as an 'embarrassment'. We shall see later that the retired and unemployed increase the amount of time spent on domestic jobs of various kinds and watching daytime TV; unemployed youth spend some of their time hanging around and get up late.

Domestic jobs may be seen as leisure but some people dislike gardening, and many dislike household chores. There is a whole sphere of activities here which are neither work nor leisure proper, including eating meals and looking after children. One way to deal with this problem is to ask people how much of the time spent on each activity they regard as leisure. This was done by Clark *et al.* (1990) in Canada, where they found amongst other things that for men with jobs 50 per cent of the time spent cooking was experienced as leisure, but for housewives only 8 per cent of it was. This means that leisure calculated as the time left over after work and domestic jobs may underestimate the amount of leisure experienced – but by different amounts for men and women for a start.

Leisure has often been calculated as the time left over from work, and understood as an activity which is contrasted with work. This may have made sense in the days of the Industrial Revolution, but both work and leisure have changed since then, and this contrast is no longer so useful. Voluntary 'work' is certainly seen as leisure, but what about those individuals who enjoy their work so much that they carry on after hours, or after they have retired? This could be regarded as a hobby activity which has many of the features of work, apart from not being paid. Most hobbies involve the use of skills commonly learnt and used at work. There are several kinds of person for whom the line between work and leisure is impossible to draw, for example academics, writers, artists and the like, and those businessmen who may need to entertain and socialize a lot with their clients, for example on the golf course.

TEN KINDS OF LEISURE

Leisure includes such a wide variety of activities that it does not make any psychological sense to try to deal with them all as a single kind of behaviour. Leisure is a general category of behaviour which has certain common themes – the enjoyment of freely chosen activities carried out for no material gain – but the psychology of playing chess is unlikely to be the same as the psychology of football hooligans, or the psychology of playing string quartets as that of all-in wrestling. There is a variety of very different kinds of leisure, which will need to be considered separately. So we need a typology, or at least a list, and no agreed typology has yet been arrived at. In this book I propose to use a provisional, working list of ten main types of leisure. Between them they cover nearly everything which is commonly regarded as leisure. In addition they will enable us to deal with the main psychological processes involved in leisure, the motivations, the origins, and so on. The ten types will be kept in mind throughout the book and then each will be discussed in more detail in Chapter 8.

The first five are activities which are mainly done at home.

1. Watching TV.
2. Music, mainly listening to it, mainly over the radio, as well as performing it.
3. Reading books, papers and magazines, and engaging in study, including taking adult education courses.
4. Social life, entertaining and visiting friends and relations; social clubs will also be included here, also sex, and eating and drinking.
5. Hobbies, such as gardening, DIY, dressmaking, pets, arts and crafts; geology, archaeology and the like may involve belonging to a club, so there is overlap with 4.

The next five are done mainly outside the home.

6. Sports, including exercise, such as walking, jogging and aerobics, and games, like tennis and football.
7. Watching sport; there is an overlap with 1 if this is done via TV.
8. Religion, including private devotions and meditation, as well as church services and other meetings.
9. Voluntary work, including collecting for charity, and work for political causes, or work to improve the environment; there is some overlap here with 4, social life, since most voluntary work involves belonging to a kind of club.
10. Holidays and tourism.

There are some inevitable overlaps; and there will be important subdivisions, for example between different kinds of sport and exercise.

Returning to the problem of the definition of leisure, most people agree that the ten activities above are forms of leisure. In a time – budget study in Canada the subjects were asked to say what proportion of each activity they regarded as a leisure, and all of these came up as being almost entirely leisure.

HISTORY AND STATISTICS

People have had different amounts of free time at different points in history, and very different ideas about how it should be spent, so we turn to the history of leisure in Chapter 2. This is an exciting story, and may help us to understand the present and the possible future of leisure. We shall be able to look at some of the great issues, which have been discussed by thinkers from Aristotle onwards. We take a brisk trip from monkeys and the Stone Age to video games and dangerous sports. For many centuries work dominated the human scene, as it dominates animal life. Work has often been unpleasant and exhausting for many; leisure was to recover from it, though the Greeks and the nineteenth-century middle class had others to do the work and had the freedom to pursue elevated and interesting ideas about leisure. And there have always been prosperous classes who spent most of their time at leisure. More recently most people have had to, or wanted to, work, and job satisfaction is one of the main sources of happiness. Can leisure satisfaction replace work satisfaction?

Sociologists have done a very good job finding out how much leisure different groups of individuals have and what they do, by means of time budgets and other methods, and in Chapter 3 we review this work. This makes it possible to answer some controversial questions, such as do women have much less leisure than men (or no leisure at all, some have suggested)? Women do have fewer hours of leisure than men, especially when they have children to look after, or a home to run as well as a job, and some of their leisure is really child-minding. Nevertheless there are still many hours of free time left, and women do more of some kinds of leisure than men.

There are major age differences in how people spend their leisure. The young are often bored and hang around with nothing better to do, and discontented and idle youth may turn to crime, drugs, or join revolutionary armies. Meanwhile the old live longer than before but are less able to get out and about and less fit than they were, so they watch a lot more TV. More could be done for both of these groups.

There are large class differences; working-class people do different things in their spare time, but also do much less, especially sport and leisure groups, and watch more TV instead.

This is all very good, but descriptive sociological studies do not enable us to understand the causes of these variations, and we need to do this if we are to be able to solve the social problems in this area. So we turn to psychology.

THE PSYCHOLOGY OF LEISURE

Perhaps the most important reason that leisure is important for psychology is that it is a major source of joy, happiness and other aspects of well-being; there are many well-designed studies demonstrating this. Leisure is one of the main sources of happiness, but it is the only one which can be altered fairly easily, unlike our jobs and personalities. It also affects physical and mental health, though different kinds of leisure have different effects; for example, sport is very good for health and for relieving depression, church for social support. Society also benefits in various ways, not only through voluntary and charity work, but also through the integration of society.

Even TV does this, by providing shared experiences and telling people what the country is doing. (This is reviewed in Chapter 4.)

In this book we are particularly interested in the social psychology of leisure, and in Chapter 5 we look at the social behaviour and relationships involved in different kinds of leisure. Most kinds of leisure are carried out with other people, with individuals or groups; we shall look particularly at leisure groups, where we have some new data, since these groups have powerful effects on well-being, and do not seem to function in at all the same way as other groups which have been studied by psychologists. Social relationships prove to be important for those activities which at first sight do not have a social component – such as TV, reading and religious devotions. However, sociability takes a great variety of forms, and existing ideas about affiliative motivation do not do justice to them.

Different individuals choose different kinds of leisure. Does this depend on personality? This is explored in Chapter 6. Eysenck's three well-known dimensions have been the basis of a lot of research here, particularly in connection with interest in and success at sport. The effect of personality is strongest for certain sports, and for the most successful performers, but overall the link between personality and leisure is quite weak. Much stronger is the effect of social learning experiences, from family and friends, and from school and college. This leads to joining a leisure group of some kind, learning the skills, perhaps going on a course of training, acquiring the equipment and clothes in many cases, gradually taking on the beliefs and ideas of that group, being accepted as a proper member of the group. This results in internalization of the leisure interest, so that it becomes rewarding in itself. These processes affect not only sport but all kinds of leisure.

The question of the motivation of leisure is a central topic in the psychology of leisure; psychologists want to know what motivates it, what the rewards are. Is it due to sex, aggression, achievement motivation, or what? We turn to this topic in Chapter 7. We shall have seen in a previous chapter that social motivation is very important, but what else is there? Other, though less well-established, forms of motivation are connected with the self-image, such as enhancing self-esteem, promoting self-actualization, or allowing self-expression. Then there are ideas about intrinsic motivation, enjoying an activity because it has become rewarding in itself, and there are various theories about this. Bandura proposed that competence at a sport leads to self-efficacy so that the activity becomes self-rewarding. We deal here with Csikszentmihalyi's theory, about the importance of challenge, producing a rewarding state of 'flow', which has generated a lot of research. Some leisure seems to be driven by a quest for excitement, the behaviour of football fans for example, but other leisure by a quest for rest and relaxation.

In Chapter 8 we try to put together the main findings about each of our ten types of leisure, to give a coherent account of the historical background, social learning, social behaviour, the motivation, et cetera of each, in order to give some psychological understanding of how they all work. We shall find that each is very interesting, and very distinctive, confirming our initial belief that it would be a mistake to try to tackle leisure as a whole. Interesting findings have come up for particular kinds of leisure, and in some cases we do not yet know their explanation. These phenomena are very interesting for the study of psychology, since they have emerged in this new field of research, and cannot yet be easily fitted into existing theories. Here are some examples. (1) Why do people watch TV so much – now the third greatest use of time after sleeping and working? The parasocial or imaginary friends idea is one, the concept of a default activity another. (2) The behaviour of voluntary workers is interesting, both for this manifestation of prosocial, altruistic behaviour, and because of the rather unreliable, authority-rejecting style in which it is often done. (3) Leisure groups are found to be major sources of well-being; they are also very different from other groups, for example in not being hostile to out-groups, and often in being quite undemocratic. (4) Music is a source of emotions, including deep emotions and deep satisfaction, but as yet we can only explain the arousal of rather simple feelings like anger and joy. (5) Sports we can understand, but dangerous sports, in which people are often killed or injured, are something of a mystery, which the theory of sensation-seeking does not really resolve.

LEISURE AND THE FUTURE

The book ends, in Chapter 9, with the practical application of leisure research. The depression and loss of purpose of the unemployed have been alleviated by sports training schemes, and there are other forms of leisure which could be introduced in the same way. The boredom and isolation of the retired can be helped by joining churches or other leisure groups, or by taking up other serious leisure activities. Sports and leisure groups of other kinds have been successful with individuals who are unhappy, lonely, or depressed; leisure therapy may be a rival to psychological treatment. It is possible to give leisure counselling to advise such people about the leisure activities which are going to suit them.

The possibility of more widespread social change will be discussed, the development of a leisure ethic to replace the work ethic, which seems to be becoming out-dated.

Implicit in some of this discussion is the idea that some kinds of leisure are superior to others. Although this is usually thought to be the domain of philosophers, some social scientists have had views about this too. For example, Csikszentmihalyi (1975) has drawn attention to the high level of satisfaction produced by absorption in serious leisure. Peiper (1963) has argued that true leisure consists of a state of contemplation, of non-activity and spiritual calm. This can certainly happen in some of our ten types: religion and music, for example. Huizinger (1939) argued that it is the play aspect of leisure which is most important, since it can lead to new developments in the culture. Aristotle distinguished between relaxation or pleasure and leisure proper, such as sport, music and philosophy. The French sociologist Dumazadier (1967) made a further division, between relaxation, entertainment and personal development.

How are the best kinds of leisure chosen? We shall have seen in Chapter 2 that at various times in history there have been positive ideas about which forms of leisure were the best, for example the ideas of the Greeks and the Victorian middle class. In both cases they were in favour of serious, constructive leisure, with other people, which they believed were better than cruder, more aggressive or drunken activities. I would support these general ideas, not on any ideological grounds, but rather because research now shows that they have better consequences. We do not need to say that collecting books is better than collecting engine numbers, or listening to Mozart better than watching football; it may be, but this remains for research to find out. Leisure can be evaluated by its effects, for happiness, health, mental health, or other benefits for individuals or society.

CHAPTER TWO

The history of leisure

INTRODUCTION

This turns out to be a most interesting and rewarding topic; it can help us understand the phenomenon of leisure, as well as the problems of leisure in our own time. I shall look first at the amount of free time in different historical periods, then at what people did with it, at the main causes of changes in leisure, such as developments in technology, or religious ideas, and, for some periods, at the positive ideas people had about leisure, where there has been a leisure ethic, a theory about what should be done in leisure time.

ANIMALS AND CHILDREN

Animals don't have much leisure – they are too busy looking for food and attending to other basic needs. The main exception is that the young of mammals play a lot, though they cease to do so when they grow up. Play is usually regarded as one form of leisure, for humans. There is more play at higher levels of the animal kingdom, which suggests that it may give some evolutionary advantage. There are a number of possibilities here, and it is widely assumed that play gives practice in motor skills, including the use of tools for primates, that it can establish social bonds and give practice in social skills, in the course of rough and tumble play for example, while exploratory play may be partly a way of increasing arousal, preventing boredom. Adult apes and monkeys don't play much, but they sit together in bodily contact, or grooming each other a lot of the time, evidently forms of affiliative behaviour, which would also serve to cement social bonds (Bruner, Jolly & Sylva, 1976).

Human children have lots of time for play of many kinds, including those described above. They also engage in a lot of fantasy play, where they pretend to be doctors and nurses, teacher and school children, or have tea parties; this may all be practice in the related social skills. Indeed games are now a common method of training for adults, in management games, war games and the like. These games would also give practice in cooperation and in seeing others' points of view. Games with rules, like marbles, tag, or with cards, give practice in following rules, an important feature of adult life (Argyle, 1991).

Huizinger (1939) thought that play is the origin of culture. He saw play as consisting of contests with rules, or as representations, for fun, and set apart from ordinary life. Play is usually not serious, but can become so, and can lead to the creation of new social institutions. Some inventions are produced by the inventor fooling about; the practice of law in Greece can be traced to a kind of ritualized contest; war can be seen as a game on a giant scale. He believed that much of life in the Middle Ages had a strong play element, with its elaborate dressing up and symbolism; he was concerned that life today has lost much of this.

LEISURE IN THE MOST PRIMITIVE SOCIETIES

During the Stone Age, down to about 8000 BC, there were communities of hunters and gatherers. These tribes were nomadic, following seasonal fruits and herds of wild animals; they did not cultivate crops or keep animals. It followed that they did not build permanent houses, or have much property. As a result they didn't have much work to do, and studies of contemporary Stone Age tribes like the Aboriginals, the Bushmen in the Kalahari desert and a tribe in Arnhem Land show that they had a lot of leisure. Some did two days' work a week, others worked alternate days, others did it in working days of two to three hours, or a third of the tribe did no work at all. Not until the late twentieth century would there be so much spare time. They had a very low standard of living, but they met the needs which they did have (Sahlins, 1974). Although there was no clear distinction between work and leisure, the hunters and gatherers did have long periods of not working, on their days and time off. The main form of leisure was what we shall call 'informal social leisure' later, that is they sat around talking, joking and telling stories. Two of our other types of leisure can also be found: there was some music, found, for example, in the Aboriginals with their didgeridoos, and there were rituals. The function of music and ritual here was probably the generation of social cohesion, as it is in more evolved societies.

EARLY VILLAGE COMMUNITIES

From about 15000 to 10000 BC people started to cultivate the land, with crops like wheat and barley, and kept domestic and farm animals like sheep and goats. This led to settled communities, with permanent houses, more material possessions, better clothes, money, and more work. Examples of such communities in the world today are the Zuni and other American and South American Indians, and Pacific Islanders. Later some of these cultures developed into more complex ones, with cities, as in Africa. There was less leisure now, because there were houses to build and look after, crops and farm animals to be attended to. There was a lot of informal social leisure at the same time as the work, which was accompanied by songs, jokes and constant chatter. Again there was no separation of work from leisure, which would continue to be the case for many until the Industrial Revolution. Leisure now took a number of quite highly developed forms, for example music, religion and sport, and we shall say a little about each.

Religion is universal to mankind, and is found in the most primitive societies. Here there is typically a priest, who wears special clothes, and is esteemed for his religious powers, such as being able to heal people. He may be a shaman and go into trances at ecstatic group meetings; such meetings are believed by anthropologists to strengthen group cohesion, and are found in tribes in which this is important in order to be able to deal with dangerous deep-sea fishing or the hunting of wild animals (Hayden, 1987).

In preliterate societies and throughout the ancient world there were races, wrestling and ball games – sometimes with sticks. Most of these were individual contests, but there is also evidence of primitive team games, defending territory. In Egypt there was hunting, archery, fighting with clubs, and primitive bowling and territorial team games. In Crete there was bull dancing, archery, throwing of discus and javelin, and boxing.

THE ANCIENT CIVILIZATIONS: GREECE

Most of the work was done by slaves, and it was believed that work was not suitable for freemen. Aristotle thought that the life of leisure was the only fit life for a Greek. The main purpose of life was the proper use of leisure, by self-development through education and contemplation, the pursuit of virtue through knowledge, and the practice of music, philosophy, ritual and athletics. Leisure was not about the pursuit of bodily pleasures; the Stoics taught that the passions should be controlled. The Greeks were the first people to have a positive doctrine of leisure, and a very interesting one – if there were someone else to do the work. Greek cities were well equipped for leisure, with parks (Goodale & Godbey, 1988).

Music was very important in Greece from 1000 BC. 'Music was an important feature of domestic celebrations, feasts and religious rituals, and musical competitions were held alongside athletic contests' (Storr, 1992). Singing and playing the lute were a regular part of education of the emotions, by the use of the calming modes. It was Pythagoras who recorded the ratios which are the basis of the series of notes still in use, and the Greeks who invented the classical and romantic styles. Music at this period was inseparable from poetry; it was only later that they became different activities.

In Greece sport was connected with military training; there was a quest for excellence and a desire for victory, in physical tests of strength and endurance, including armed combat, which carried honour and financial rewards. The Olympic Games, which started in 776 BC, were ahead of their time in being rule governed and well organized; they were only for men, who performed naked. However there was a lot of violence in some of these games – boxing and wrestling, for example – and contestants could be injured or killed. The rules were not laid down in detail, and while honour was important, fairness was not.

At first there were few spectators for these athletic events, which took place close to gymnasia, but later on stands were erected, spectators came, and some of them were rowdy and drunk. There was, however, a religious link to these games, which were held in honour of the gods.

In many ways the Greeks had similar leisure activities to those today – sport, music, social life with drinking and talk, theatre, but not much reading or gardening.

THE ANCIENT CIVILIZATIONS: ROME

Rome was the centre of a vast empire, and was more concerned with military conquest and administration than with philosophy. However, the Romans too had slaves; again manual work was regarded as degrading. The state took an active role in directing leisure. Athletics were encouraged for military training and for health reasons. Many leisure facilities were built – baths, resorts, and for sport. Colosseums for spectacles and circuses for chariot races were to be found everywhere (British Museum, 1929), and there was often free food, to keep the public content. There was less concern with music, theatre or dancing than in Greece. There was a lot of free time; the middle class did little work, and there were up to 200 holidays a year.

Informal social life was important, and houses and cities were built to facilitate it. The houses of the well-to-do had large, elegant dining-rooms and elaborate formal gardens with statues, pools and garden furniture. Those who could afford it had very elaborate banquets, with many courses. The cities had agoras, parks and baths, where hours of conversation could take place. Public life was conducted out of doors in the agora.

Races and other sports were organized partly to promote the fitness of the participants, partly to entertain the public. It was in Rome, and later in Constantinople, that really large crowds of spectators became common. The Colosseum could hold 50,000 to watch gladiators kill each other or be killed by animals. There was little crowd violence, however, though the audience became worked up into a bloodthirsty frenzy. As in Greece, there was a religious dimension, in that images of the gods were displayed and the blood of the dead offered to them. It was Christians, outraged by the idolatry as well as the violence, who succeeded in stopping these performances in AD 339. Chariot races in the Circus drew larger audiences, and the

Circus Maximus could hold a quarter of a million. There was much more crowd violence here, as well as political protest; and sometimes buildings were burnt down. This suggests that there is little or no relation between violence on the field and among the spectators. Here, as in the Colosseum, there was a lot of sexual activity, and prostitutes were busy.

The Greeks couldn't do much foreign travel because of the wars, but the Romans controlled very large territories, so they were able to travel long distances, by road, to seaside resorts, summer villas, religious shrines and historical sites, for their pleasure, health, education or spiritual life. Many had second houses in cooler places; some travelled to Greece and Egypt, and the Holy Land, to see the same things tourists see to-day. Rome itself was a popular tourist spot. Inns, spas and travel arrangements developed to meet the needs of tourists, as did tour guides and sellers of souvenirs. All this tourism was made possible by the wealth, roads and political stability of the Roman empire.

The Romans did a lot of writing, of different kinds. There were important historians such as Livy and Tacitus; there was oratory; there were essays and letters, for example by Cicero; and there were novels with myth-like plots about how two lovers were ultimately united. There were many famous Roman writers and, we deduce, many readers of what they wrote (Boardman, Griffin & Murray, 1986).

THE MIDDLE AGES

This is the period from the end of the Roman empire, by about 500 AD, to the end of feudalism, and the Black Death in 1381. Ninety per cent of the English population lived in the country, in small villages, on the estates of landed gentry, the lords of the manor. The peasants had to do work and military service for the land owners, as well as cultivating their own strip of land.

The church was an important influence on leisure during this period. Saint Benedict founded the first of many monasteries in the sixth century; his monks had to do six hours of manual work a day, as well as attend many services, though he taught that religious and intellectual work was superior to manual work. The Benedictines developed clocks, in order to keep the times of services. The church disapproved of many of the pleasures which had been popular for the Romans: gambling, drinking, theatres and most music. It believed that the purpose of life was preparation for the next world, and that lower desires should be controlled. The church was particularly against bear-baiting and other sports at the expense of animals.

The peasants had a hard life, and often experienced famines, but kept up their spirits with cheerful, though unsophisticated, singing and dancing, creating the tradition of 'Merrie England'. There was dancing, for example, round the maypole, and the songs and festivals were derived from earlier pagan traditions, some of which were taken over by the church. There were theatrical performances, such as miracle plays.

Sport was very rough, indeed dangerous, for the peasantry, consisting of wrestling, fighting with staves, and brawling in ale houses, together with a violent form of football, where whole villages would have a violent and uncontrolled contest, in which old feuds could be pursued. There were some basic rules, for example players should not hit each other below the belt, and only one player should attack another at a time (Elias & Dunning, 1986). There was no separation of the spectators, if any, from the players.

The feudal nobility and the knights did a lot of hunting of deer, wild boar and other animals. They had extravagant feasts, at which there would be drinking, singing and gambling; they had mock battles at tournaments, with jousting, which the lower orders were allowed to watch; the peasants were not allowed to go hunting, though many did. The craftsmen and other middle-class folk had many days off, only working 200 days a year by the end of the period. They had their own sports, such as archery; and anyone could swim or skate.

A new form of music appeared from the seventh century: Gregorian and other plainchant for unaccompanied voices, which reached its height in the twelfth century. There was also secular music in the Middle Ages, from the troubadours for the gentry and the jongleurs for the peasants. Churches adopted organs partly to distance themselves from the roisterous jongleurs.

In the Middle Ages travel was more difficult, but there were pilgrimages, to as far as the Holy Land, and again there were routes, inns and even guide books. The regular resting places became tourist spots with feasting and entertainment (Coulton, 1938).

THE RENAISSANCE AND REFORMATION

The Renaissance started in Italy in about 1350 and was at its height in England in the 1500s, the age of Queen Elizabeth and Shakespeare. It was a time of great activity in painting, music, literature and science, and of a decline in the moral influence of the Catholic Church. Rabelais thought that games, dancing, physical exercise, singing and painting were important, and should be part of education. This was a new humanism. Creative human expression was of value for its own sake and the achievement of full human potential, it was believed, included development of mind and body, leisure as well as work (Glyptis, 1989).

However, this was all for a small section of the privileged classes. For the common people most of their leisure was based on the alehouse, which played a central part in village life. It not only provided ale and bread, but it was also a public meeting place where they met kin for weddings and funerals, neighbourly help, and where some met for courtship. It was the drunkenness, the disorderly entertainment and the resulting crime which led the church and authorities to control or suppress alehouses by frequent prosecutions and withdrawal of licences (Wrightson, 1981).

There were more frequent country fairs and festivals, at which there was eating and drinking, and a great variety of entertainment, including disreputable ones like bear-baiting and cock-fighting. There was a lot of drunkenness, sexual promiscuity and fights between individuals and groups, though these sometimes took the form of aggressive games. Hostility to authority could be expressed but there was also some mixing of the classes, and the generation of group pride and cohesion. Esteem could be gained by doing well at sports or by dressing up well (Malcolmson, 1973).

There was more dancing and music. At higher levels of society there was court dancing, like the galliard, and for other people there was folk dancing of several kinds, including English country dancing, Morris dancing, Scottish and Irish dancing, and there were dancing schools. From the 1500s onwards the social élite preferred dancing to

sport. Ballet developed, though the aristocrats also took part in tournaments. The middle class still engaged in archery.

From 1450 there was a considerable increase in music in churches
and banqueting halls in England, first polyphonic church music, then
music for voices and lute, and madrigals. New stringed instruments
appeared, and the names of Byrd, Tallis, Dowland, Morley and
Gibbons were well known. A greatly increased range of activities
and entertainment became available, and there were many actors,
dancers, singers, musicians and other performers. It was the aristocracy who were mainly responsible for building theatres, parks and
gardens. The Globe and many other theatres were the settings for
plays by Shakespeare and Marlowe. There was also mumming, in
which dancers and singers in costume would parade to visit a noble-
man's house. Some of the gentry were patrons of the arts; a few were
creative themselves, as writers or artists; some were scientists, like
Roger Bacon; this was of course leisure for them. This is a good
example of Huizinger's idea that play is the basis of culture.

Those who lived in the country, the majority of the population
still, engaged in country sports. The upper classes hunted deer or
wild boar, engaged in falconry, horsemanship, fencing and duelling.
They had real tennis, bowls, cards and chess. Other people hunted
smaller beasts, practised archery, as well as running, jumping and
wrestling, but also bear-baiting, dog-fighting and cudgelling. Football took the form of contests between whole villages, sometimes
1,000 a side. Gradually these violent and disorganized sports became
displaced by more controlled and less violent ones: for example
football became somewhat more orderly. Horse races became fairer.
Golf came from Scotland in the fifteenth century.

The Reformation began in the 1500s with the ideas of Luther and
Calvin, who had a very different view of leisure. Luther thought that
salvation was by faith, but that we are judged by the effect that faith
has on our lives; work was the main purpose of life, and we should
be devoted to the worldly duties of our calling. Calvin had a different
view, that we are all predestined to be saved or not, but that the elect
can be recognized by a life of good work, self-denial and devotion to
duty. These ideas became the basis of what was later known as the
Protestant work ethic. This proclaimed that work was the purpose of
life, leisure was unimportant; indeed much leisure was thought to be

wicked, especially gambling and drinking, and most leisure activities on the Sabbath. The Protestant ethic was an important source of the Industrial Revolution, and is still alive today. The belief that leisure is of no value, in comparison with work, is also still alive today.

From the sixteenth century Britain initiated several kinds of tourism. The grand tour became popular for aristocratic youth, with educational and cultural goals, and was on a sufficient scale to lead to hotels and regular routes. Spas were established, for the pursuit of health, relaxation and pleasure, first of the wealthy and the middle classes; seaside resorts also appeared, but these rapidly started to cater for the working class too, though different places catered for different social groups (Malcolmson, 1973).

THE INDUSTRIAL REVOLUTION

From the 1600s most crafts, weaving and spinning in Britain were done by the domestic system, in which master craftsmen put work out to families in town and country who did it at home and were paid by piece-work. From the 1750s there was a great change, mainly due to the discovery of steam power and inventions in the textile industry. The result was that since work was increasingly done in factories, which could provide the steam power and new machinery, instead of at home, many had to move to the towns, and had to work regular hours. Moreover they had to work very long regular hours, often twelve hours a day for six days a week, followed by three services on Sundays. There were very few holidays. The conditions of work in mines, iron works and textile factories were often unpleasant; people were not used to these hours or conditions and had to be made to work by fear of the sack or even corporal punishment, in the case of apprentices. Work was now very sharply distinguished from leisure, though there was little time or energy for leisure, apart from recovering from work and its frustrations.

In the eighteenth century many industrialists and mine owners didn't want their workers to have any leisure, which they saw as idleness and drunkenness. The churches, especially the Methodist Church, were against most forms of working-class leisure, with its baiting of animals, prostitution and drunkenness. The result was a massive suppression of much working-class leisure. This came about in several ways. The enclosure of the land, and the move to the towns, removed much common land, which could no longer be used for recreation, apart from village greens. Laws were passed to prohibit the playing of football and other games in the streets. Working-class blood sports, like cock-fighting, were prohibited in a similar way, though the hunting and other sports of the gentry were exempted. Finally the many holidays and wake days of previous times were gradually abolished. Observers at the time commented that the working people had almost no facilities for recreation. For the gentry it was very different, and their whole lives, particularly those of the women, were devoted to leisure; they had land for country pursuits, and large houses for entertainment, eating and drinking, concerts, games and reading (Walvin, 1978). This was the way of life which Jane Austen described, with visits to Bath, elegant balls, and girls looking for rich husbands.

All that was left for the working people was the tavern, which was the main social centre for working-class men, and drink was perhaps necessary for doing arduous work, and to cope with a frustrating life situation, particularly in times of economic hardship. Many working-class women turned to prostitution in order to eat, their clients often coming from a higher social class. The leisure of the working people was rough and violent: drinking in taverns, bear-baiting and dog-fighting, cudgelling and wrestling. The gentry kept their distance from such leisure, and had their own country sports and grand social life; whole towns began to be devoted to leisure. By the nineteenth century the urban middle class had their own leisure, including theatres, reading and seaside holidays (Clarke & Critcher, 1985).

The period of the Industrial Revolution is very interesting for the study of leisure. The less enlightened factory owners thought that the leisure of the workers should be abolished, in order to get more work out of them, and because of moral disapproval of their kind of leisure. Meanwhile the rich spent most of their time at leisure, and could be said to have a clear leisure ethic, though, as in Greece, this depended on someone else doing most of the work (Cunningham, 1980).

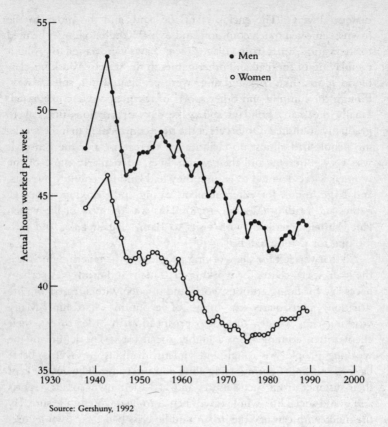

Source: Gershuny, 1992

Figure 2.1a: Full-time manual workers in manufacturing – hours/week

THE NINETEENTH CENTURY (1830–1914)

From the 1830s onwards the leisure situation gradually improved: hours of work became shorter (see Figures 2.1a and 2.1b), bank holidays and holidays with pay were introduced, Saturday afternoons were made free and wages increased.

There was a change of attitudes towards leisure, so that it was now

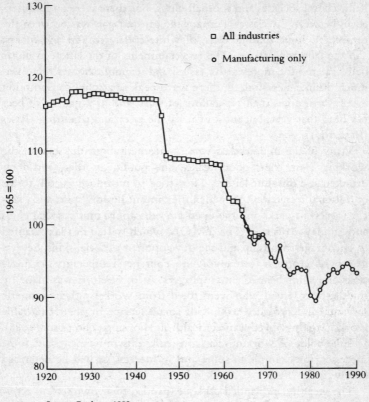

Source: Gershuny, 1992

Figure 2.1b: Hours of work 1850–1990

thought that people had a right to leisure, and that the means for it should be provided. Disraeli said in 1872, 'Increased means and increased leisure are the two civilizers of man.' There was considerable expansion of leisure facilities of all kinds: parks, theatres, concert halls and libraries, for example, sometimes provided by the working class themselves.

Things were different in town and country. In the villages there were a lot of very enjoyable occasions, such as feasts, fairs and harvest suppers. In the towns there were new developments such as music

23

halls, choral societies and football clubs, but there were large differences between the classes. Perhaps the greatest gap was between the respectable lower middle class, of white-collar workers and others, and the labouring classes. The entertainments of the latter, in music halls, catered for more earthy tastes, and in public houses there was much drunkenness. Indeed, there was a peak of alcohol consumption in 1875 of no less than 1.3 gallons of spirit and 34.4 gallons of beer per head that year, but most of it by the poor and labouring classes (Best, 1971).

Many of the middle class were concerned about the state of the working class, their poor health, the public disorder, and their drunken and dissolute leisure. They tried to introduce various forms of 'rational recreation', by which they meant healthy sport and exercise, access to parks and the open air, education, music, social clubs and Sunday tea parties. The YMCA, which started in 1844, wanted to encourage friendship and the development of social skills. Several groups of reformers were involved – churches, temperance organizations and some benevolent employers. A lot of effort was made by middle-class wives, who were freed from work by their domestic servants, and provided a kind of social service by their charitable works, to help with education, health and housing (Thompson, 1988). Despite a lot of working-class mistrust, this movement had some successes, for example in sport and in literacy, as will be described below.

The wealthy and landed classes expanded their own leisure activities, and some of these, such as sports, spread to other groups. The churches ceased to be so hostile to leisure pursuits, and there was a move to 'muscular Christianity', the encouragement of healthy outdoor sports. Local authorities decided that they should provide swimming pools, libraries and parks out of the rates. Commercial interests provided music halls, though drink in them was now illegal. There was some growth of leisure activities and facilities indigenous to the working class, such as brass bands and choirs, and working men's clubs, some of this encouraged by the more benevolent employers (Clarke & Critcher, 1985).

The nineteenth century showed a complete transformation of organized sport, much of it taking place in Britain, as will be described later. Organized sport became a worldwide leisure activity. Furthermore, this development of sport was very much a British middle-class phenomenon. Working-class sport was promoted by churches, who often fielded church football teams, and by firms likewise. Not since ancient Greece had athletic and other contests been so well regulated.

By the early nineteenth century cricket and football became the most popular sports, and watching sport had become a major leisure activity. Cricket crowds, who were mainly middle class, in the South as least, were well behaved. In Australia they were more working class and often rioted and invaded the pitch. Soccer soon emerged as the proletarian sport; there were audiences of up to 50,000 by the 1890s, mostly working-class men, who sometimes behaved badly, for example by invading the pitch. From the 1840s travel to football matches was made much easier by the railways. People also went to the races, and to boxing matches, which now drew large crowds, even to public executions, for which the railways offered cheap day returns.

Middle-class families went to the seaside, working-class families on day trips; whole resorts like Blackpool grew up, offering not only sea bathing, believed good for health, but also many other entertainments. They became pleasure centres. The rich had been going on the grand tour for some time; now they could also spend the summer at the seaside, though at different resorts from those used by the lower orders. Thomas Cook invented the package tour, first for visits to the British seaside and later to Europe.

There was a great deal of music in this period; there were many choirs, which sang the *Messiah* and other religious works, and there were working-class brass bands, which often played in the open air and at spas. Middle-class ladies played the piano. However, the most popular kind of entertainment was the music hall, which had developed out of the earlier singing saloons. These were the result of commercial enterprise, built up the performances to new heights of sophistication, were patronized mainly by working- and lower-middle-class clients, and had a very noisy and gregarious atmosphere.

Church attendance declined during this period, but religion was still an important part of life. Sunday schools were very important; they provided the only education for many working-class children, and in particular they taught them to read and write, and gave other instruction, as well as providing enjoyable outings, and some leisure for them and their families (Walvin, 1978).

During the nineteenth century in Britain there was a rapid growth in literacy and reading. There had been a high rate of illiteracy: 49 per cent of women and 33 per cent of men could not sign the marriage register in 1840. This was partly because many working-class children did not go to school. Church Sunday schools, and an increase in primary education, made a great difference; in addition, hours of work became shorter, giving more time for reading; lighting in houses improved, as did the space in houses, so that reading became more possible. There was a great expansion of public libraries and mechanics' libraries for the poor, and of subscription libraries for the middle class. Publishers realized the commercial possibilities of appealing to a mass reading public, so books and magazines became cheaper and more numerous, and were targeted at different sections of the population. There was a similar expansion of newspapers, and these too became cheaper (Altick, 1957).

Veblen (1899) thought that the leisure of the rich, at the end of the nineteenth century, was motivated by the desire to impress other people by their conspicuous consumption, lack of need to work, and clothes which were obviously expensive and unsuitable for work. The purpose of their leisure, he argued, was to display their wealth and add to their social status, for example by women wearing high heels, men wearing tall hats, the employment of servants, and engaging in the study of dead languages and other useless scholarship. No doubt some of the rich at this and at other times did behave in this way but, as Reisman (1953) pointed out, some of the rich and their wives at this time did a lot of charity work, supported the arts, and were concerned with politics and reform. And some of my Oxford colleagues might contest his interpretation of the purpose of classical scholarship.

There was still a great gulf between the classes at leisure. The leisured class had no problem with leisure, they had been doing little else for years. They kept themselves apart, by going to resorts which were too expensive for anyone else, and by playing sports like golf, mountaineering, rugger and tennis, from which others were excluded, and by spending a lot of leisure in their grand houses. The rich were certainly idle and they were sometimes drunk. The working class lived in a totally different world, of pubs, working-men's clubs and the music hall. They were far from idle and they were often drunk too.

The middle class rejected both styles of leisure; they were serious and morally concerned people, much influenced by evangelical Christianity, believers in chastity, sobriety, piety and charity; they thought that leisure should be more than pleasure or rest, that it should have some moral legitimacy. They decided that sport was all right and favoured muscular Christianity, strongly supported by their schools. They established a lot of clubs for sports, social reform, voluntary work, indeed any common interest. They went on foreign travel but took this seriously and spent their time in churches, art galleries and the rest, unlike the frivolous aristocracy (Thompson, 1988).

Another aspect of middle-class idealism at this time was the hope that the classes which had been separated by work might come together at leisure, that leisure could be a source of social integration. Although some middle-class folk were helpful in promoting working-class clubs and sport, on the whole the classes kept apart at their leisure, indeed made considerable efforts to do so. There was some mixing of classes, however, in choirs, and to a small extent in attending football, the races, and going to the seaside. In the end most working-class leisure was not the result of middle-class help, but of spontaneous growth from the working class itself, of working-men's clubs, brass bands and football teams (Bailey, 1978; Cunningham, 1980).

THE TWENTIETH CENTURY

The amount of free time has increased gradually during this century in several ways. As we saw in Figure 2.1b the hours of work had already declined a lot since the 1850s, though this had levelled off, so that by the end of the present century it is just over forty-three hours a week for male manual workers. There has been an increase, starting in 1980, and there are now many who work longer hours than this, such as the self-employed, some doctors, lawyers and other professionals, and workaholics of all kinds. The working life became shorter: education and training continued after sixteen for many, and a lot of people retired early, at sixty or before, with an average working life for men of about thirty-seven years. The average working life for women has increased, because more of them are working, though mainly part time. There are more holidays; where there were almost none in the last century, most workers now have over four weeks' paid holiday per year. The average length of life has increased; those born at the beginning of the century could expect to live to forty-eight for men and fifty-two for women; the corresponding figures towards the end of the century are seventy-two and seventy-four, so that they have a lot of free time after retirement. Perhaps the largest source of free time, though not always of leisure, has been the increasing level of unemployment. This reached a peak in the early 1930s, with 3 million unemployed, 22 per cent of the working population. Their enforced free time was not experienced as leisure but as an embarrassment; they were distressed and apathetic, stayed in bed and hung around street corners, though some did manage to go to football matches, pub or cinema. Churches, trade unions and voluntary organizations did what they could for them, by organizing clubs, education, craft work and holiday camps. Unemployment reached a later peak of 13.1 per cent of the labour force in 1986, or 3.29 million. It is now less, partly through changes in who is counted as unemployed, but the figure is between 7 and 13 per cent for most industrialized countries. Most labour economists doubt whether it will ever become less, and believe that it will probably become more, as a result of the relentless increase in the use of computers and automation to do the work. The increased unemployment of men has been partly due to the decline of whole industries like mining and steel; there has been increased employment of women, in quite different jobs, but most of them part time. Women who have jobs and also look after husbands and children have very little spare time. A final source of increased leisure has been the widespread introduction of central heating, washing machines, and other labour-saving devices. For the middle class at least this has meant them doing more of the domestic work themselves, where servants had done it before (Glyptis, 1989). And there has been increasing prosperity for most people during this century, which means that they have more money to spend on holidays, sports and every kind of leisure.

The ways in which people spend their leisure in the present century have changed out of all recognition. Turning to the first of our list of leisure activities, *television*: this replaced the cinema from 1948 on-wards, just as the cinema had earlier, in the 1920s, replaced the music hall, and rapidly became the main use of leisure time. The history of TV watching is very short, indeed the rise of TV is the most dramatic development in the history of leisure. Much of the population of the developed world now watch for one and a half to three hours a day or more, and this came about in a very few years.

People continued to listen to *music*, on the radio – later on tapes and discs. Most people listened to the radio at home, some to the new dance music and jazz from America, others to classical music on hi-fi. Young people went to pop concerts, and successive youth movements were associated with new styles of music with more or less rebellious messages. The new dance halls had a great appeal to women, and to all social classes.

There has been more to *read*. In the twentieth century publishers combined commercial acumen with the intention to improve what people read. Mills and Boon, Penguin Books and others started publishing readable fiction and other materials, the public libraries improved and reading was stimulated by adult classes.

The latest twist in the history of reading is of course the introduction of television, which has resulted in a drop in the amount of time spent reading books and magazines, but not in reading the paper. On the positive side, when some serious novel, like *Middlemarch* or *Brideshead Revisited*, has appeared on TV, there have been greatly increased sales of the book.

Meanwhile study has increased, on the part of adults, through local authority classes, for non-vocational subjects, and through the Open University.

There has been a great increase in prosperity, so that many now own their homes, have filled them with material possessions as in the USA, looked after them with DIY and gardening, and spent a lot of time at home with these activities, needlework and other *hobbies*. A new domestic hobby, for the young, has been computer games.

Social life has been decreased by the time spent watching TV, but there have been many clubs and leisure groups, for many different purposes, or just for sociability. People still go to pubs, some to night clubs, working-class women to bingo. For public entertainment, the cinema rose to be the most popular activity, fell rapidly when TV came, and has now started to rise again.

For *sport* there have been two interesting developments. Many more people now engage in exercise than in sport, i.e. many walk, run, jog, swim, cycle, do aerobics, work out in the gym, or in other ways keep fit. There has been a large increase in indoor sport, due to the building of new sports facilities. Keeping fit has been something of a social movement, which started in the USA, and was fuelled by news of medical research on how to avoid heart attacks and the like. The second development has been in the growing popularity of dangerous or 'vertigo' sports, such as hang-gliding, parachuting, bungee-jumping, white-river rafting, scuba-diving and off-piste skiing. These dangerous sports really are dangerous: scuba-diving kills about 120 a year in the USA alone, but it is the risk which makes them exciting.

For *spectators*, football gradually became the most popular sport in the world. It reached a peak of popularity in Britain in 1977, since when there has been a fall in attendance, mainly due to fear of violence (Canter, Comber & Uzzell, 1989), though the large numbers watching on TV may also be a factor. The working classes went to football matches and greyhound races, and took part in the associated gambling. While Britain is widely believed to have invented football hooliganism, some of the worst riots have been in South America, where 300 were killed in 1964 in a game between Uruguay and Peru.

For *religion* there was a continuous decline in church attendance during the century, but recently there has been an increase in charismatic activity in the main churches, and a rise in membership of small sects and cults.

There has always been *voluntary work* in Britain, mainly done by upper- and middle-class women in the past. The scale of this work has increased, and it was extended to supplement the welfare state in the 1950s. It was broadened so that younger and working-class individuals also take part.

Holidays and *travel* have increased greatly as the result of greater prosperity, holidays with pay, more cars, and the development of air travel and package holidays. There have been new commercial developments such as theme parks and indoor 'tropical' pools. If tourism, hotels and sport are included, the leisure industry is now one of the largest employers.

A FINAL COMMENT ON WHAT WE CAN LEARN FROM HISTORY

Leisure has shown extraordinary variations from one historical period to another, in the amount of leisure people had, what they did with it, and what they believed they should do. At some periods large sections of the population had little to do but leisure, like the Greeks and the landed gentry later. We are now moving into a period when most people are going to have more leisure than before, so that the question of a leisure ethic becomes important. Several ethics have been influential in the past. The main ones have been: (a) Aristotle thought that leisure was for moral and spiritual education, the growth of virtue and wisdom; the Greeks had slaves to do the work; (b) the Romans thought that leisure was to promote fitness, for military and health reasons; (c) several Christian groups thought that leisure was to prepare for the next world, by religious and charitable duties; (d) the leisure classes everywhere had no difficulty in spending time at leisure, by country pursuits, sport and elegant social life, but they didn't have an ethic exactly, since no moral justification was offered for their leisure; (e) the Victorian middle class believed in rational recreation for themselves and others, i.e. education, exercise, music and helping others. All of the groups which had a definite leisure ethic were against idleness, the pursuit of pleasure, and drunkenness. We shall examine current ideas about the leisure ethic in the final chapter of this book.

Another historical issue is what the causes were of these changes in the amount and nature of leisure. Most recently some of the main causes have been technological – the cinema, radio, TV, computer games, trains and aeroplanes. In the last century commercial activity was the major factor – music halls, big sports meetings, holiday travel. It has been important in this century too – package holidays, with airlines and hotels, commercial TV, pop concerts, sports facilities and equipment. Government action has sometimes been import-ant, when it has decided to provide leisure facilities: in the USA, state parks created a widespread interest in the 'wilderness', now a major leisure activity. Government has also restrained some kinds of leisure, such as animal-baiting. In Britain local authorities have been one of the greatest sources of leisure facilities – swimming pools and other sports settings, public libraries, parks and evening classes.

The state of the economy and the organization of work were major influences in the Industrial Revolution, and still are in the present day, when increased prosperity and increasing unemployment are important parts of the leisure scene. Churches, reform movements, philanthropists and philosophers have all had their influence, for example the Puritans and the Temperance movement.

CHAPTER THREE

Leisure statistics: effects of gender, age, class, unemployment and retirement

Here we discuss how many people engage in different kinds of leisure, how much time they spend on it, and how this varies between men and women, young and old, and other groups. Some groups are of special interest – women, the retired and the unemployed, for example. We discussed the meaning and definition of leisure in Chapter 1, and decided that leisure consists of 'the activities which people do because they want to, for their own sake, for fun, entertainment or self-improvement, or for goals of their own choosing, but not for material gain'. But we still have to decide on the range of activities which fall under this heading.

One way round this problem is to ask people whether they regard various activities as leisure or not, or what percentage of them they see as leisure. Clark, Harvey and Shaw (1990) did this in a time-budget study in Canada. Nearly all of the obvious forms of leisure, like watching TV and sport, were regarded as leisure. However, there were some large gender differences in that, for example, for employed men 50 per cent of their cooking was seen as leisure, but for housewives only 8 per cent of cooking time was so seen. We shall return to this problem when we come to gender differences.

This problem has been tackled by the General Household Surveys in another way, and I shall make use of the 1990–93 surveys of 17,574 people (in 1993) in Great Britain aged sixteen and over. These surveys of leisure have been built up over the years. They now ask if respondents have done various things during the past four weeks and during the past year; results are reported for four quarters of the year, and a prompt card is shown with a long list of possible leisure activities. This made a big difference: in 1973, when the prompt card was not used, only 11 per cent reported home repairs/DIY, but in 1977, when the card was used, the figure was 37 per cent. The prompt card almost amounts to a definition of leisure, and it is one with which many would agree. However, the list does not include shopping, going for a short walk, or sitting or hanging around (Smith, 1987). I shall also make use of earlier GHS surveys which asked about the frequency of engaging in different leisure activities.

Another source of data is time-budget studies, in which samples of people have been persuaded to keep diaries for a period. The results are then categorized, and the time spent on different kinds of leisure is found. I shall make use of the 1983–4 study by Gershuny and Jones (1987) of an Education and Social Research Council (ESRC) survey of 474 men and 691 women in 1983, using time budgets for a week, and of some international comparisons.

A third source of data is the amount of money spent on different leisure activities, and this has been obtained in the General Household Surveys.

THE TOTAL AMOUNT OF LEISURE

The Henley Centre for Forecasting reported the hours of leisure, or free time, for different kinds of people in 1992–3 as shown in Table 3.1.

Free time is what is left over after work, eating and the rest; this is the time which is available for leisure, though some of it may be spent doing nothing very much. Men in full-time work have almost as much free time as they spend on work and getting to work; women in full-time work have less free time, but they have 8.2 hours a day at weekends; the retired and the unemployed of course have a great deal of free time.

LEISURE ACTIVITIES

We will now look at the amount of leisure in each of the ten areas which were introduced in Chapter 1. The percentages who had engaged in each of these in the 1990 survey are shown in Table 3.2. I shall also draw on a number of more specialized surveys, for example of reading and church attendance.

Time-budget studies tell us how much time is spent on each of

Table 3.1: Time use in a typical week: by employment status and sex, 1992–3

Weekly hours spent on:	Full-time employees		Part-time female employees	Housewives	Retired	
	Males	Females			Males	Females
Employment and travel†	47.1	42.2	20.8	0.4	0.5	0.6
Essential cooking, shopping and housework	13.0	25.5	32.5	38.1	17.0	33.0
Essential childcare, personal hygiene and other shopping	13.2	20.1	25.2	29.4	10.0	14.0
Sleep‡	49.0	49.0	49.0	49.0	49.0	49.0
Free time	45.7	31.4	40.6	51.1	91.5	71.4
Free time per weekday	5.0	3.0	4.7	6.6	12.8	9.7
Free time per weekend day	10.3	8.2	8.5	9.0	13.8	11.5

†Travel to and from place of work.
‡Seven hours per night.

Source: The Henley Centre for Forecasting

Table 3.2: Participation in leisure in last 4 weeks (percentage of adult population)

1. TV	99
2. Radio	93
3. Reading books	62
4. Social life: visit or entertain friends or relations	97
5. Hobbies: gardening	48
DIY	44
dressmaking etc. (females)	44
hobbies	51
6. Sport: any, except walking	48.5
walking	41
7. Watching sport: any	8
football	4
8. Church	20
9. Voluntary work	15 (1987)

Source: *Social Trends*, 1993–4

these activities, and Table 3.6 gives some of the Gershuny and Jones data for 1983, re-arranged under our ten categories. I have given the figures for employed men and for women with full-time jobs and women without jobs, generally known as housewives.

We also know how much was spent on all these things, and this is given in Table 3.3, which shows, amongst other things, that 16.6 per cent of domestic budgets was spent on leisure, as generally understood.

A number of studies have shown how the amount of leisure and the use of leisure are affected by certain variables. These are gender, age and point in life cycle, and social class. The leisure of the retired and the unemployed is of particular interest. All these variables will be discussed in later sections of this chapter.

TV watching

Nearly 100 per cent of the population watch TV in Britain and other countries which have it, and this is now the third greatest use of time

are not known. Table 3.2 shows the numbers who do garden-
8 per cent), DIY (51 per cent of men, 24 per cent of women),
ressmaking, needlework or knitting (44 per cent of women).
er 57 per cent did arts, crafts or other hobbies. Other studies
ound that those who do these things do them two to three
week and spend 3.5 to 4.5 hours a week on them. Adolescents
moment play computer games a lot, 30 per cent daily, and
34 per cent more than once a week; a further 8 per cent
me at fruit machines in arcades. But after a year or so they
more interested in other pursuits such as the opposite sex or

d exercise

turn to five kinds of leisure which are done outside the
rting with sport. The GHS has asked about sport in some
latest being 1990, and some of the results are shown in

ws that walking (for more than two miles at a time) was
opular form of exercise: 41 per cent had done it in the last
, usually twice a week. Next most popular is swimming,
in four weeks; keep fit or yoga 12 per cent, but 16 per
men; and snooker, if this can be regarded as sport, 12 per
st one activity was reported for the past four weeks,
alking, by 48.5 per cent. Competitive and team sports,
, cricket and tennis, were less common than individual
rcise.

us surveys respondents were asked how often they did
In most cases the average was once a week, for football,
a, but walking was done twice a week, as was keep fit/
ning or jogging, and cycling was 2.5 times. Swimming
e a week, though there were some who swam every
ame was true of jogging.

ort

t of men and 5 per cent of women had watched sport
four weeks, usually once a week, and usually football

Table 3.3: Expenditure on leisure (£ per week per household)

1. TV purchases and rentals	7.59
2. Radios, music, cinema and theatre	0.74
3. Books, magazines and papers	3.84
4. Meals out, alcohol	13.89
5. Home repairs etc.	3.96
hobbies	0.07
home computers	0.61
6. Sports	2.02
7. Spectator sports	0.24
8. Church (for attenders)	c.3.00
9. Voluntary work	—
10. Holidays	11.21
Total £	**45.04**

As a percentage of household spending 16.6%

Source: *Social Trends*, 1994

after sleeping and working: 3.92 hours a day for women, 3.27 for men. The TV sets in many houses are left on for much longer than this; these are the hours when people said they were watching. For about 60 per cent of this time they are also doing something else, mainly eating, talking or reading as the primary activity, but with half an eye on the set. Sometimes there is less than half an eye on the set: Collett (1987) devised a way of filming people while watching and found that they were sometimes asleep, making love or not in the room at all. The time when TV is the main focus of attention is about an hour and a half on average. There is increasing use of video-recorders, rented or borrowed videos, and computer games; the latter will be discussed under hobbies. TV is watched mainly between 6 and 11 in the evening, when over 40 per cent of the population is watching. The most popular programmes are soap operas, for reasons which will be explored later.

Music and radio

Table 3.2 showed that most people listen to the radio, and many to records or tapes. Although the Gershuny and Jones study only found three to four minutes a day, other work shows that a truer figure is an hour and a quarter (Reid, 1989), but that people are doing something else at the same time, like housework or driving to work. A high proportion of this broadcasting is music – most broadcasts on Radios 1, 2 and 3 in Britain consist of music of three different kinds, i.e. pop, popular music including popular classics, and classical proper. Some sections of the population listen much more, especially teenagers.

A smaller number go to concerts: 12 per cent say they go to classical concerts, 5 per cent to opera, and 5 per cent to jazz. A smaller number still make their own music: 3 per cent report doing amateur music or drama. More detailed information on music and the other main categories of leisure will be given in Chapter 8.

Reading and study

In the GHS survey 62 per cent said they read books, but other research suggests that this may include magazines and some very lightweight books. About 5 per cent can't read. It seems that about 50 per cent do read books regularly, and 26 per cent had been to the public library in the previous four weeks. The Gershuny and Jones study found that men read for twenty-four minutes, women for twenty-one, plus another three and two minutes for study. A twelve countries study found that their 25,000 subjects read books for an average of 8.3 minutes, magazines for 3.9 and papers for 15.2, 27.4 in all, quite close to the British figure (Robinson, 1990). Sixty eight per cent in Britain read a national daily, and 74 per cent a Sunday paper, but far fewer read the serious papers, e.g. 6 per cent read the *Daily Telegraph*, and 3 per cent *The Times*.

However, the twelve countries study found a much higher figure for study, 15.7 minutes, much higher than the British figure of three minutes for men, 1.5 for women. This may be because study is used in a more restricted sense in Britain. Study is the main work done by children and students, but at a later age it becomes a form of leisure. There is a difference between those studying for qualifications related to their jobs, and those going to evening classes in art history or Italian, just out of interest or for self-development.

It is estimated that 5 million in England and Wales, 14 per cent of

the adult population, take courses of some ki[nd] them for leisure, not for any qualification, through LEA evening classes (Woodley *et al.*,

Social life

Nearly everyone spends time in conversation with family, friends, neighbours and others budget study, men with jobs spend eighty this way, women without jobs 118 minut with other family members but a lot of child care, et cetera, which isn't leisure, covered already. Informal social life can default activity, which is done when th Some people meet their friends at pubs cent of women do this two to three times in other shared leisure. Or they may m groups, and about 37 per cent of the p and 16 per cent were office holders o clubs in Young and Willmott's survey

Most people see something of thei round for a chat or are visited once cent once a week or more (MORI,

The main activity in these soci accompanied by eating or drinking. dancing (16 per cent in last four we 5 per cent of men), or any of th dancing and conversation can lea ment of sexual relationships, espec

Hobbies

In hobbies I shall include a var carried out alone, using manua like gardening, DIY, needlewo ing after pets, bird watching, g computers, collecting things, aspects of the environment. T

thing ing (4 and d Anoth have f times a at the another spend t become football

Sport a

We now home, sta years, the Figure 3.1 This sh the most four week 15 per cen cent of wo cent. At le excluding v like football forms of exe In previo these sports. golf, et ceter yoga and rur averaged on day, and the

Watching sp

Eleven per cer in the previous

Table 3.3: Expenditure on leisure (£ per week per household)

1. TV purchases and rentals	7.59
2. Radios, music, cinema and theatre	0.74
3. Books, magazines and papers	3.84
4. Meals out, alcohol	13.89
5. Home repairs etc.	3.96
hobbies	0.07
home computers	0.61
6. Sports	2.02
7. Spectator sports	0.24
8. Church (for attenders)	c.3.00
9. Voluntary work	—
10. Holidays	11.21
Total £	**45.04**

As a percentage of household spending 16.6%

Source: *Social Trends*, 1994

after sleeping and working: 3.92 hours a day for women, 3.27 for men. The TV sets in many houses are left on for much longer than this; these are the hours when people said they were watching. For about 60 per cent of this time they are also doing something else, mainly eating, talking or reading as the primary activity, but with half an eye on the set. Sometimes there is less than half an eye on the set: Collett (1987) devised a way of filming people while watching and found that they were sometimes asleep, making love or not in the room at all. The time when TV is the main focus of attention is about an hour and a half on average. There is increasing use of video-recorders, rented or borrowed videos, and computer games; the latter will be discussed under hobbies. TV is watched mainly between 6 and 11 in the evening, when over 40 per cent of the population is watching. The most popular programmes are soap operas, for reasons which will be explored later.

Music and radio

Table 3.2 showed that most people listen to the radio, and many to records or tapes. Although the Gershuny and Jones study only found three to four minutes a day, other work shows that a truer figure is an hour and a quarter (Reid, 1989), but that people are doing something else at the same time, like housework or driving to work. A high proportion of this broadcasting is music – most broadcasts on Radios 1, 2 and 3 in Britain consist of music of three different kinds, i.e. pop, popular music including popular classics, and classical proper. Some sections of the population listen much more, especially teenagers.

A smaller number go to concerts: 12 per cent say they go to classical concerts, 5 per cent to opera, and 5 per cent to jazz. A smaller number still make their own music: 3 per cent report doing amateur music or drama. More detailed information on music and the other main categories of leisure will be given in Chapter 8.

Reading and study

In the GHS survey 62 per cent said they read books, but other research suggests that this may include magazines and some very lightweight books. About 5 per cent can't read. It seems that about 50 per cent do read books regularly, and 26 per cent had been to the public library in the previous four weeks. The Gershuny and Jones study found that men read for twenty-four minutes, women for twenty-one, plus another three and two minutes for study. A twelve countries study found that their 25,000 subjects read books for an average of 8.3 minutes, magazines for 3.9 and papers for 15.2, 27.4 in all, quite close to the British figure (Robinson, 1990). Sixty eight per cent in Britain read a national daily, and 74 per cent a Sunday paper, but far fewer read the serious papers, e.g. 6 per cent read the *Daily Telegraph*, and 3 per cent *The Times*.

However, the twelve countries study found a much higher figure for study, 15.7 minutes, much higher than the British figure of three minutes for men, 1.5 for women. This may be because study is used in a more restricted sense in Britain. Study is the main work done by children and students, but at a later age it becomes a form of leisure. There is a difference between those studying for qualifications related to their jobs, and those going to evening classes in art history or Italian, just out of interest or for self-development.

It is estimated that 5 million in England and Wales, 14 per cent of the adult population, take courses of some kind, three-quarters of them for leisure, not for any qualification, most of these being through LEA evening classes (Woodley et al., 1987).

Social life

Nearly everyone spends time in conversation or other social activities with family, friends, neighbours and others. According to the time-budget study, men with jobs spend eighty-three minutes a day in this way, women without jobs 118 minutes. A lot of time is spent with other family members but a lot of this is housework, eating, child care, et cetera, which isn't leisure, or TV, which has been covered already. Informal social life can be regarded as a kind of default activity, which is done when there is nothing else to do. Some people meet their friends at pubs – 26 per cent of men, 8 per cent of women do this two to three times a week – or may meet them in other shared leisure. Or they may meet them in clubs or leisure groups, and about 37 per cent of the population belonged to these, and 16 per cent were office holders or members of committees of clubs in Young and Willmott's survey of London (1973).

Most people see something of their neighbours; 17 per cent call round for a chat or are visited once a day or more, another 30 per cent once a week or more (MORI, 1982).

The main activity in these social events is conversation, often accompanied by eating or drinking, though there are others, such as dancing (16 per cent in last four weeks), bingo (9 per cent of women, 5 per cent of men), or any of the other activities of clubs. And dancing and conversation can lead to the establishment and enjoyment of sexual relationships, especially for young people.

Hobbies

In hobbies I shall include a variety of activities, most of which are carried out alone, using manual or technical skills, usually at home, like gardening, DIY, needlework, arts and crafts, photography, looking after pets, bird watching, geology, making or operating radios or computers, collecting things, restoring old railways, canals or other aspects of the environment. The total numbers of those who do these things are not known. Table 3.2 shows the numbers who do gardening (48 per cent), DIY (51 per cent of men, 24 per cent of women), and dressmaking, needlework or knitting (44 per cent of women). Another 57 per cent did arts, crafts or other hobbies. Other studies have found that those who do these things do them two to three times a week and spend 3.5 to 4.5 hours a week on them. Adolescents at the moment play computer games a lot, 30 per cent daily, and another 34 per cent more than once a week; a further 8 per cent spend time at fruit machines in arcades. But after a year or so they become more interested in other pursuits such as the opposite sex or football.

Sport and exercise

We now turn to five kinds of leisure which are done outside the home, starting with sport. The GHS has asked about sport in some years, the latest being 1990, and some of the results are shown in Figure 3.1.

This shows that walking (for more than two miles at a time) was the most popular form of exercise: 41 per cent had done it in the last four weeks, usually twice a week. Next most popular is swimming, 15 per cent in four weeks; keep fit or yoga 12 per cent, but 16 per cent of women; and snooker, if this can be regarded as sport, 12 per cent. At least one activity was reported for the past four weeks, excluding walking, by 48.5 per cent. Competitive and team sports, like football, cricket and tennis, were less common than individual forms of exercise.

In previous surveys respondents were asked how often they did these sports. In most cases the average was once a week, for football, golf, et cetera, but walking was done twice a week, as was keep fit/yoga and running or jogging, and cycling was 2.5 times. Swimming averaged once a week, though there were some who swam every day, and the same was true of jogging.

Watching sport

Eleven per cent of men and 5 per cent of women had watched sport in the previous four weeks, usually once a week, and usually football

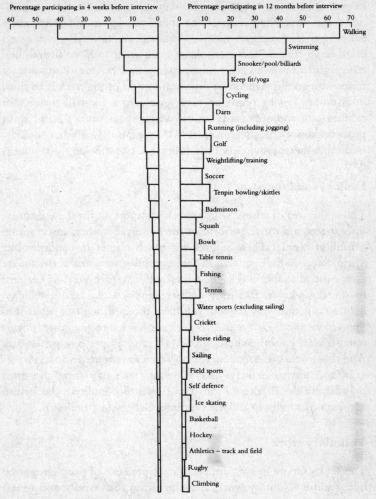

Percentage participating in 4 weeks before interview

Percentage participating in 12 months before interview

Walking
Swimming
Snooker/pool/billiards
Keep fit/yoga
Cycling
Darts
Running (including jogging)
Golf
Weightlifting/training
Soccer
Tenpin bowling/skittles
Badminton
Squash
Bowls
Table tennis
Fishing
Tennis
Water sports (excluding sailing)
Cricket
Horse riding
Sailing
Field sports
Self defence
Ice skating
Basketball
Hockey
Athletics – track and field
Rugby
Climbing

Note: Participation in sports in the 12 months and 4 weeks before interview
Persons aged 16 or over: Great Britain, 1990

Source: General Household Survey, 1990

Figure 3.1: Participation in sports

41

(6 per cent of men, 1 per cent of women). Football is now, world-wide, the most popular spectator sport, though in the USA more people go to American football or baseball. Several other sports draw large crowds, for example 393,000 went to Wimbledon, and many go to horse racing, motor racing and boxing. For some of those who go this is the most important event of the week, and most of Saturday can be taken up with going to a football match, for example. In addition many more watch sport on TV, and sport provides some of the most popular TV programmes. TV has popularized some sports previously little followed, like snooker.

Holidays and tourism

This is the area of leisure which is most important for the economy, since it accounts for 12 per cent of the British economy, and employs 3 million people. These figures are much higher in countries like Spain. Seventy-four per cent of those in full-time work in Britain are now entitled to four weeks' holidays with pay each year, 93 per cent to three weeks. In fact only 60 per cent actually take a holiday, defined as going away for four nights or more, though 15 per cent of them have two holidays and 10 per cent have three or more. Forty-one per cent go somewhere in the UK, and 27 per cent go abroad. And those who go abroad increasingly go to remote destinations.

In addition to holidays many people take day trips; the most popular are the Blackpool Pleasure Beach (6.5 million), the British Museum (6.3 million) and the National Gallery (4.3 million).

Voluntary work

The GHS survey in 1987 found that 15 per cent of people reported doing some voluntary work in the previous four weeks, and 10 per cent in the past week (Matheson, 1990), but other surveys have found a little more than this, about 13.5 per cent each week. The activities reported in the GHS survey were, in order of frequency, raising or collecting money, committee work, helping at a club, helping with entertainments, administration, teaching or training, talks or canvassing, visiting institutions and giving advice. This does not seem to cover the large number of volunteers used by the social services to visit, befriend or help the elderly and handicapped. Nor does it include those who are engaged in various pressure groups to promote peace, racial equality, the preservation of the countryside et cetera. Gershuny and Jones (1987) in their time-budget study found that for those who did some voluntary work, the women put in 2 hours 40 minutes a week, the men an hour and a half.

Religion

Some may not like this to be classified as a leisure activity; however, belonging to a church is quite similar to belonging to a tennis or amateur theatrical club in a number of ways. About 13 per cent of the population in Britain go to church once a week or more, and another 10 per cent go once a month or more. Attendance may not be the best measure, and an index of other aspects of religious commitment such as prayer, acceptance of beliefs, and drawing comfort and strength from religion found that about 20 per cent had what was interpreted as a high score.

However, church is a little different from belonging to a tennis club, because for many it involves daily prayer, and because it is supposed to affect the whole way the members behave and how they think about things. If going to a football match can affect the whole of Saturday, church may affect the whole week.

GENDER DIFFERENCES

Total amount of leisure

There is an influential theory about this topic, due to a number of feminist writers, that women have very little or no leisure, because of the demands of domestic work and the barriers due to husbands who want them at home, because they have less money to spend on it, or because of the men who control sport won't let them do it, or the other men who make it dangerous to go out. It is asserted that women have little choice in what they can do in their leisure; they have to do it mostly in the home, and to squeeze it in the intervals between cooking and child-minding, or at the same time. It is also said that women's leisure is mainly in the home. Most radical of all is

Table 3.4: Effect of children on leisure

	Younger, no children	Children < 5	Children 5–14	Older, no children
Outside the home	133	85	91	95
Inside the home	245	209	241	265
Total	**378**	**294**	**332**	**360**

Source: Gershuny & Jones, 1987

the idea that leisure is a concept which applies only to men, if it is regarded as a reaction to or contrast with paid work (for example, Deem, 1986; Green, Hebron & Woodward, 1990; Smith, 1987). These ideas have been supported by sociological research in the form of interviews and case studies rather than by any quantitative research.

Women have less free time than men on weekdays if they have full-time jobs, about the same if they have part-time ones, and more than men if they don't have jobs at all, as Table 3.1 showed. Women with full-time jobs had about two hours less free time a day than men with similar jobs.

How much leisure time women have also depends on whether they have children. Gershuny and Jones (1987) found the hours of leisure per day for parents, of either sex, with children of different ages. Table 3.4 gives these results.

This shows that couples have less leisure the younger their children, though the effect is greater for women. However, other, less quantitative, research has found that women actually have less leisure than these statistics suggest, because domestic work never stops, and 'having a swim' or 'going to the park' may really be babysitting, while a lot of social life is really looking after relatives or others, a form of unpaid social work (Reid & Stratta, 1989). Taking children to the park is less like true leisure than going to a dance or an evening class, but it is also very different from working at a supermarket or in the office.

One solution to this problem is to say that women have a lot of semi-leisure. Horna (1989) found that play and games with the chil-

Table 3.5: How much domestic work is seen as leisure?

	Employed men %	Employed women %	Non-employed women %
Cooking	50	17	8
Home chores	18	6	2
Child care	45	33	28
House	40	19	27
Laundry	0	6	4
Shopping	33	35	35

Source: Clark, Harvey & Shaw, 1990

dren were mostly seen as leisure by fathers but as only semi-leisure by mothers. Or both sexes can be asked what proportion of various activities they regarded as leisure. This was done by Clark, Harvey and Shaw (1990) with a sample of sixty couples in Halifax, Nova Scotia, and some of their results are shown in Table 3.5.

It is cooking, home chores and laundry which are seen by women as mostly not leisure. Husbands see cooking, child care and work round the house as semi-leisure. However, these domestic activities are all in addition to the free time shown in Table 3.1.

Different kinds of leisure

We shall start with an overview of male and female leisure using the times found by Gershuny and Jones (1987) for employed men, full-time employed women and non-employed women.

Table 3.6 shows both the differences between men and women when both are working full time, and the differences between women with jobs and housewives.

We then look in more detail at the main areas of leisure, together with other findings from the General Household Surveys and elsewhere, using the ten categories of leisure we have been thinking about.

Table 3.6: Time budgets for leisure: gender differences (minutes per day)

	Employed males	Full-time employed females	Housewives
1. TV	129	102	147
2. Radio	4	3	5
3. Reading books and study	27	22	29
4. Social: conversation at home	14	21	26
friends and relatives	24	28	45
clubs	5	2	3
pubs	13	10	4
5. Hobbies: hobbies	12	11	14
dressmaking etc. (females)	0	7	18
6. Sport etc: sport	10	1	3
walking	9	4	9
dancing	5	7	7
7. Watching sport	2	1	1
8. Church	2	6	4
9. Voluntary work	13	21	17
(Relaxing	16	14	32)

Source: Gershuny & Jones, 1987

TV watching
Women watch more than men, on average, but this is mainly due to the high rate for housewives – working women watch twenty-seven minutes a day less than working men. And older women, over fifty, watch a lot. However, some of them may be doing more of other things at the same time than men, such as serving meals, looking after children and doing the housework. Women watch more soap operas, and these programmes are written with a female audience in mind; some are shown in day time, they are about close relationships and emotional problems, and the central characters are usually assertive women (Livingstone, 1990).

Music and radio
The differences here are small. The main one is that women are more interested in music, especially classical music and ballet, but also pop

music, while men listen more to jazz and rock. Women go dancing more often, and they play the piano and other instruments more than men. They go to more concerts, cinema and theatre when they can.

Reading and study

Housewives read more than men, women with jobs less, the same pattern as with TV. More women read books (68 as against 56 per cent). The books they read are different: more are fiction, especially romance, and there are many books only read by women, for example those published by Mills and Boon. Men read adventure stories, thrillers and spy stories. Women read more magazines: 26 per cent read weekly women's magazines, and 33 per cent read monthly ones; this is far more than any male equivalent, such as books about cars, gardening or sex.

Women also go a lot to adult education classes, partly as a route to employment, partly as an acceptable form of escape from the home, it is suggested. About three times as many women as men go to non-vocational interest courses; there are more men on vocational ones, but this isn't really leisure.

Social life

Women with jobs put in forty-nine minutes a day with friends and relations, housewives seventy-one minutes, men with jobs thirty-eight. The pattern for conversation at home is similar. So women have more social life, especially housewives. Sociologists have noted that women have a great capacity for establishing informal contacts with other women, at the school gates, in the shops, but particularly through their common concern with babies and children, in the course of which a lot of advice and mutual help is generated. Women see a lot more of their relatives and their neighbours than their husbands do, especially working-class women, for whom kin and neighbours are important. Women form closer friendships with other women than men do with other men, with a lot of intimate disclosure of emotional problems and trouble with relationships (Argyle & Henderson, 1985).

Women belong to women's clubs, like the Women's Institute, Weight Watchers and voluntary organizations, which are quite different from men's clubs, which tend to be based on sport and drink. They go much less to pubs than men, but many working-class women go to bingo in the afternoon, and women go to more discos, dances and parties than men, despite the problems of getting there, and dangers in the streets (Deem, 1986; Green, Hebron & Woodward, 1990).

Hobbies

These are strongly sex-linked. Women do a lot of dressmaking, needlework and knitting, while men rarely do such things. Many more men report hobbies, 13 as against 3 per cent for women, and these are often activities like repairing motor bikes, working with radios and computers, or making things in the workshop, in all of which they are using skills similar to those used by skilled male manual workers. Curiously it is class 1, professional-class men who have hobbies, far more than any other class. Men also do more gardening and DIY than women, though women do these too. Both sexes collect things in childhood, but it is mainly men who return later to collect in adulthood.

Sport and exercise

Men do more sport and exercise of nearly every kind. The only exception is keep fit and yoga, reported by 16 per cent of women and 6 per cent of men for the previous four weeks, and women swim a little more than men. Many more men play competitive sports like squash, tennis or golf, and many more men play team games like football or cricket. The most popular competitive sport for women is badminton (3 per cent but 11 per cent for the sixteen to nineteen year olds), and young women play quite a lot of darts and snooker. Women's sport is mainly individual exercise, walking, swimming, keeping fit and cycling. Women do play some rough games like hockey and lacrosse, mainly at school and college, and some have recently taken up rugger and boxing, but these appear to be minority interests, and the stereotype that only certain kinds of sport are suitable for women may be correct.

Watching sport

Men watch sport more (11 per cent in last four weeks as against 5 per cent for women), and they mainly watch football (6 as against 1 per cent for women). Women go to football to accompany their men folk; there are no female football hooligans. Women watch tennis, gymnastics, swimming and skiing, partly because these are the sports they play themselves, though it is often their own children that they are watching.

Holidays and tourism

There is no objective evidence of any gender differences here, since most families go on holiday together. However, it has been pointed out that women on holiday are often still looking after children or even doing the catering, so that it may be less of a holiday for them. Furthermore they may have less say in planning the holiday, if they are not going to pay for it (Deem, 1986).

Voluntary work

Slightly more women report doing regular voluntary work than men (9 as against 7 per cent) and time-budget studies find that they spend on average 2 hours 40 minutes a week compared with an hour and a half for men. This may be a serious underestimate of women's voluntary work, however, since there are about 300,000 single women who look after elderly parents or relatives (Reid & Stratta, 1989).

Religion

Women in Britain go to church about 50 per cent more than men do, and the same ratio is found for all other measures of religious activity, such as saying daily prayers, reporting religious experiences and holding religious beliefs (Argyle & Beit-Hallahmi, 1975).

These gender differences are a little different at different ages, though for most families it is stage of life cycle which has most effect. When there are young children under five, there is less leisure for both sexes, but particularly for women. They become more house-bound, can go out less, but even inside the house have less time for reading and TV, less space for themselves. Men still go to the pub, though women do not; women go more to cinema, theatre and dancing, and any physical activity is tied up with the children, such as swimming. When the children are five to fifteen, however, women do more sport, and working-class women now do as much as middle-class. For sport and several other kinds of leisure women are most active during the period from thirty to thirty-nine, and for clubs and voluntary work from forty to fifty-nine (Smith, 1987). Women take very little exercise when over seventy, apart from walking; men keep going a lot longer. Some of the male activities do fall quite fast with age; the pub-related games, cycling, running and weights are only done by the young.

Some of these gender differences depend on social class too. In the reanalysis of GHS data by Smith (1987) it was found that women of all classes engaged in less leisure than men, but the basic manual/non-manual divide made a difference. Working-class males went to the pub a lot, and took part in the associated darts, snooker and betting; they were the least likely to go dancing, while the women of all but the professional class played bingo. The latter engaged in most cultural and civic activities, but it was clerical-grade females who were most physically active.

Summary and explanation

Do women have less leisure than men? If both partners work full-time, part-time, are unemployed or retired, the female has fewer hours of leisure, about one and a half hours a day, and this can be accounted for by the fact that women do most of the housework, especially the child care, shopping, cooking and cleaning. Both partners have less leisure if there are young children. And for women the distinction between leisure and non-leisure is unclear and for them the same domestic activities seem less like leisure than they seem to men. However, many women have a lot of spare time; for example housewives have seven hours a day on weekdays and nine on weekends, and even women in full-time work have 8.3 hours at weekends. So the theory that women have no leisure is not confirmed.

How about the theory that women are so constrained in their leisure that all they can do is to squeeze in a little reading or TV watching between the household jobs? Women have one and a half to two hours a day of leisure outside the home, and they do more of some kinds of such leisure, such as going to church, doing voluntary work and seeing their friends; they go to the pub less, but they go to bingo and they go to dances, discos and parties more than men. However, women do spend more of their leisure in the home, watching TV, reading, knitting and chatting to friends and neighbours. The sphere where there are said to be the greatest barriers to female leisure is sport, and women certainly do less overall. But they do more keep fit and yoga, swim a little more and, overall, 39 per cent of women engage in regular sport or exercise apart from walking (58 per cent for men), so this is not negligible.

What is the explanation of these gender differences in leisure? The demands of domestic work, and especially of child care, do reduce leisure hours for women, and result in more home-bound leisure; it is more difficult for mothers of small children to get out. However, there are the positive motivations which lead women to engage in close relationships with other women, and to engage in church and voluntary work activities which, we shall see later, are great sources of social support and satisfaction.

AGE DIFFERENCES

We would expect that many leisure activities, like sport, will be done less by older people. And it is often said that older people gradually withdraw from activities and social contacts outside the home. However, for more sedentary and home-bound forms of leisure we would expect a high rate of participation at all ages, i.e. watching TV, listening to the radio, reading, and seeing friends, and that more time will be spent in these ways with age. Older people have more free time, if they are retired, and after their children have left the home, so it will be interesting to see how they spend their time, and whether they make good use of it.

Again we will look briefly at the effects of age on the ten types of leisure which we have chosen to follow. Later we will look at the main stages of life and try to form an overall picture of how leisure is spent in each of them.

Another line of thought was introduced by Rapoport and Rapoport (1975), who produced an influential book in which they claimed that the stage of life is the main determinant of leisure activities. If this is true, then leisure depends less on chronological age than on whether individuals are married, have young children, are retired, et cetera. Retirement is of special interest to students of leisure and will be discussed in the following section.

The total amount of leisure certainly changes with age, or perhaps with life cycle. Young couples, without children have, on average, 133 minutes a day of leisure outside the home and 245 inside it. When they have children under five they have forty-eight minutes less leisure outside and thirty-six minutes less inside the home. This is due to the 104 minutes extra domestic work (Gershuny & Jones, 1987). These figures are averages for husbands and wives; we have already seen that it is wives who do most domestic work and have less leisure.

Watching TV

The General Household Surveys show that 99 per cent of all age groups watch TV. However, they watch for different amounts of time each day. Children watch a lot, they like it and parents use TV as a kind of babysitting; teenagers watch less, since they prefer being out with their friends to watching TV with the family. For married couples TV watching is a central activity of family life, and the time spent increases from age thirty-five to forty-four onwards. Different age groups watch different programmes too; children watch children's programmes, of course, and old people watch more news and non-fiction material.

Music and radio

Babies are taught to sing at mother's knee; some children are taught to play an instrument. Music plays an important part in the life of teenagers, since pop music is about dancing and love; it is also about protest, and every rebellious youth movement has its own special kind of music. Adolescents listen to music via records, tapes, or the radio, often for several hours a day. Interest in classical music increases with age, and older people prefer it to the loud, aggressive and erotic music of the young.

Reading and study

Most people read books, papers and magazines at all ages. Children read a lot – comics and stories like those of Enid Blyton; adolescent girls read about romance and fashion, boys about adventure. The content of magazines changes gradually with the age being catered for. Young women read about grooming, the presentation of self at work, and conforming to the peer group; young mothers seek practical advice and escapism. When the children are older their parents no longer need advice or escapism, and develop more sophisticated interests and read more specialist journals. Those over fifty-five use the public library more, but read the papers a little less.

Children and students study, but various kinds of study are leisure for many adults, especially older ones taking courses not for any qualification but just out of interest. The peak age for these is thirty to fifty-five.

Social life

The time spent with friends varies greatly over the lifespan. Adolescents may spend several hours a day with their immediate circle of friends, and this dominates their leisure time. Marriage and job reduce time spent with friends drastically, and they may be seen monthly or yearly instead of daily. Married couples see their joint friends together, more formally in middle-class circles, though they may also see them at clubs, pubs and bingo. During the period of family life mothers see their women friends informally at crèche, school and elsewhere, while their husbands see their cronies at the pub or the golf club according to class. Social activities in public places, meals and drinks out, dances and bingo, peak at twenty to twenty-four and decline after this age. Leisure groups are very popular with the middle-aged, and in later life people have a greater need for friends, and find them in church or leisure groups. Working-class people continue to see their kin during the period of family life, but middle-class people do so more rarely.

Hobbies

Children take up hobbies, such as collecting things like stamps, dolls or soldiers, but this falls off in adolescence. Males may take up collecting later in life. Children's hobbies are sex-linked as we have seen, for example radios or pets. Computer games are very popular with children and adolescents. Most hobbies develop later; more women take up dressmaking later, and participation peaks in the sixties. Gardening also grows in popularity with age, and peaks at forty-five

Table 3.7: Age and leisure (percentages who participated in previous 4 weeks)

	16–19	30–44	60–69
1. TV	99	99	99
2. Radio	97	92	86
3. Reading books	62	62	66
4. Hobbies: gardening	15	53	58
DIY	25	54	40
dressmaking etc. (female only)	19	43	53
5. Social: visit, entertain friends or relations	98	97	95
6. Sport: walking	45	43	42
any sport except walking	82	59	28
swimming	25	21	7
cycling	24	11	6
soccer	20	4	0
keep fit/yoga (female only)	29	19	8
snooker	41	14	4
7. Watch sport: football	7.9	4.6	7.9
		(Source: Young & Willmott, 1973)	
8. Church (weekly)	11.9	8.5	11.9
		(Source: Brierley, 1991)	
9. Voluntary work	24	33	22 (1987)
	Source: General Household Survey, 1990		

to sixty-nine. Many retired people spend their time with hobbies, as we shall see, and they look like a substitute for work.

Sport and exercise

Participation in every kind of sport falls off with age, very fast for football and other team games. The one which is kept up most is walking, and 42 per cent of the sixty to sixty-nine group still do it (they also keep up gardening). Swimming, cycling and keep fit fall off a little faster (see Table 3.7).

Watching sport

The peak age for watching football is sixteen to nineteen, when 8 per cent watch it. Football hooligans are drawn entirely from this age group. The same ages also watch rugby football and motor racing the most, but cricket is watched most by the twenties to thirties and the forty-five to sixty-four age group.

Holidays and tourism

Children go on holidays with their families, and later in life may return to the places they enjoyed as children. Adolescents feel increasingly constricted by family holidays and want to go off with others of the same age, first to organized camps and the like, later more independently. Students travel a great deal, often to exotic, Third World places, in search of adventure or, as they say, 'to find themselves'. Other 'under-thirties' may be in search of sex, along with the sea, sun and sangria. Family holidays are often on package deals to the seaside, in Britain, Spain, Greece or elsewhere. Older couples may go on bus tours, cruises, et cetera, according to income, often of a cultural or educational character. The old now have the time and money for such things, but may be in poor health.

Voluntary work

The most active age for doing voluntary work is thirty-five to forty-four, although it is done by those of all ages, and teenagers do quite a lot. The old do it too, and when they do they put in a lot of time. Older people do more visiting, young people do more active things, and they choose activities which may teach them new skills. Older helpers say that they volunteer as part of their religious beliefs or philosophy of life.

Religion

The church attendance statistics show that the young and old go most, those in their early thirties least. Adolescence is a time of great concern with religion, both emotional and intellectual; young people are concerned with the meaning of life and the existence of God, and they may be converted and deconverted back again, ending up with a less simple faith or none. Perhaps it is the pressures of family and work which keep those in their thirties away from church, though there is a lot of interest in sects and cults by those in their twenties. After thirty there is a continuous increase in religious practices and beliefs to old age; 100 per cent of those over 90 believe in the after life, though there is less church attendance by the infirm (Argyle & Beit-Hallahmi, 1975).

LEISURE AT DIFFERENT AGES

We will now try to present a more coherent picture of the main themes of leisure at different stages of life.

Adolescence

This has been described as 'a peak time of leisure needs' by Hendry *et al.* (1993), who carried out a survey of 10,000 young people in Scotland, aged between ten and twenty; I will use this survey as one of the sources for this section. Adolescents have a lot of time for leisure, and their leisure activities are of central importance to them.

Their social life is perhaps the most central of their concerns; early in this period they make close friends with one or two of their own sex, this develops into forming peer-group gangs or cliques, and it is the peer-group culture which helps them become independent of home. Adolescent sub-cultures have been very influential since the Second World War; each has had its own style of music, clothes and hair, and an ideology. Music, i.e. pop music, is of central importance at this age, since it is about love and protest, and adolescents spend many hours with their transistor radios or Walkmans. Ideologies have embraced political protest about peace, race relations, et cetera. Delinquent peer groups have sometimes taken to drugs and delinquent activity. Teenage groups meet outside the home, first in adult-organized youth clubs, then in more commercial settings, such as discos, dances, bowling alleys and fruit-machine arcades, or they may just hang around street corners. These commercial venues provide just the kind of environment where young people can meet and engage in the forms of interaction they seek. There is a great common interest in the world of entertainment, especially pop singers, but also TV personalities (Smith, 1973). Teenagers spend less time in front of the family TV but, while they are at home, more time with computer games. The older age groups spend less time at youth clubs, less time at home, more at pubs, discos and parties. Although most teenagers spend a lot of time with their friends, and about 60 per cent say they have many friends, 10 per cent admit to finding it difficult to make friends, and presumably 30 per cent find it somewhat difficult (Hendry *et al.*, 1993). Church is important during early adolescence, and conversion and confirmation common, but later there is a big fall-out rate from church attendance.

Less time is spent with the peer group after age sixteen, because heterosexual interests become more important. First boys and girls meet in mixed groups, but soon they have dates, which become increasingly steady. 'For some girls, thinking, talking about, preparing, then actually going out with boyfriends become virtually the whole of leisure' (Roberts, 1983). The sexual revolution of the past fifty years had led to 43 per cent of sixteen year olds and 70 per cent of those in their twenties being sexually experienced, though often only with a steady partner who may be the final mate (Fife-Shaw, 1995). Boys are not so single-mindedly concerned with sex and social life; they keep up their earlier interests, in football, fishing, motor bikes and the rest (Rapoport & Rapoport, 1975).

Sport is important throughout adolescence; it is taught and organized at school and college but falls off after, or even before, leaving. Over 90 per cent take part in weekly sport at thirteen to fourteen, and this falls to 67 per cent for males and 49 per cent for females at nineteen to twenty, though this is still a high rate of participation. Competitive sport and team games are soon replaced by exercise, i.e. walking, swimming, running and aerobics. Girls drop out faster, especially from competitive and team sport, perhaps because of concern with their bodily changes. Middle-class young people keep up an interest in organized and team sport longer. In the USA sport is a more central common interest to teenagers than it is in Britain (Smith, 1973).

We said that teenagers move away from their families, and indeed they become more concerned with their teenage friends and their good opinion. However, they still see a lot of their families, and spend a lot of leisure time with family at age fifteen and about the same amount as with peers at eighteen. They still watch TV, a central family activity, but less than any other age group.

Students form an interesting group for the study of leisure. Like teenagers they have a lot of time for leisure; they also have exceptional facilities for it. They can play a great variety of sports, and there are clubs for every possible form of leisure. They can try out new leisure activities, and instruction is available; they can engage in journalism, acting, music, politics, or pursue a great variety of interests. This is all part of social life; indeed they may join primarily to make friends, but at the same time they are acquiring leisure interests. We have seen that students have high levels of going to dances, the cinema, and they do a lot of foreign travel.

Adult life, until children leave home

We have seen that having children leads to a sudden drop in the number of hours of leisure, especially for women, and there are more findings of a similar kind. When there are children in the home, especially pre-school children, leisure has to be fitted in around child care, or combined with it, for example in family outings or joint visits to pool, park, cinema, et cetera. During this time of life leisure is home-centred, so that TV, car, garden and looking after the home are all important. There are family holidays to seaside or Spanish resorts, and mothers read magazines about how to look after their children, or escape to adult education to get a break from the home.

For men this is also a period when work is very important and takes up a lot of time and energy, especially in some middle-class careers like those of doctors, or for the self-employed; this further reduces possible leisure. Social life with friends is much reduced; women see female friends and acquaintances when they can, at the crèche, for example; men see theirs at or after work, often still at the pub or golf club. Although meals and drinks out, dancing and bingo are done less often, the rate of participation falls quite slowly with age, as Figure 3.2 shows. Participation in sport falls a lot faster; shortage of time combines with falling vigour and fitness. Walking, swimming and keep fit are the main forms of exercise left.

Later adult life, after children have left

There is now more time for leisure, the children are gone, careers may be less demanding, and there is usually more money, though perhaps less energy. Many take up new hobbies and interests; there is more gardening, dressmaking and DIY, more voluntary work and church activity; middle-class men take up skilled interests. Couples may try to re-invigorate their marriages, and may travel or go to classes together. Satisfying leisure is a major source of life satisfaction for old people, as we shall see in Chapter 4.

Explanation of age changes

We introduced two theories of the effects of age: one, the effects of age as such, for example on physical vigour and social energies; and two, the effects of stages in the life cycle. We have seen evidence for both theories. The effects of age on physical vigour can be seen in the decline in sports, and indeed in every aspect of leisure, as shown in the following graphs of GHS data (see Figure 3.2).

The life-cycle point of view is most evident in the effects of having small children in the home, the return to previous leisure when they grow up and, above all, in the effects of retirement, to be studied next. The preoccupation of teenagers, especially girls, with sex may be primarily an effect of ageing, but to this is added the current teenage sub-culture, which gives a life-cycle effect.

Retirement

This is a very interesting time of life from the point of view of leisure. To begin with the retired have far more time for leisure. Table 3.1 showed that they have over eleven hours of free time a day during the week and nearly thirteen hours a day at weekends. They have also lost their work and all the satisfactions it can provide – income, the work itself, the company of work-mates, achievement and recognition, role and status in the community, and a feeling of contributing to it. Leisure could be used to replace these forms of satisfaction, but is it used in this way? And if it isn't, could we help the retired to do so? Retirement could be the time for realizing dreams and ambitions, doing things you have always wanted to do; but many actually fear the prospect of retirement (Puner, 1974).

In a recent British survey, Parker (1982) found that 31 per cent did not feel happy to retire, 35 per cent were looking forward to it, while the rest had mixed feelings. Respondents were asked what

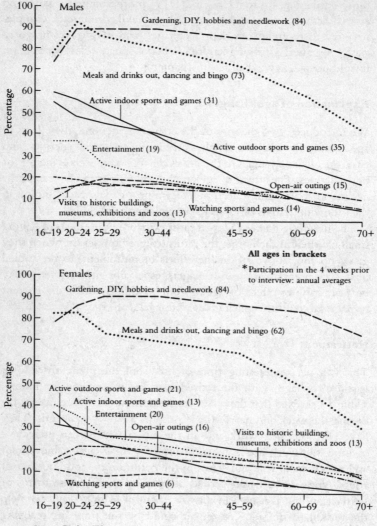

Figure 3.2: Grouped leisure activities: participation* by age and sex, 1977, Great Britain

Table 3.8: Aspects of work missed by the retired

	Workers	*Retired*
Would or did miss most:		
The money the job brings in	48	31
The people at work	24	36
The feeling of being useful	10	10
The work itself	8	11
Things happening around	3	5
The respect of others	2	3
Other things	5	4

Source: Parker, 1982

they thought they would miss, and what they did miss, with the results shown in Table 3.8.

Loss of income was the greatest worry, followed by loss of the social contacts at work; feeling useful and the work itself were worries for only about 10 per cent of them. In another survey Beveridge (1968) found that 74 per cent missed the companionship of other workers, 27 per cent the money, 20 per cent the job itself, and 14 per cent the routine of working life. These surveys have all been of men, partly because it has been assumed that retirement involves less change for women.

Retirement has often been regarded as a stressful life event. How far is this correct? It is found that about a third of British retired have difficulty in settling down during the first twelve months, but that most of them did so later (Parker, 1982). Some wished they had carried on working. How well the retired adjust varies with their previous work. Managers often find it difficult, since they miss the position of responsibility and can't replace their jobs by anything similar. Professionals and academics are better placed, as will be shown later. Manual workers may be better off, if they had tiring or unsatisfying work.

There is no evidence that mental health is any worse, and if anything it is a little better than for those at work, because of the removal of job stresses. Some of the retired are in poor health, but careful follow-up studies have found that this is because some retire as a result of poor health; retirement does not affect health (Kasl,

1987). The retired are, on average, happier than those still at work, although some feel bored, and some lonely. They are certainly a lot happier than the unemployed (Argyle, 1987).

Do the retired take up any new leisure activities? Follow-up studies in several countries show the same thing, that they carry on with the same leisure as before. The main new things they do are watch more TV and do more jobs around the house. Long (1987) followed up 105 Scottish men after they had retired. For 58 per cent there was no change, 8 per cent did more housework, 7 per cent took up bowls, 4 per cent education, 3 per cent photography and 3 per cent sport. A very different picture came from a study by McGoldrick (1982) of 1207 men who had retired early, at forty-five to sixty-four, because they wanted to, and who were in good health, under a company scheme which gave them good pensions. They and their wives were very active in retirement and did a lot of new things. There were several main groups:

1. Resting and relaxing, i.e. watching TV, walking, gardening et cetera. This aspect of retirement was appreciated by most of the group.
2. Time spent with home and family; over two-thirds appreciated this.
3. Hobbies, such as music, DIY, golf, bird watching, fishing or stamp collecting; 37 per cent said this was a major benefit of retirement.
4. Social life and travel, having a good time; 42 per cent did more of this.
5. Committees and clubs; 24 per cent increased this kind of leisure and it was a major activity for 3 per cent.
6. Voluntary work, done by 3 per cent before and 19 per cent after retiring.
7. Further education was pursued by 9 per cent.
8. Part-time jobs, done by 15 per cent and another 6 per cent occasionally.
9. New jobs which were slower or easier, done by 18 per cent.

This study is of interest since it shows what can be done in retirement, but the findings are far from typical, since these men retired under somewhat ideal conditions. They retired early, with good pensions, in good health, and were from good jobs, so were probably above average in education and motivation to achieve things. Clarke and Critcher (1985), writing about working-class people, give a much more negative picture of retirement, as a period of 'excess of time and deficiency of resources', and of 'enforced dependency on a home life progressively more difficult to manage and increasingly isolated from the context of extended family and community' (p. 155). We shall see what a wider range of retired people do with themselves shortly.

The usual findings are that people carry on with the same leisure as before, though they are more passive and more house-bound, and do not take up much new leisure (for example, Kremer & Harpaz, 1982). However, the leisure of the retired is very important since life satisfaction is higher if they are more active (Peppers, 1976). How far do the retired meet any of the needs which were previously met by work? A number do so by carrying on working, often at a slower or easier job, mainly in order to earn some more money. Many do unpaid work, not only their own DIY and house repairs, but also bartering with others, including gardening, French lessons, babysitting, et cetera (Parker, 1982). In some professions it is possible to carry on much as before, though usually unpaid; many academics can continue with their research, writing or teaching, continue to see their colleagues, or do committee work, at their own pace. The same applies to writers, artists and others. Those who are strong in the Protestant work ethic may want to work because this is what they value most, and feel that leisure has to be earned and is indeed defined by its contrast with work. As we shall argue later, this is an attitude which may be changing, as we come to value leisure for its own sake.

Some of the main things that the retired do will not help much to replace the satisfactions of work, i.e. watching TV, sleeping and doing more housework. There are several common retirement activities which meet more work-related needs. Education is one, and the University of the Third Age and the Open University are two of a number of schemes worldwide which are much appreciated by retired people. Voluntary work is done by many retired people and is often taken up at the point of retirement; it provides a valuable social service and gives those involved a sense of purpose and contribution to the community. A third activity which the retired often take up is increased participation in leisure groups, and they may do some of the administrative work, using their managerial or other skills, as treasurers for example.

We will now look at the leisure of the retired in more detail. There is a problem that the retired are also old, and it is not always clear which is the key variable, though we shall, where possible, take studies which have compared people before and after retiring.

Old and retired people spend an increasing part of the day doing nothing whatever, in a state of 'semi-somnolent idleness'. Another sphere where the retired do more is housework, including doing up the house. Most of this is not leisure in the usual sense.

TV watching
This is the main activity which increases with age; the hours of watching increase after retirement, and the elderly watch more than any other age group.

Music and radio
Ninety-three per cent listen to the radio; they like classical music and the popular music of previous years, but they are not as devoted to music as young people are.

Reading and study
This also increases with age, and a proportion of retired people read more, partly in connection with further education or study. Those over sixty-five use the public library a lot; 66 per cent read books, 54 per cent the paper.

Social life
Those who are retired and have lost their work-mates may also be widowed and live alone, in which case they can be rather isolated. Friends may also have died or moved away, so they have real social needs. Life satisfaction is greater for those with good social contacts. They prefer the company of friends their own age, and may find them in church, voluntary work, educational or other leisure groups; there is increased membership of clubs, though only a minority make use of clubs for old people. They often keep in close touch

with their own grown-up children or other kin. In traditional working-class culture and in the Third World old people are looked after by their extended family.

Hobbies

We have seen that some retired people take up new interests, especially if they retire early and have plenty of money. Gardening, dressmaking and DIY stay at a high level of participation, but the proportion who take up new hobbies is quite small.

Sport and exercise

As Figure 3.2 showed there is a continuous decline in physical activity with age. The main forms of exercise which are kept up are walking and gardening. However, a few when they retire take up bowls or other sedate forms of exercise.

Watching sport

Retired men continue to watch sport, though increasingly on TV.

Holidays

Old people have plenty of time but may not have the money or the health for holidays and tourism. They go increasingly in groups and on package deals where they are well looked after and comfortable. Not for them the back-packing through Afghanistan which some did in their youth.

Voluntary work

In the McGoldrick study 19 per cent of early retirees took up some voluntary work, where only 3 per cent were doing it before. Between 17 and 22 per cent of retired people do some voluntary work, and as many as 14 per cent of the over-seventies still do some. This is something where such people can use their skills, meet their friends and feel useful. Often the people being helped are other old people, with whom the workers perhaps have most sympathy.

Religion

This is another activity which increases with age, and which is an important source of satisfaction. Retired people may take up some new duties, in some cases becoming ordained as non-stipendiary ministers.

Theories of retirement

According to the disengagement theory, it is inevitable that old people break their links with others in society. This often happens as the result of retirement, widowhood and ill-health, but is by no means inevitable; there are many who do not disengage (Parker, 1982). The 'activity theory' says that in order to adjust to retirement people must find substitute activities to meet the goals which were achieved in work. We have seen that a proportion of retirees miss their work-mates and the work itself. However, there are those who miss nothing, and those who spend a lot of time either doing nothing or watching TV. Research on satisfaction shows that they would be happier if they had more active leisure and better social contacts.

A final comment concerns some cultural differences in response to retirement. Many more in Japan continue to work after retirement, both because the retirement age is fifty-five, and because the meaning of life is almost entirely derived from work. In America, on the other hand, leisure is being taken more seriously, and 'activity is so valued by older Americans that the pastimes of retirement take on the aspects of work' (Shanas et al., 1968).

SOCIAL CLASS

Social class is one of the main variables which affect every aspect of life, and so is of great interest to social scientists. Indeed I find it so interesting that I recently wrote a book about it (Argyle, 1994a). The GHS and other surveys usually define class in terms of the occupation of the respondent or of the main earner in the family, from 'professional' to 'unskilled manual' in the most recent GHS surveys, and we shall make use of the results. However, there is a problem here in that this is not the way the man or woman in the street thinks about class. If you ask him or her how they tell which class someone is they think that 'style of life', 'appearance and behaviour' and 'the way they spend their money' are as important as occupation. The way people spend their money is as important as the way they earn it. It looks as if leisure is more than a consequence of social class, it is part of its definition. This is partly because leisure is a major factor in who people's friends are, the circles they move in, and thus affects their social status. Two families with the same jobs and the same income may be regarded as of different social classes because of their lifestyles; one may drink red wine, the other may take brown sauce; one goes to Blackpool or Majorca, the other to Turkey or Italy; one plays squash, the other plays darts.

We saw in the last chapter the immense differences in leisure between classes in earlier historical periods. For example during the early nineteenth century in this country there was a landed leisure class, most of whom did no work at all, a hard-working middle class devoted to serious and sober rational recreation, and a working class with no time or energy for any leisure at all apart from recovering from work in the pub. The effect of class on leisure is now far smaller, indeed some American sociologists think it has disappeared, that it is simply a matter of 'sitting in different seats at the opera'. That is going too far; there are many who don't want to go to the opera and who couldn't afford it anyway (Kraus, 1971).

Which class has the most time for leisure now? There is not much difference between occupational groups in actual hours of work, though professional and managerial workers have a longer journey to work, in London at least (Young & Willmott, 1973). Manual workers have work which is more physically demanding, so they are probably more tired when they get home. The Gershuny and Jones time-budget study found that they had six minutes a day less leisure than non-manual workers. The self-employed, who run small shops or businesses, work very long hours. And some financiers, lawyers and other professionals work long hours and bring work home. The unemployed have the most free time, and the rate of unemployment is much higher for the working class – 21 per cent of unskilled male workers, compared with 2 per cent of professionals in 1981. We shall discuss their leisure later in the chapter. There is a small 'leisure class' of idle rich individuals living on inherited wealth, but death duties have reduced them to a small group, highly visible to the newspapers but, unfortunately for us, ignored by social scientists. The main differences between classes in leisure are not in how much they have, but how they spend it, to which we now turn. The differences in leisure activities reported for the four weeks before the interview are given in Table 3.9; here we report the rates for professional class and unskilled workers and their families; the other occupational groups usually fall in between them.

TV

There are very large class differences here: classes A and B (professionals and managers) report that they watch on average 2.79 hours a day, while classes D and E (semi-skilled and unskilled workers and their families) watch far more, 4.56 hours a day (GHS, 1992); we saw earlier that the periods of attending to TV as the main activity are about 40 per cent of these figures. There are also class differences in the programmes which are watched: 24 per cent of middle-class and 15 per cent of working-class people watch soap operas. American studies find that lower-class and black families like aggressive and action/adventure programmes more than sitcoms and family series. Working-class American women like portrayals of upper-class families like *Dallas* as a form of escapism, but think that programmes about working-class life are unrealistic (see Argyle, 1994a).

Music and radio

There are large class differences in the radio stations which are listened to. Classes A and B spend on average twenty-eight minutes a day listening to the classical station Radio 3, compared with four minutes a day for classes C2 (skilled manual) and below; for the popular music station Radio 1, it is the other way round. In America middle-class people listen more to classical music, jazz and folk music, working-class ones to hard rock and blues. Middle-class people in Britain go to more classical concerts (28 per cent as against 4 per cent), jazz concerts (14 per cent as against 5 per cent) and opera (13 per cent as against 2 per cent). Classical music, as with other fine arts and 'high' culture, is almost entirely a leisure activity of the professional classes. Amateur music is pursued by 6 per cent of class A and 1 per cent of unskilled (Reid, 1989). The most active dancers are in class D.

Reading and study
There are substantial class differences here. Middle-class people read, borrow and buy more books than working-class. For example 81 per cent of middle-class people had read a book in the last four weeks, compared with 38.5 per cent of working-class; public libraries were visited by 43 per cent of graduates and 18 per cent of those without qualifications. The serious papers, like *The Times*, are read only by classes A and B, and there is a sudden drop to C1, white-collar. The *Sun* and the *Daily Mirror* are read by classes C to E. Many more middle-class people take adult education courses and classes; for those taking qualifications this is usually job-related, and many have been socially mobile already. For leisure courses, class A women are over-represented 4.5 times, class A men 2.9 times; classes D and E scarcely go at all.

Social life
There is a lot of social life in all classes, but with different kinds of people. Middle-class individuals have more friends, about twice as many as working-class, though the latter see theirs twice as often. Working-class people see much more of their kin, because they live much nearer to them than the middle-class kind usually do, and they see more of their neighbours. In classes D and E 21 per cent call round for a chat daily or more, versus 9 per cent in A and B; 16 per cent of DE visit neighbours daily or more, versus 6 per cent in AB.

A second big class difference here is that many more middle-class people belong to clubs and leisure groups – about 69 per cent of classes A and B are active members of at least one such club – and most belong to several, compared with 36 per cent of D and E. And more middle-class individuals are officers or committee members. Furthermore they are quite different kinds of club. Middle-class clubs usually have a definite activity, for example sport, theatre, geology or music, while working-class clubs are mainly social clubs, that is the members just drink and talk.

Two traditional forms of working-class social life are pubs and bingo. Pubs were for a long time centres of working-class male sociability. The situation has now changed so that all classes go, as do women, though the most frequent drinkers in pubs are now skilled manual workers. For women who do not feel at home in pubs bingo is a female haven, and is almost entirely a working-class activity (Dixey, 1987).

Hobbies

The largest difference here is in hobbies, arts and crafts, which were reported by 21 per cent of class A, and much fewer by members of any other class, for example 9 per cent of B and 2 per cent of class F, for the past four weeks in the 1983 GHS survey. DIY showed a smaller difference in the same direction, 61 per cent of class A and 23 per cent of F. Gardening was similar, 61 per cent of A and 38 per cent of F (this survey used six classes). However, dressmaking, needlework and knitting showed the opposite pattern, 28 per cent of class 6 and 10 per cent of class A, while the highest level was for class C at 42 per cent.

Sport and exercise

Middle-class people engage in more sport and exercise, as the 1992 GHS results show (see Table 3.9).

So 65 per cent of professionals did some sport or exercise, other than walking, in the previous four weeks, compared with 28 per cent of unskilled manual workers. The same pattern is found for most forms of sport, but there are some exceptions. As Table 3.9 shows, classes D and E do more dancing, darts and fishing.

Watching sport

All sections of the population watch football, though the rate is greatest for social class 3, i.e. routine non-manual and skilled manual workers. Football hooligans, however, come almost entirely from class 5 and the unemployed. Otherwise the two main classes go to different sports. The middle class go to rugby football, golf, tennis and horse racing. The working class go to boxing, wrestling and greyhound racing.

Holidays and tourism

In 1991 55 per cent of classes D and E did not go away for a holiday, nor did 15 per cent of members of A and B. However most of the 85 per cent of these classes that went away had two or three holidays. And the middle-class holiday makers were more likely to go abroad, to more remote places, to hotels and to more expensive hotels.

Table 3.9: Leisure and social classes (percentages participating in previous 4 weeks)

	Professional	Unskilled manual
1. TV	98	98
2. Radio etc.	98	83
3. Read books	80	42
visit public library	43	18
4. Hobbies: gardening	63	40
DIY	56	32
dressmaking (female only)	43	35
5. Social: entertain or visit		
friends and relations	97	92
social clubs	69	36
on committee	28	4
bingo	1	11
6. Sport: walking 2 miles	51	31
any sport except walking	65	28
swimming	24	6
snooker	14	8
keep fit/yoga	11	6
golf	13	1
squash	9	0
7. Watching sport: football	9	3
8. Church	17	9
9. Voluntary work	20	11
10. Holidays and trips: out for a meal	65	32
visit forest etc.	78	32

Sources: General Household Survey, 1990, supplemented by other sources, see text

Working-class people go more often to holiday camps, go camping, or on package tours to certain places in Spain specializing in sex, sea and sangria.

Middle-class families make far more trips in their cars to the countryside, for a picnic, or to visit stately homes or beauty spots. They have more cars and drive greater distances than other classes.

Voluntary work

Class is a major predictor of who will do voluntary work. In the 1987 GHS survey, 34 per cent of class 1 had done some voluntary work in the previous four weeks, compared with 4 per cent for class 6. They also did different things. The middle-class people did a lot of committee work, giving advice, talks, teaching and coaching, while the working-class people did transport, repairs, gardening and domestic help. And different voluntary work groups all have their social niches; some are more exclusive than others.

Religion

Middle-class people in Britain go to church much more, 17 per cent weekly compared with 9 per cent for classes D and E. However, other measures of religiosity have found that working-class individuals hold more traditional, fundamentalist beliefs, engage more in prayer and contemplation, and draw more comfort and strength from religion. Perhaps working-class people don't feel at home in churches because the churches are felt to be too middle-class. Different classes go to different churches to a large extent, for example working-class people go a lot to fundamentalist sects. The exception is the Catholic church, which appeals to all sections of the population.

Summary of class differences

We have seen that there is little difference between classes in the number of hours of free time which they have, but there is a great difference in the amount of leisure carried out: middle-class people do more of nearly every kind of leisure, except for watching TV. Working-class people watch much more TV; middle-class people see more of their friends and belong to more clubs, while working-class people see more of kin and neighbours; only classes A and B listen to classical music; middle-class people read more books and more serious papers, and have more hobbies, especially class A; they take more exercise and do more of most kinds of sport; everyone watches football, especially class C, otherwise classes watch different sports; middle-class people have more holidays and trips, and to more distant places; they go to church more, but the others believe more; middle-class people do more voluntary work, and of different kinds.

The explanation of class differences

There are several possible explanations. Some of the differences could be due to money. For example, having a car opens up a lot of sporting and other possible leisure activities. Young and Willmott (1973) found that having a car in London in 1970 added 3.23 leisure activities; having a larger income, apart from the car ownership, added 1.71 activities. This is partly because those with more money can afford babysitters and other domestic help. Roberts (1978) compared more and less affluent workers and found that, for the white-collar ones, being better off resulted in more active leisure activities and less time on socializing. For blue-collar workers, however, the effect was the opposite – affluence led to more of the traditional working-class leisure pattern, with less active leisure, but more socializing in the pub. It could also be pointed out that many leisure activities cost little or nothing – reading public library books, church, many clubs, walking and running, and voluntary work, for example. On the other hand some forms of leisure are only open to the rich, like yachting and polo, or to the fairly prosperous, like skiing and golf; we discuss later whether doing these things is a form of 'conspicuous consumption'.

Another theory is that leisure depends on acquiring the necessary skills, knowledge and interests, and this often happens in the course of education, which middle-class individuals have more of; colleges and universities have many clubs at which new interests can be explored. When we discuss the socialization of leisure later (Chapter 6), we shall see that leisure interests are usually acquired in the company of other people. Middle-class people also have work which gives satisfaction from the use of skills, cooperation to attain goals and the pursuit of excellence; they assume that leisure will be the same; this is less true of much manual work. Sometimes there is a spillover from work to leisure. Voluntary work shows this pattern, where middle-class people do committee work, teach and give advice, and manual workers contribute technical skills.

This still does not explain why one class plays cricket, and another football, why one bets on horses and the other on dogs, or why they go to different places for their holidays. These are simply cultural differences; people learn what is the 'right' sport, because different sports and other forms of leisure have become accepted by different strata. If you play the right sport and go to the right places you will meet people like yourself. And you will identify yourself as a member of a particular social group (Argyle, 1994b).

UNEMPLOYMENT

This is another very interesting topic for the psychology of leisure, since it is a major social problem which can be alleviated by leisure, though normally it isn't. The level of unemployment is now high in all industrialized countries and shows little sign of falling. It is mainly due to the growth of automation and computing, whereby workers are replaced by machines. It has been estimated that by early in the next century all our needs for agriculture and manufacturing may be provided by 10 per cent of the population. There has been an increase in the number working in the service sector – education, entertainment, medicine, holidays, banking, et cetera, but some of these jobs are in turn being automated. Unemployment reached its height in Britain in 1986 at 13.1 per cent of the labour force; it has fallen since then, partly as a result of earlier retirement and more part-time work. There are two general solutions: sharing the work, by shorter hours, less overtime, earlier retirement, et cetera; and 'workfare' schemes, where the unemployed are paid to do public work. Both are beset by serious practical difficulties (Argyle, 1994b).

Meanwhile it is well documented that unemployment creates a great deal of distress for those involved. Compared with those at work there is: (1) a higher mortality rate, partly caused by (2) a much higher suicide rate; (3) poorer health, especially from heart disease and strokes; (4) poorer mental health, especially depression and alcoholism; (5) lower levels of happiness and life satisfaction; (6) lower self-esteem; and (7) boredom and apathy. In these ways those who are out of work are not only different from those working but, even more, from the retired, who are also technically unemployed.

Like the retired they have a great deal of free time. What do they do with it? A time-budget study in Halifax, Nova Scotia, reported the time spent in 1971 and 1981, for people who were still working in 1981 and those who were not (Elliot & Elliott, 1990); I have corrected the changes in time use by the subsequently out of work by

vidence of this, though in the Halifax study the women spent
ten minutes a day on church activities.

LUSIONS

nemployed have much more time for leisure than those at
but take part in less leisure of nearly every kind, apart from
ng TV. They engage in mainly passive pursuits, and the older
re largely house-bound. Furthermore, participation in leisure
shes over time for the long-term unemployed. The reasons for
activity are only partly economic, since many forms of leisure
e or nearly free. We have seen that active participation in
has very beneficial effects for the unemployed, and that there
en success with schemes to provide training in sport for young
. There are many other kinds of leisure which could have
benefits, some of them a lot cheaper. This appears to be an
where the introduction of leisure facilities could make a very
tant contribution to one of the greatest social problems of our

any changes for the others, to allow for the effect of ageing and
cultural change. The main effects of job loss on time use were more
TV watching (65 minutes more), reading (57 minutes), study (30),
home chores (28), shopping (22), conversation at home (21), social
life (19) and cooking (16). A great deal of the time formerly spent at
work is occupied by domestic jobs of some kind; as we saw earlier
most domestic work is not usually defined as leisure. A British study ✳
by Kelvin, Dewberry and Morley-Bunker (1984) found that unemployment led to increased time spent watching TV, housework,
reading and hobbies, less on social activities and less time on several
kinds of sport; overall there was an increase in home-based, solitary,
passive and inexpensive activities. Some studies have found a lot of
time is spent doing nothing, by getting up later, sleeping longer, just
sitting around, or in the case of young people 'hanging out' on the
street corner (Glyptis, 1989). There is evidence that time is perceived
differently, as an unstructured continuum, as a result of having no
engagements or timetable. Very few unemployed people take up any
new leisure activities; indeed they see barriers to participating in
leisure, through being short of money, being too depressed, or feeling
that they are not socially acceptable. In sum, the unemployed spend
most of their new free time watching TV, doing housework or
doing nothing. Furthermore this inactivity increases over time, for
those who continue to be out of work (Glyptis, 1989).

However, there is plenty of evidence that leisure could help with
their problem. The first indication of this came from the study by
Fryer and Payne (1984), who found a number of people who were
happier unemployed than they had been when at work. They had
found more interesting things to do, such as running a community
project, where they could use their skills, be useful, and enjoy a high
degree of autonomy. Several studies have found that active and
social leisure is a good predictor of the well-being of the unemployed.
A large study in Adelaide found that low self-esteem, depression,
negative mood, hopelessness and anomie were all much higher for
those who did nothing a lot of the time, and lower for those who
engaged in gregarious activities; watching a lot of TV had a weak
adverse effect and individual activities like hobbies had a weak
positive effect. This was found for the unemployed, and for people
at work who didn't enjoy their jobs, but not for those who did

(Winefield, Tiggemann & Winefield, 1992). Evidence that leisure has a causal influence on well-being is provided by experience of a number of schemes which have been set up in Britain by local authorities and the Sports Council to provide facilities and training in sports for young unemployed. Several thousand in each area took part, and a follow-up study in Leicester found that there was an increase in out-of-home activities; they became more involved not only with sport but also study, voluntary work and politics, a range of purposeful non-work activities; they found a new sense of purpose, sometimes just in child care or personal health; and these various purposeful activities became more important for them than the sport (Kay, 1987, cited by Glyptis, 1989). A study in Israel found that unemployed individuals with a strong Protestant work ethic or work involvement scores watched less daytime TV, the men did more voluntary work and read more books, while the women did more home improvement, more study, met and helped their friends more (Shamir, 1985).

TV watching
We have seen that there is a large increase in TV watching. The Halifax time-budget study found an increase of sixty-five minutes a day for men, but much less than this for women. A British study by Kelvin, Dewberry and Morley-Bunker (1984) found that they spent two to three hours watching TV as the main activity and a further two hours while doing something else. One of the main differences from those at work is that the unemployed watch daytime TV, which is perhaps more likely than evening TV to produce that state between sleeping and waking reported in some TV research.

Music and radio
There is little to report here, except that the out of work are less likely than others to attend cultural events.

Reading and study
The Canadian survey found substantial increases in time spent on reading and study. In Britain this is more characteristic of the middle-class, more educated unemployed. It is also characteristic of individuals with a strong work ethic, as was found in the Israeli study (Shamir, 1985).

Social life
The unemployed spend more time in socia[...] in the home, visiting friends and relative[...] informally on the street. The young are [...] spend a lot of time in pubs; there is more [...] Heather & Robertson, 1986). But they ca[...] entertainment. Older unemployed are more [...] of their time at home. Few join clubs. One [...] not want to be members of or identified wit[...] like themselves, the unemployed, and are hopi[...]

Hobbies
They spend some time gardening, and a lot o[...] house, some of it on DIY; Kelvin, Dewberry an[...] (1984) found some increase in hobbies by a minority[...]

Sport and exercise
The General Household Survey for 1980 found that th[...] did less sport than those at work; the main things [...] walking, swimming, darts, billiards and snooker, the [...] nected to pub life. However, this is the main sphere in [...] ful interventions have been carried out, as described ab[...]

Watching sport
They watch sport, mainly football, at a lower rate [...] work.

Holidays
There are fewer trips and holidays, for financial reaso[...]

Voluntary work
Few of the unemployed do any voluntary work, [...] do. This was one result of the sports training schem[...] and has also been found for those with strong wor[...]

Religion
From the psychology of religion it might be expe[...] ment would lead to more religious activity. H[...]

much e[...]
an extr[...]

CON[...]

The u[...]
work[...]
watch[...]
ones [...]
dimin[...]
this i[...]
re fr[...]
eisure[...]
as be[...]
eople[...]
mila[...]
ea v[...]
po[...]
ne.[...]

any changes for the others, to allow for the effect of ageing and cultural change. The main effects of job loss on time use were more TV watching (65 minutes more), reading (57 minutes), study (30), home chores (28), shopping (22), conversation at home (21), social life (19) and cooking (16). A great deal of the time formerly spent at work is occupied by domestic jobs of some kind; as we saw earlier most domestic work is not usually defined as leisure. A British study ✳ by Kelvin, Dewberry and Morley-Bunker (1984) found that unemployment led to increased time spent watching TV, housework, reading and hobbies, less on social activities and less time on several kinds of sport; overall there was an increase in home-based, solitary, passive and inexpensive activities. Some studies have found a lot of time is spent doing nothing, by getting up later, sleeping longer, just sitting around, or in the case of young people 'hanging out' on the street corner (Glyptis, 1989). There is evidence that time is perceived differently, as an unstructured continuum, as a result of having no engagements or timetable. Very few unemployed people take up any new leisure activities; indeed they see barriers to participating in leisure, through being short of money, being too depressed, or feeling that they are not socially acceptable. In sum, the unemployed spend most of their new free time watching TV, doing housework or doing nothing. Furthermore this inactivity increases over time, for those who continue to be out of work (Glyptis, 1989).

However, there is plenty of evidence that leisure could help with their problem. The first indication of this came from the study by Fryer and Payne (1984), who found a number of people who were happier unemployed than they had been when at work. They had found more interesting things to do, such as running a community project, where they could use their skills, be useful, and enjoy a high degree of autonomy. Several studies have found that active and social leisure is a good predictor of the well-being of the unemployed. A large study in Adelaide found that low self-esteem, depression, negative mood, hopelessness and anomie were all much higher for those who did nothing a lot of the time, and lower for those who engaged in gregarious activities; watching a lot of TV had a weak adverse effect and individual activities like hobbies had a weak positive effect. This was found for the unemployed, and for people at work who didn't enjoy their jobs, but not for those who did

75

(Winefield, Tiggemann & Winefield, 1992). Evidence that leisure has a causal influence on well-being is provided by experience of a number of schemes which have been set up in Britain by local authorities and the Sports Council to provide facilities and training in sports for young unemployed. Several thousand in each area took part, and a follow-up study in Leicester found that there was an increase in out-of-home activities; they became more involved not only with sport but also study, voluntary work and politics, a range of purposeful non-work activities; they found a new sense of purpose, sometimes just in child care or personal health; and these various purposeful activities became more important for them than the sport (Kay, 1987, cited by Glyptis, 1989). A study in Israel found that unemployed individuals with a strong Protestant work ethic or work involvement scores watched less daytime TV, the men did more voluntary work and read more books, while the women did more home improvement, more study, met and helped their friends more (Shamir, 1985).

TV watching
We have seen that there is a large increase in TV watching. The Halifax time-budget study found an increase of sixty-five minutes a day for men, but much less than this for women. A British study by Kelvin, Dewberry and Morley-Bunker (1984) found that they spent two to three hours watching TV as the main activity and a further two hours while doing something else. One of the main differences from those at work is that the unemployed watch daytime TV, which is perhaps more likely than evening TV to produce that state between sleeping and waking reported in some TV research.

Music and radio
There is little to report here, except that the out of work are less likely than others to attend cultural events.

Reading and study
The Canadian survey found substantial increases in time spent on reading and study. In Britain this is more characteristic of the middle-class, more educated unemployed. It is also characteristic of individuals with a strong work ethic, as was found in the Israeli study (Shamir, 1985).

Social life

The unemployed spend more time in social activity and conversation, in the home, visiting friends and relatives and, for young people, informally on the street. The young are less socially isolated and spend a lot of time in pubs; there is more heavy drinking (Winton, Heather & Robertson, 1986). But they can't afford other kinds of entertainment. Older unemployed are more isolated and spend most of their time at home. Few join clubs. One problem is that they do not want to be members of or identified with the group of people like themselves, the unemployed, and are hoping to leave it.

Hobbies

They spend some time gardening, and a lot of time around the house, some of it on DIY; Kelvin, Dewberry and Morley-Bunker (1984) found some increase in hobbies by a minority.

Sport and exercise

The General Household Survey for 1980 found that the unemployed did less sport than those at work; the main things they did were walking, swimming, darts, billiards and snooker, the last three connected to pub life. However, this is the main sphere in which successful interventions have been carried out, as described above.

Watching sport

They watch sport, mainly football, at a lower rate than those at work.

Holidays

There are fewer trips and holidays, for financial reasons.

Voluntary work

Few of the unemployed do any voluntary work, but a small group do. This was one result of the sports training schemes described above, and has also been found for those with strong work motivation.

Religion

From the psychology of religion it might be expected that unemployment would lead to more religious activity. However, there is not

77

much evidence of this, though in the Halifax study the women spent an extra ten minutes a day on church activities.

CONCLUSIONS

The unemployed have much more time for leisure than those at work, but take part in less leisure of nearly every kind, apart from watching TV. They engage in mainly passive pursuits, and the older ones are largely house-bound. Furthermore, participation in leisure diminishes over time for the long-term unemployed. The reasons for this inactivity are only partly economic, since many forms of leisure are free or nearly free. We have seen that active participation in leisure has very beneficial effects for the unemployed, and that there has been success with schemes to provide training in sport for young people. There are many other kinds of leisure which could have similar benefits, some of them a lot cheaper. This appears to be an area where the introduction of leisure facilities could make a very important contribution to one of the greatest social problems of our time.

CHAPTER FOUR

The benefits of leisure

To say that leisure makes people happy, or puts them in a good mood, is almost a tautology. If leisure is what people do when they can choose freely, it would be very odd if they didn't enjoy it. And if leisure is motivated in the ways described later, it would be very odd if it didn't provide satisfaction. But if we define leisure in terms of the usual range of spare-time activities or in terms which allow people to define the word as they will, it is possible to enquire whether it does, in fact, have such positive effects.

LEISURE SATISFACTION

Andrews and Withey (1976) asked an American national sample a number of questions about this, and the results are shown in Table 4.1.

The answers to the first question show that about 43 per cent were pleased or delighted with their leisure; only 8.5 per cent were dissatisfied, though 11.5 per cent weren't sure. How does satisfaction compare with satisfaction from work? Veroff, Douvan and Kulka (1981), in a similar American survey, asked about this, and some of the results are shown in Table 4.2.

Men and women with jobs obtained more satisfaction from their work, though for a third work and leisure gave similar amounts of satisfaction. But for housewives, and no doubt for the unemployed and the retired, leisure is the greater source of satisfaction.

Which kinds of leisure give the most leisure satisfaction? In an early American survey Robinson (1977) found that the percentages of the population who reported 'great satisfaction' with various activities were as set out in Table 4.3.

Table 4.1: Satisfaction with leisure

How do you feel about:	Delighted	Pleased	Mostly satisfied	Mixed	Mostly dissatisfied	Mostly Unhappy	Terrible	Mean*
The way you spend your spare time, your non-working activities?	11	32.5	36.5	11.5	6	1.5	1	5.25
The amount of time you have for doing things you want to do?	6	24	33.5	16.5	13	5	2	4.7
The sports or recreation facilities you yourself use, or would like to use – I mean things like parks, bowling alleys, beaches? (14% chose not to answer this question)	9	32	33	12	7	4	3	5.0

* 1–7 scale; 'delighted' scores 7

Source: Andrews & Withey, 1976

Table 4.2: Satisfaction from work and leisure

	Employed men %	Employed women %	Housewives %
work > leisure	49	45	34
work = leisure	32	36	32
work < leisure	19	19	34

Source: Veroff, Douvan & Kulka, 1981

Table 4.3: Satisfaction with leisure activities

Activity	Great satisfaction %
your children	79
your marriage	75
your home	40
religion	34
being with friends	33
helping others	33
reading	32
being with relatives	27
making or fixing things	27
sports or games	26
housework	25
relaxing, sitting around	27
car	25
cooking	23
shopping	17
TV	17
clubs	13
politics	9

Source: Robinson, 1977

Some of these results are quite surprising. The low score for TV doesn't match the hours people spend on this activity and the low score for clubs is at odds with the high level of satisfaction later research has found for this. Research by Csikszentmihalyi and colleagues (see p. 165) has obtained subjective ratings on several aspects of leisure. Their favourite dimension is called 'flow', based on a combination of high levels of both challenges and skills, and associated with a high degree of concentration and low levels of boredom, apathy and anxiety. The percentages of time spent in flow for several kinds of leisure were as follows:

art and hobbies	47.2
socializing	32.2
sport and games	26.3
reading	24.6
TV watching	2.8

Again TV comes out with a very low score; we shall see later that this activity is satisfying, but in a very low-key way.

We shall look at the effects of leisure on positive moods, happiness, health, mental health and social integration. In each case we shall look first at the overall effects of leisure, then those of social relations, sport, religion, and of any other areas of leisure when good research is available.

POSITIVE MOODS

We start with the question of whether leisure has short-term benefits for moods; longer-term effects on happiness, health and mental health will come later. This is a more straightforward research problem too. Moods are often measured by self-report scales like:

not happy ——————— very happy

or

relaxed ——————— tense.

I asked respondents to rate their mood 'by the end of a typical meeting of the club', and some of the results are shown in Figure 4.1. A fairly high level of 'joy' is reported for a number of different kinds of leisure groups, though dancing had the highest score. The results for excitement and frustration are also given here.

In a survey of students in five European countries, the main causes of joy were said to be relationships with friends, food, drink and sex, and success experiences (Scherer et al., 1986). A number of other surveys have found different sources of joy, based on leisure experi-

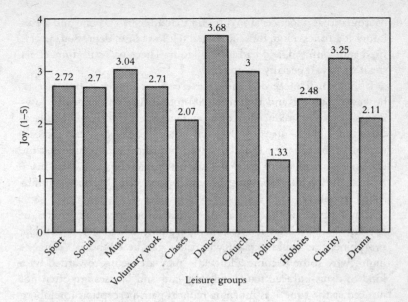

Figure 4.1: Ratings of joy at end of meeting

ences. A study of girls in several countries found that their main sources of happiness were sports and games (swimming, tennis and cycling), and cultural activities (music and reading) (Barschak, 1951). Lewinsohn and Graf (1973) compiled their Pleasant Events Schedule of 320 pleasant activities, of which forty-nine were said to affect mood for the whole day by 10 per cent of their subjects. Many of these events were social ones rather than specific leisure activities, but there were a number of items about being in the country, enjoying the scenery, as well as music and reading.

A more rigorous research procedure is to administer such scales immediately before a leisure activity, immediately after, and at one or more later intervals; the effects of different leisure activities can be compared. This has been done for the effects of sport, to which we now turn. A number of studies have found that after running, swimming or aerobics people say that they are 'feeling better', or have a greater sense of well-being. Thayer (1989) found that a rather small amount of exercise, a ten-minute brisk walk, led to less tiredness, more energy and less tension two hours later.

Maroulakis and Zervas (1993) found that after half to one and a half hours at a fitness club, those involved felt less tense, depressed, angry, tired and confused, and had more vigour. There was still some effect the next day, especially on anger.

It looks as if more demanding exercise has longer-lasting effects; however, Steptoe and Bolton (1988) found that moderate- or low-intensity aerobics reduced anxiety, and increased vigour and exhilaration, but a high-intensity class did not. The exercise can increase tension at the time; we found in a student project that people became less anxious and more relaxed during the exercise, but even more relaxed during the following hour (G. Seere & J. Marlow, unpublished, 1994).

It has been suggested that the explanation for these effects of exercise may be that it releases endorphins, which act rather like morphine; this could explain why there can be euphoria, 'runner's high', why some become addicted – they are being rewarded by a kind of drug-induced state, and why cuts and bruises are often not noticed at the time – as morphia reduces pain-perception (Steinberg & Sykes, 1985). Many studies, mostly with trained runners, have found that exercise does produce increased endorphin levels. Bortz *et al.* (1981) recorded the highest levels on record in a group of thirty-four marathon runners who ran 100 miles up and down mountains in California. Some recent studies with more modest levels of exertion have not confirmed this theory, and there are other, psychological explanations which we shall discuss in connection with happiness.

Some of these apparent effects of exercise may really be due to social interaction with friends. Whiting (unpublished, 1994) found more positive mood increase after rowing in a crew than after solitary training. In a 'bleeping' study, in which subjects were electronically paged, Larson (1990) found that subjects were happiest when with their friends. One reason for this is that friends do nice things together, and another is the frequent exchange of smiles and other social signals while they are doing them. At the bowling alley they frequently smile at each other, whether they have hit or missed, but they rarely smile at the skittles (Kraut & Johnston, 1979). And we saw above the high level of joy reported after meetings of a range of different kinds of leisure group.

People watch TV for several hours a day, on average. If asked why they watch TV one of the main reasons given is 'relaxation' (Comstock *et al.*, 1978). We shall discuss later the finding by Csikszent-mihalyi and Kubey (1981) that, while watching TV, their subjects were in a particular emotional state: they were relaxed, cheerful and sociable, but also more drowsy, weak and passive than for reading or other kinds of leisure; but we shall see that nevertheless individuals may use TV to induce a desired mood.

We saw that music is often mentioned as a source of joy; music has been used successfully in the lab for inducing moods; both joy and depression can be generated quite easily by means of suitable choice of music. Music offers a very wide and subtle choice of moods, and it seems very likely that it is often used to control moods in this way. We shall investigate how music has these effects in a later chapter.

Going on holiday is mentioned spontaneously in several of the surveys cited earlier, and studies of people on holiday find that they are less tired or irritable, less worried, and have fewer headaches (Rubenstein, 1980). Perhaps the main effect of holidays on mood is greater relaxation. The countryside, the wilderness and the great outdoors are often mentioned in American studies, especially those carried out in western states, like that of Lewinsohn and Graf (1973) in Oregon, and by Driver, Brown and Peterson (1991) in Colorado. Zehner (1976) found that satisfaction was affected by the proximity to nature of where individuals were living. Part of the explanation is that interesting natural scenes have an immediate positive effect, which has been measured by physiological measures of facial muscles (Ulrich, Dimberg & Driver, 1991). It is also found that some people have religious experiences, or something like them, in wilderness settings (McDonald & Schreyer, 1991). This is familiar in Britain, in less wild settings, as nature mysticism and the inspiration of poets like Wordsworth. Surveys of religious experiences show that they are often of this kind (Hay, 1982).

HAPPINESS

Some of the famous early studies of life satisfaction found correlations between leisure satisfaction and overall life satisfaction. When Camp-bell, Converse and Rogers (1976) described leisure as 'hobbies and things like that' the correlation was quite small, but when introduced more broadly as 'life outside of work' it was the strongest predictor of life satisfaction (correlation, $r = .21$), though this would be confounded with satisfaction with family and friends to some extent. Headey and Wearing (1992) in Australia found that reported satisfaction with leisure correlated quite strongly with life satisfaction, positive affect, and with the absence of anxiety and depression, i.e. with all of the main components of happiness. Job satisfaction correlated with subjective well-being in a similar way (see Table 4.5). Winefield, Tiggemann and Winefield (1992) studied 603 unemployed young people in Australia, and found a strong relation between subjective well-being and leisure; those who spent a lot of time doing nothing in particular, or watching TV, had lower self-esteem, felt hopeless and had a high level of anomie. This is one of a number of studies in which watching TV has been found to have negative effects.

However, these correlational studies do not tell us which is the true direction of causation, do not demonstrate that leisure is a cause of happiness. A stronger design is the use of multiple regression to find whether leisure still predicts well-being when work, income or other variables have been held constant. Riddick (1985) carried out a path analysis of the effects on the life satisfaction of older people of leisure activities, employment, health, income and transport. These variables accounted for only 25 per cent of the variance in life satisfaction, but leisure activities were the strongest predictor. In a similar study Allen and Beattie (1984) looked at the predictors of community life satisfaction and again leisure activities were the strongest predictors.

A stronger method is the use of longitudinal data, which gives rather more convincing evidence of causality. Headey and Wearing (1991) studied 600 Australians at two-year intervals and found that enjoyable activities with friends did affect later subjective well-being. The strongest method of all is the use of experiments; for example Reich and Zautra (1981) found that students who had been asked to take part in either two or twelve pleasant activities for a month reported a better quality of life and degree of pleasantness than control subjects.

We look now at the effects of different aspects of leisure on well-being. The greatest effects have been found for social interaction and relationships. London, Crandall and Seals (1977) surveyed 1,297 adults and found that satisfaction with life as a whole was greater for those who had greatest satisfaction with things done with friends and with family, though this did not work for working-class or black subjects. There is extensive evidence of the benefits for happiness and mental health of 'social support', i.e. the availability of a sympathetic and helpful confidant (Veiel & Baumann, 1992). However, Rook (1987) showed that 'companionship' has an even greater effect, i.e. taking part in joint, mainly leisure, activities with other people, usually friends. Palisi (1985) surveyed adult men in London, Sydney and Los Angeles; he found that the strongest predictor of well-being was joint companionship with spouse. Companionship affected well-being at low levels of stress as well as buffering the effects of higher levels. Argyle and Lu (1990) found several factors of participation in leisure – that is activities grouped together because the same people did them; two of them were related to happiness – belonging to teams and clubs, and going to parties and dances. The five types are shown in Table 6.2 later (p. 138).

A number of theories have been offered to explain these effects, including distraction, pleasant activities, gains to self-esteem and the exchange of positive non-verbal signals.

In a later chapter we shall discuss the ideas of Csikszentmihalyi, who argues that deeply absorbing forms of serious leisure produce what he called 'flow', a state of loss of self-awareness, brought about by facing challenges with the necessary skills. This is found in the more serious and committed versions of some of the activities described so far, such as in sport, music or religion. It is presumably *not* found in TV watching, except perhaps in the case of professional TV critics. Flow could be found on holiday, but only if something serious and demanding were being done. In a study of this problem, Lu and Argyle (1994) compared two groups of adults who did or did not have such committed leisure activities. Those who did found them more stressful and challenging, but also more satisfying, and they were happier. These results are shown later in Figure 7.2 (p. 168). In the survey of leisure groups reported in Figure 4.1, it was found that great satisfaction was derived from voluntary and charity work.

It might be suggested that intrinsic leisure satisfaction would be produced by the same kinds of activity as intrinsic work satisfaction. This idea was tested by O'Brien (1981) with 301 Australian retired people. However, he did not find that leisure satisfaction was much affected by use of skills, variety of skills, or social influence, as job satisfaction is. The main predictor of leisure satisfaction here was the number of leisure activities. It is possible that this kind of intrinsic satisfaction with serious and skilled leisure activities is confined to a minority of the population.

We turn to the effects of sport on happiness. A number of studies have found that athletes, and those who engage in regular exercise, have higher scores on POMS (Profile of Mood States), i.e. are less depressed, anxious, tense, angry and confused, but are more vigorous. But Rosenberg and Chelte (1980) found little difference in life satisfaction between members of leisure groups which did and did not engage in sport. So we turn to experimental studies to settle the issue. In the last section we looked at experiments on the short-term effects of exercise on mood; similar studies have been done on a longer term, for example to study the effect of eight- to ten-week courses of running, aerobics, et cetera, two or four times a week. These have found similar positive effects, though it has been pointed out that, as experiments, they can be criticized since there is some degree of self-selection: the subjects will only do what they want to do or are prepared to do (Biddle & Mutrie, 1991). However, a number of studies have found that although sport and exercise do not affect personality traits, they do lead to increased self-esteem and to a more positive body image (Folkins & Sime, 1981). We shall see later in this chapter that exercise has a strong effect in reducing depression.

Watching TV is probably the most widespread form of leisure activity in the modern world, certainly in terms of hours spent on it, but TV is never mentioned spontaneously in these surveys as a source of happiness or joy. Robinson (1977) found that 17 per cent of an American national sample said that TV gave them 'great satisfaction', but this compares with 25 per cent for housework, 26 per cent for sports and games, and 34 per cent for religion (Table 4.3). We found that those who watch a lot are less happy, on the Oxford Happiness Inventory, than those who watch less; the reason may be that those who watch most haven't anything better to do, because they are ill, socially isolated, or simply have no leisure interests. Watching may have a positive effect for them, but they would do better to do something more active and more social. We also found that heavy

Table 4.4: Happiness and church membership

	Church leaders	Other church members	Non-church members
Married	15	15	12
Widowed	15	11	7
Single	12	8	5
65–70	18	14	10
71–79	15	12	7
80 +	13	8	6
Fully employed	18	18	17
Partly employed	16	16	13
Fully retired	15	12	7
Health (self-rated)			
Excellent	17	14	13
Good	15	14	11
Fair	17	6	8
More active in religious organizations			
than in fifties	16	13	9
Less active	14	11	7

Source: Moberg & Taves, 1965

soap opera watchers were *more* happy than those who watched them less (Figure 8.2, p. 190). We suggest later that this may be because they have acquired a new, though imaginary, social circle.

Religion was a common source of happiness in the Robinson (1977) survey. A number of surveys in Europe and the USA have found that religious people are happier. A Eurobarometer survey in 1982 found that 25 per cent of those who said they were 'a religious person' said that they were 'very happy', compared with 19 per cent of those who were not a religious person, and 16 per cent of atheists (Inglehart, 1990). The effect is particularly strong for old people. Moberg and Taves (1965) studied 1,343 elderly people in Minnesota, and found that belonging to churches was associated with greater subjective well-being. The effect was stronger the more actively people participated in church activities, and was greatest for those who were widowed, retired, or socially isolated in other ways.

Church is evidently a very important source of well-being for older people. Cutler (1976) studied the effects of belonging to seventeen different kinds of groups for old people; church was the only one to have an effect on psychological well-being, and the effect was still present after income, occupation and health had been taken into account.

Other work has confirmed the benefits of church membership for the elderly; it makes them feel less lonely, gives higher self-esteem, and greater meaning and purpose in life; the effect is greater than for any other group or organization. In my survey of leisure groups it was found that the level of social support reported was higher for churches than for any other group; 37 per cent said that their church friendships were closer than their other friendships – this is higher than for any other kind of group. The subjects here were not the elderly but students and young adults.

However, religion may produce benefits in a second way. Ellison, Gay and Glass (1989) analysed an American national survey and found that devotional intensity had a little more effect on well-being than frequency of attending religious meetings, with a number of other variables controlled; intensity was assessed from reported frequency of prayer and feeling close to God. Ellison (1993) studied 2,000 black Americans and found that both church involvement and private devotions were correlated with self-esteem; he suggests that they feel themselves to be accepted and well regarded by the other church members, and can also see themselves as God sees them, as loved and forgiven, and believe that God has a plan for them.

The leisure-based sources of life satisfaction are different at different ages. Kelly, Steinkamp and Kelly (1987) studied a sample of Americans over forty and found that from ages forty to fifty-four travel and culture were most important, from fifty-five to sixty-four social life, culture and travel, from sixty-five to seventy-four social life and travel, and from seventy-five home-based, family and church.

MENTAL HEALTH

There is a strong relation between mental health and leisure participation or satisfaction, so much so that active leisure has sometimes been regarded as part of the definition of positive mental health. Headey and Wearing (1992), in their Australian study, found high correlations between leisure satisfaction and the absence of anxiety and depression (Table 4.5).

Again we have the question of which causes which. It may be that anxious or depressed individuals are less keen to engage in leisure. Cunningham (1988) found that the induction of depressed moods in the laboratory led to lower interest in social and strenuous leisure, while positive mood induction had the opposite effect. However, when we come to examine particular forms of leisure, we shall see that some of these can have powerful effects in reducing depression and anxiety.

Coleman and Iso-Ahola (1993) argue that leisure can buffer the effects of stress on mental health, and does so in two ways. Firstly leisure generates social support, by creating companionship and new friendships. Secondly, since leisure is experienced as free and autonomous, and invites meeting challenges, it enhances feelings of personal control and mastery. We shall see how far these processes operate in particular spheres of leisure.

We shall start with the effects of friends and companionship. Stress increases the level of mental distress, but social support can prevent this happening. Williams, Ware and Donal (1981) surveyed 2,235 adults in Seattle, and found that community attachments and other ties were associated with better mental health at all levels of stress. In a study of people from the American-Chinese community in Washington, such support from friends and neighbours had as much effect as marriage (Lin et al., 1979). Palinkas, Wingard and Barrett (1990) surveyed 1,615 people over the age of sixty-five and found that depression was predicted by friends and organizations after a number of controls had been applied, while marriage had no effect. The effects for depression are clearer than those for anxiety (Brown, 1992). There is some evidence that such networks operate at all stress levels, while more intimate relations only work when there is stress (Cohen & Wills, 1985).

What appear to be benefits due to sport may really be due to social integration; Vihjalmsson and Thorlindsson (1992), in a study of 1,131 Icelandic adolescents, found that belonging to sports clubs was associated with low depression and anxiety, but that individual sport was not. The crucial factor may be 'social integration', the 'benefits

Table 4.5: Relationship of domain satisfactions with well-being and psychological distress

Domain satisfaction	Life satisfaction index	Positive affect	Anxiety	Depression
Leisure	.42	.28	− .29	− .29
Marriage	.39	.17	− .29	− .32
Work	.38	.26	− .27	− .36
Standard of living	.38	.20	− .18	− .26
Friendships	.37	.19	− .15	− .12
Sex life	.34	.17	− .19	− .33
Health	.25	.11	− .23	− .14

Source: Headey & Wearing, 1992

received from regular and sustained contacts with others: a sense of purpose and behavioral guidance, and perhaps a global sense that support is available' (Thoits, 1985). Again there is evidence that companionship is more effective than social support. Some forms of social support can have negative consequences. Nolen-Hoeksema (1987) asked subjects, 'What do you do when you are feeling depressed?' Women were more likely to say that they had a moan about it with a friend, while men engaged in physical activity with their friends and forgot about their troubles. Bolger and Eckenrode (1991) found that social integration buffered the effect of examination stress on anxiety; and they found that social contacts from leisure and religious groups were effective but that kin and work- or college-based contacts did not, perhaps because the former are seen as based on genuine affection.

How does such companionship work? We have seen that distraction may be part of the explanation. In addition the experience of cooperation is in itself a source of positive emotions, probably for evolutionary reasons (Argyle, 1991). Being chosen and accepted by others for freely chosen leisure activities is itself a source of status and satisfaction. We saw earlier that social interaction with friends is usually accompanied by the exchange of positive non-verbal signals, and the enjoyment of pleasant activities.

The effects of companionship and social support on mental health are so clear that groups and networks have been used as a form of treatment. Alcoholics Anonymous was the first of many such support groups, in which those with similar problems have regular meetings to help one another. Social workers may direct such people and others who are simply lonely to these groups, or form new ones. However, it is reported that the meetings of groups of this kind can be rather repetitive and boring, and it might be better to join a regular leisure group, where some interest could be pursued and attention directed away from the self to other people and the goals of the group. Some leisure groups, such as church house groups, provide a high level of intimacy and social support.

Membership of leisure groups may also lead to enhanced social skills; in all groups there are leaders and usually other committee members; there may be practice and training in dealing with clients in the case of voluntary work, in making speeches for political groups. Indeed this is seen by sociologists as one of the main functions of leisure groups (Sills, 1968).

Exercise, sport and fitness all correlate with good mental health. Tucker (1990) studied a sample of 4,032 adults; the greater the level of fitness the better the mental health. Other studies have found that individuals who exercise regularly are less depressed than others. In the field of sport and exercise there is clear evidence of the direction of causation, since a number of experiments have been carried out in which subjects have been given experimentally varied periods of exercise. These can be looked at as experiments on exercise as a form of therapy. Greist et al. (1979) compared the effects of running three times a week for thirty to sixty-five minutes, for ten weeks, with cognitively or behaviourally based psychotherapy, on depression in clinic patients; all three groups improved equally. In another study, Klein et al. (1985) allocated seventy-four depressed patients to twelve weeks of either group psychotherapy, meditation or running, and equated the time in contact with the therapist; at a nine-month follow-up all three groups had improved equally. In another study it was found that counselling plus running three times a week had more effect than counselling alone. This study was followed by a number of others which used improved controls, and all of which found that exercise has a strong effect on depression in patients, out-patients or in-patients, that the effect lasts for at least a year, and is as good as counselling or psychotherapy. Some of these studies found that aerobic exercise had more effect than other kinds, but other studies found there was no difference (Biddle & Mutrie, 1991).

The effects of exercise on anxiety are less clear. We have seen that there is often a short-term reduction in anxiety. Steptoe *et al.* (1988) compared a twice-a-week aerobic exercise programme over ten weeks, for anxious subjects with a non-aerobic exercise schedule, and found that the first group showed a greater reduction in anxiety and confusion. There has also been some success with treating phobic patients with exercise. However there is a much smaller body of evidence about the effects of exercise on anxiety compared with the effects on depression (Biddle & Mutrie, 1991).

These studies of the effects of exercise on mental health have led 80 per cent of American doctors to prescribe exercise for patients with depression, and 60 per cent for those with anxiety (Greist, 1984). A number of employers have introduced exercises for their staff. Falkenburg (1987) reports that the effect of such programmes has been to reduce anxiety, depression and tension, especially on exercise days, and that there has been improved work performance, as well as improvement in bodily health. Exercise has other positive effects on personality. Jasnowski and Holmes (1981) studied the effect of fifteen weeks' aerobic training, twice a week. It led to less inhibition, more imagination, greater self-assurance, being more easy-going and lower on type-A personality. A number of other studies have found that self-confidence and related dimensions are enhanced by exercise and fitness (Folkins & Sime, 1981).

Why does exercise have this positive effect on mental health? One widely held view is that aerobic exercise has a buffering effect, that it enables people to cope with stresses. A meta-analysis by Crews and Landers (1987) combined the results of thirty-four studies of this phenomenon and found that subjects who were aerobically fit did have a reduced response to stress, with an effect size of half a standard deviation. Steptoe *et al.* (1988), in the study already reported, found that the aerobically trained group improved more in self-reported coping. And Weidenfeld and colleagues (1990) trained subjects for two hours to deal with snakes, using a graduated series of tasks; this resulted in greater immune system activity, as assessed by several physiological indicators. This all confirms the ideas of Coleman and Iso-Ahola (1993) that leisure has positive effects by increasing the sense of mastery and self-determination. Another reason for the effects of exercise may be the social integration, as we saw above.

Religion is an area of leisure which also has implications for mental health. There have been many studies of the relation between church attendance or other measures of religiosity and mental health. Batson, Schoenrade and Ventis (1993) reviewed sixty-seven such studies; some showed positive results, some negative, some neutral. However, if measures of 'intrinsic religiosity' were used, i.e. going to church for devotional reasons, the relation was usually positive. There is evidence that perceived social support from God can work in a similar way, and that this is a buffering effect, helping those under stress (Maton, 1989). Williams, Larson and Buckler (1991), in a survey of 720 American adults, found that religious participation acted as a buffer against stress. People may use religion as a form of coping with stress, for example by taking part in a kind of joint problem-solving with God (Pargament et al., 1988). A study with American students found that those high in intrinsic religiosity, and those who engaged in religious coping to deal with their problems, actually became *less* depressed and anxious when experiencing uncontrollable stressful life events; the other students became more depressed and anxious (Park, Cohen & Herb, 1990). Some people find that religious beliefs help them to find meaning in very stressful events, such as the death of a child (McIntosh, Silver & Westman, 1993). Beliefs, such as in the afterlife, can have positive effects, especially for those about to go there. Religious individuals, when terminally ill, are found to be looking forward cheerfully to what is to come (Swenson, 1961).

Religion can have negative effects too. Intense forms of evangelism can be very disturbing and produce many mental patients. At the time of the Millerite revival in New England, as many as 24 per cent of mental patients were diagnosed as having 'religious excitement'; a similar diagnosis is used in Jerusalem today to describe the state of some religious visitors. It has been widely believed that joining strange and fanatical sects is bad for mental health. On the whole the opposite is the case, mainly because those who join are usually in such a poor state already, for example they are often on drugs.

However, sects like those at Waco and Jonestown have led to the deaths of many of their members.

Caltabiano (1994) asked subjects to rate eighty-three kinds of leisure for their stress-reducing properties, and found three factors, i.e. three types of leisure, which were thought to do this – outdoor and active, social, and cultural and hobby activities. We have seen that TV, music and sport can reduce tension, and that sport can buffer the effects of stress on health. We have seen that holidays reduce irritability and headaches, and that most people say that they go on holiday in order to relax. There has been a lot of research interest into American 'wilderness experiences'. Viewing videotapes of natural scenes, after subjects had seen a stressful film, led to lower heart rate, skin conductance and blood pressure than scenes of traffic or a pedestrian mall. It is widely believed that camping, canoeing and other wilderness activities are relaxing; those who go on these trips give relaxation, 'escaping the pressures of work', et cetera as the main reasons (Ulrich, Dimberg & Driver, 1991). The more active kind of course of the outward-bound type has often been found to develop greater self-confidence, and related changes in the self-image, as a result of coping successfully with the challenges provided (Easley, 1991).

HEALTH

Health can be looked at as the absence of disease, and possible benefits of leisure can be studied through the effects on rates of illness or length of life. However, we can also look at positive aspects of health, such as cardiovascular fitness, muscular strength and endurance, flexibility, the state of the bones and lack of obesity (Wankel & Berger, 1991). We can also ask people how well they feel, which is interesting and important, but may be little related to physiological health; the reason for this is that subjective health is greatly affected by neuroticism and depression, which lead people to worry about their bodies, while they may be unaware of, for example, their blood pressure (Watson & Pennebaker, 1989).

There is probably a direct link from leisure and leisure satisfaction to health. There is clearly a relation with subjective health, since leisure produces happiness and happy people think that they are in

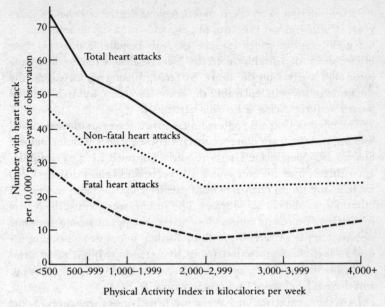

Source: Paffenbarger, Wing & Hyde, 1978

Figure 4.2: Heart attacks and physical activity

better health. Health is one of the strongest predictors of subjective well-being, especially for the elderly. Willits and Crider (1988) studied 1,650 men and women aged between fifty and fifty-five and found that health satisfaction was the strongest predictor of overall satisfaction, stronger than friends or marriage.

The clearest effects of leisure on health are from exercise. Paffenbarger *et al.* (1991) carried out some very well-controlled studies, for example of 16,936 Harvard alumni, over sixteen years. Those who took more exercise had a lower death rate from heart attacks and strokes; a small effect on cancer was not significant. The effect was greatest for taking part in sports, rather than walking or stair climbing, and the maximum effects were obtained by about thirty minutes' exercise a day (Figure 4.2).

The effect consisted of a 31 per cent reduction in deaths over the sixteen years, but only to 1.25 years' greater longevity. However, there were a number of other factors which would be associated with an active lifestyle, and taken together would give over seven extra years of life – blood pressure, obesity and smoking. Indeed, one of the main ways in which exercise gives its benefits is through these other aspects of a healthy lifestyle. Nevertheless, exercise does have some direct effect on the heart, by strengthening it, increasing the thickness of its walls, enlarging the coronary artery and reducing the heart rate (Froehlicher & Froehlicher, 1991).

The effects of exercise on cardiovascular diseases are the most well known, but there are other important consequences. Wannamethee, Shaper and Macfarlane (1993) recently followed up 7,735 middle-aged British men for nine and a half years, and found that (lack of) exercise and (high) heart rate both predicted deaths from cancer and other non-cardiovascular diseases. The authors suggest that the reason is that low heart rate reflects low stress and hence strong immune system activity. Exercise produces further widespread benefits for health, including protection from: hypertension (high blood pressure); obesity; diabetes; osteoporosis (weak bones); low back pain; and there is heightened immune function.

However, exercise can have some negative consequences. Sport which is too violent can be fatal; middle-aged men sometimes have heart attacks on squash courts, and it is type-A personalities who are likely to take squash very seriously, as a suitable outlet for their aggressive competitiveness (Robertson et al., 1988). Girls who exercise too much may become anorexic. And there are a lot of knee injuries in runners, mainly in those who are overweight and who run long distances (Biddle & Mutrie, 1991).

Lamb et al. (1988) studied 4,441 adults and found that those who engaged in the more demanding sports, and more often, were in the best state of health. However, these results could be due to 'reverse causation' – that is, those in good health feel more like taking part in sports. The same applies to the finding of Roberts et al. (1989) in a study of 4,554 individuals: those with the most active involvement in a variety of sports were more likely to be in excellent health. The only real check on this is to look at the effect of persuading people to enrol for exercise programmes. There have been many studies with students to study the effects of courses of aerobics, swimming or jogging; such courses show clear before-and-after effects on cardio-vascular measures (Williams & Getty, 1986). Industrial schemes have found that introducing exercise programmes has led to improved health, weight reduction, reduced tension, greater energy, reduced absenteeism and greater productivity (Feist & Brannon, 1988). Experiments on the introduction of more exercise in schools have had similar effects (Biddle & Mutrie, 1991).

Exercise also acts as a buffer; it is found to reduce the effects of stress on health. Kobasa, Maddi and Puccetti (1982) found that stress had no effect on illness for individuals who took a lot of exercise and who were also 'hardy', i.e. high in internal control and other personality factors. Brown (1991) found that objective, aerobically assessed, fitness buffered the effect of stress on the number of visits to the doctor, and on self-reported health. Wheeler and Frank (1988) studied a range of possible buffers for the effects of stress on physical and mental health, and found that the most important ones were leisure, exercise, a sense of competence and a sense of purpose; each of the last two can be produced by leisure. Another mechanism is via the sense of control or efficacy; Weidenfeld et al. (1990) found that training for snake phobia produced such a sense of self-efficacy, and a strengthening of the immune system.

How much exercise do people need to reap these benefits? In the Paffenbarger study, thirty minutes a day of exercise more vigorous than walking produced the maximum results, but other studies have found that less than this may be enough, and that four to five times a week of vigorous walking or the equivalent may be sufficient (Froehlicher & Froehlicher, 1991).

A second area of leisure important for health is social support and companionship. A widely repeated study was carried out by Berkman and Syme (1979), who followed up 4,725 Californians over a nine-year period. A social network index took account of marriage, contact with friends and relatives, church membership and other group memberships, so it had a strong leisure-group content. A number of other variables, including self-reported health and health behaviour, were held constant. Those with higher scores on the social network index had a lower death rate over the nine years, as is shown in Figure 4.3.

Since so many variables were held constant, it is likely that social support was a true causal factor in health. However, initial health was obtained only by self-report; a later study of House, Robbins

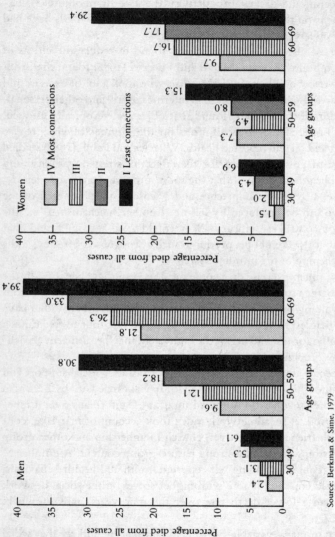

Figure 4.3: Mortality and social networks

Source: Berkman & Sime, 1979

and Metzner (1982), with 2,754 adults, used an objective medical examination, and still found the effect of social integration. Men lived longer if they were married, attended leisure groups and engaged in other forms of active leisure; women lived longer if they went to church and did not watch much TV.

A clear causal effect of social support is demonstrated by the effect of bereavement; this increases the death rate of the survivor during the first year, especially for husbands, and especially from heart attacks. The reason that women are affected less than men is probably that they have a better supportive network outside the home. Social isolation has negative effects on health; it has been suggested that one reason that type-A personalities become ill is because their aggressively competitive behaviour leads to isolation from colleagues (Syme, 1984).

The most convincing demonstration of the effects of social contacts on health comes from laboratory experiments. Experiments with animals and humans have shown that stress has less effect on heart rate, anxiety and other aspects of arousal if there is another person present – in the case of animals, a familiar animal of the same species (House, Landis & Umberson, 1988).

Family may be more important than friends as a source of social support against stress. However, the social network of friends is also important. The importance of friends for health was shown by Reis et al. (1984), who found fewer visits to the doctor for students who had contacts with their friends which were reported to be intimate, pleasant, involved self-disclosure, and especially if they were female friends.

How does social support affect health? It is partly because married people have better health behaviour, because they look after each other, and the same may apply to other supportive relationships. McClelland (1987) found that individuals with a high need for affiliation (who would form intimate relationships) had stronger immune systems, lower blood pressure and reported less illness. He also found that immune system activity could be raised experimentally by showing subjects a film about Mother Teresa, which presumably aroused prosocial and other positive social emotions. It has also been found that loneliness or social isolation lead to reduced immune system levels (Kennedy, Kiecolt-Glaser & Glaser, 1990). Social

Table 4.6: Disease and church attendance

	Once or more per week	Less than once per week	Infrequent attenders
Arteriosclerotic heart disease			
Females, death in 5 years per 1,000	8.52	18.12	2.1*
Males, deaths per year, per 1,000 (smoking, social status and water hardness held constant)	4.9	8.7	
Lung emphysema			
Deaths in 3 years per 1,000	0.74	1.70	2.3
Cirrhosis of the liver			
Deaths in 3 years per 1,000	0.21	0.82	3.9
Tuberculosis			
New cases in 5 years per 100,000	57	84	138
Trichomoniasis			
Females incidence %	12.4		17.8
Cancer of the cervix			
Females incidence %	0.64		1.88

*Unreliable, since numbers small   Source: Comstock & Partridge, 1972

support puts people in a good mood, and this may be the route to better health. It also provides resources, so that people think that they can cope with their problems.

Going to church affects health. Comstock and Partridge (1972) studied mortality rates for part of Maryland and found that those who went to church once a week or more had substantially lower death rates, especially from heart disease, emphysema and cirrhosis of the liver, as is shown in Table 4.6.

There could be a reverse causation problem here, in that those who are too ill would be less likely to get to church. However, Dwyer, Clarke and Miller (1990) compared church membership and illness rates in 3,060 American counties. There were lower rates of cancer, especially respiratory and digestive, in areas of frequent church membership. It is likely that these results are partly due to church members drinking less, smoking less, and perhaps having a plainer diet. These effects would be expected to be particularly strong for those sects with stricter rules. And it has been found that male

American Adventists live an extra four years, the females an extra two years; there are similar effects for Mormons (Jarvis & Northcott, 1987). However, Kune, Kune and Watson (1993) in Australia found that self-reported religiousness was a protective factor for cancer of the rectum and colon, with diet and drinking held very carefully constant.

The benefits of religion for heart disease could be explained by other factors in addition to the better health behaviour – the social support of the church community, including a lot of actual help, or the peace of mind and relief from stress produced by religious beliefs; we accounted for the effects of church on happiness and mental health in this way.

TV watching can scarcely be good for health, apart from some benefits from relaxation. Holidays and other aspects of leisure also provide relaxation, especially for those with stressful jobs or demanding family duties. It is found that minor symptoms are at a much lower level while people are on holiday; Rubenstein (1980) found that the levels of constipation, indigestion, headaches and insomnia were much lower. Programmes of relaxation and meditation have been introduced into some places of work, and have led to reduced absenteeism; similar courses have been introduced to help type-A personalities to relax more. Relaxation during leisure would probably have much the same effect.

SOCIAL INTEGRATION

Leisure may do a lot for the welfare of individuals, but does it do anything for society – in particular for the cohesion of groups and of the community as a whole? Many primitive societies are very cooperative, share their possessions, help one another with their farming, something which has been lost in modern society, especially in the West. This is sometimes maintained by song and dance. Something similar on a smaller scale was noticed by Homans (1951), writing about industrial working groups. He pointed out that in these groups there were a lot of games, joking and gossip during the rest periods, and that this carried over to the work; those who played games together later cooperated over the work. We carried out a study of industrial workers and found that those who were closer friends

Table 4.7: What is the attitude of the group to other relevant groups?

	%
Hostile	
Social	3
Total	1
Competitive	
Sporting	37
Musical	33
Total	17
Friendly	
Religious	95
Voluntary work	86
Dancing	80
Total	75

engaged in a lot of jokes and gossip apparently irrelevant to the work, as well as helping one another over the work (Henderson & Argyle, 1985).

We show later how in leisure groups of a variety of kinds there are very close social bonds, often closer than other friendships, and that there is a lot of acceptance of others from different classes and ages. This is partly because such groups meet the precise require-ments of the 'contact' hypothesis, that people will accept others from a different race or background if they meet under equal status, and in rewarding and intimate conditions. However, positive atti-tudes to the in-group are sometimes accompanied by negative atti-tudes to the out-group. Does this happen here? For most kinds of leisure groups it does not, as Table 4.7 shows.

With the partial exception of sports and political groups, a high degree of acceptance of out-groups was expressed. In the case of churches and voluntary work groups this is, of course, one of their central goals.

Does sport promote social integration? It is widely believed that sport is good for people in 'socializing' them, teaching them to cooperate, play fair and keep to the rules. But several sports seem to promote not only intense competition but actual violence, for example in ice hockey, and the various forms of football, especially at international level. There is sometimes increased cooperation within teams, especially when the team wins, but there can also be strong rivalries and hostility within teams, as well as between them. Perhaps the greatest contribution of sport to social cohesion is among the followers. Supporters, for example, of football teams form a very cohesive group, united in their dedication to their team, but also in their hostility to the supporters of rival teams (Wankel & Berger, 1991).

Leisure can draw families together. There is greater marital satisfaction when couples share their leisure activities. This has been found in several countries, and longitudinal studies have shown that the effect is a causal one. Parallel leisure, such as watching TV, has a weaker, though positive effect; high levels of watching can reduce direct family conflict. On the other hand, conflict over leisure in the family, such as which TV channel to watch, is very common; indeed it is the most common source of conflict in the family (Orthner & Mancini, 1991).

Does religion contribute to social cohesion? We have seen that the church is one of the strongest sources of social support and of close friendships, especially for older people. But do church members accept outsiders? They say that they do, and they do give a lot of money away to deprived groups. However, there is quite a high level of racial prejudice on the part of church members, though this is not found in the devout. Church members also have rather negative attitudes to 'sinners' of a variety of kinds, such as unmarried mothers, drug addicts and homosexuals. This is ironic, since they are supposed to love such people. The explanation may be that such out-groups are seen as not even trying to lead a good life; the contrast is enhanced and the out-groups rejected. It is also notorious how many wars, past and present, are partly based on religious differences; again this is ironic since in most religions the followers are supposed to love their enemies.

However, religion does seem to produce prosocial, altruistic behaviour. When we discuss voluntary workers later we shall see that one of the motivations is because 'It's part of my religious belief or philosophy to give help'. Churches often engage in voluntary work which they organize themselves. In an American survey 44 per cent of those who were 'highly spiritually committed' said that they were at present working among the poor, infirm or elderly (Gallup, 1984). Surveys of how much people give to charity and good causes have found that non-attenders in the USA gave about 1 per cent of their incomes, those attending once or twice a month gave 1.5 per cent, and those going weekly gave 3.8 per cent (Myers, 1993). This is partly at least because churches encourage their members to make regular contributions to the church, and American churches expect quite large contributions.

CHAPTER FIVE

Social life with friends, family and leisure groups

Social life is one of the ten kinds of leisure which are being given special attention in this book. The main findings about the other nine are brought together in Chapter 8, but social life plays such an important part in leisure that it is dealt with here, earlier and in more detail. There are two aspects of this: 'pure' sociability, where the focus is on conversation or other social interaction, and leisure which is carried out at home or with friends. There is no clear boundary between the two. Social life overlaps all the other kinds of leisure in different ways, since much leisure is done with friends, family or in groups, or is about imaginary others. And social motivation is one of the most important motivational roots of leisure as a whole.

STATISTICS

People spend quite a lot of time, every day, with members of their family, neighbours, relatives, kin and work-mates. This takes place at home, in the homes of others, in the street, at work, at pubs, clubs, bingo and other meeting places. Time-budget studies show how much time is taken up in this way. Here are some of the results of Gershuny's analysis of 1987 GHS data.

	Employed men	Non-employed women
Conversation in the home	14	26 (mins per day)
Entertaining visitors	24	45
Pubs, clubs, restaurants	22	11
Visiting friends	18	29
Discos, dances, parties	5	7
Total	83	118

Source: Gershuny & Jones, 1987

Young and Willmott (1973), in their survey of married, middle-aged adults in London, found that they spent on average 46 minutes a day with friends, 5 hours 35 minutes with people at work, and 6 hours 40 minutes with family, though much of the latter would not be leisure, for example housework and child care.

LEISURE IN THE FAMILY

The family is often said to create barriers to leisure, but there is also a positive side. Most people think that the family is an important source of leisure (79 per cent); eight out of ten of the most popular forms of leisure are done with it, and three-quarters of those which are not done alone are done in the family (Holman & Epperson, 1984). As we showed earlier, many forms of leisure are home based, and therefore connected with the family. New and very enjoyable forms of leisure are taken up which otherwise would not have been, and many new social contacts established.

The first stage of the family is courtship, and one of the main places where couples meet is at church, tennis, or other leisure settings. It is the shared leisure interest which brings them together in the first place, and provides one of the main things which they do together. As well as playing tennis, courting couples spend a great deal of time in conversation, on a wide range of increasingly intimate topics, and on increasingly intimate sexual activity. They need to be alone, and the appropriate leisure settings are long walks, meals, drinking, dancing, the cinema and, in the USA, the car.

Getting married affects leisure. Most leisure is now based in the home, and much leisure is done as a couple, rather than as individuals. We studied the distinctive activities of spouses, things which they did with each other more than with anyone else. These included several leisure activities: watching TV; chess and other indoor games; intimate conversation; going for a walk; tennis or squash (Argyle & Furnham, 1982).

We shall see later that watching TV, which is the leisure activity which now consumes more time than any other, plays a central part in family life. There are a number of common topics of conversation, some to do with running the household and therefore not really leisure, but also discussion of quite intimate personal problems, which may be met with social support or amateur psychotherapy. In addition, couples after marriage keep up those leisure activities which brought them together in the first place. And the more they share their leisure, the more successful the marriage is likely to be. Locke (1951) found that happily married couples, compared with those which ended in divorce, more often shared the following leisure activities: reading; sports; parties; music and radio.

Other studies have found that shared social life is also associated with marital satisfaction (Blood, 1972). A great deal of leisure is home based, indeed the first five of our ten categories – TV, music and radio, reading and study, social life (especially conversation with family and friends) and hobbies – while most of the other activities are often done with family, for example holidays.

Having children has a great effect on leisure, especially while there are children under age six in the home. Parents of young children report that they are no longer able to do some of the leisure activities they would like to do, and this has been seen as 'constraints on leisure'. There is certainly less free time: we showed earlier that couples with young children had on average one and a half hours less free time available for leisure per day than those without children. A whole range of activities is now impossible or done much less often: golf, tennis and most kinds of sport, most social activities, music, reading and study, travel, going to the pub or the cinema. However, couples with children do *more* of certain other leisure activities – things done with children, such as going to the park, beach, swimming pool, playground, picnics and camping. But is this leisure? Fathers see it as leisure but mothers see it as 'semi-leisure' (Horna, 1989). American studies find particular increases in camping, picnics (American style) and trips in motor caravans. Some of these outings are most suitable for children of certain ages; camping is done most when the children are between six and twelve (Cheek & Burch, 1976). Apart from these outings, there is more leisure at home, and more time spent on home-based activities, like gardening, DIY and hobbies, and there are more visits to relatives. Having children leads to more community work (Stockdale, 1987), and to more contacts with neighbours and others with children. Overall there is less travel to other locations, and less use of commercial facilities. And there is less individual leisure, more done as a family unit.

The impact of children on leisure is greater for women, and as we saw earlier, a lot of their leisure is bound up with child care, and they are less able to engage in leisure outside the home. We also saw that for the elderly and the unemployed the home is the main setting for leisure, both for active leisure, like hobbies and gardening, and for passing the time with watching TV and sitting around.

These changes have been interpreted as effects of the family life cycle, which was introduced earlier; the changes in family leisure with stages of the family fit this theory quite well (Rapoport & Rapoport, 1975). However, a difficulty with this idea now is that so many people do not live in traditional families, in particular there are many one-parent families, and others where both parents have jobs. So other important variables are the number of parents and whether they are employed. A parent who has a job will have less time for leisure, and when both have jobs there is less time still. In this case it is found that they spend *more* time reading to the children, and helping with their homework, but less time playing with them. Family life cycle is also confounded with age; for example, after the children have left home parents on the whole do not take up active sport again, but this is mainly due to age. When family life cycle has been looked at as an explanatory variable, it does work – for example there is an inverted U-shaped curve of constraint – but it accounts for quite a small percentage of the variance (Witt & Goodale, 1985) (see Figure 7.3, p. 179).

Women spend more time in the home and have more to do with the children; some husbands come home late from work and scarcely see them. It is women who hold the kinship system together, a 'female trade union', mainly through the female–female links of mother–daughter and sister–sister. They are the ones who know about birthdays and arrange meetings. In the past it was mainly men who were at work; now many women are also at work, many of them part-time. For most couples, however, it is still the case that it is the husbands who are most involved and concerned with their work-mates and careers, although in some cases it is the other way round, and there has been a lot of pressure from women to have careers which are as important as those of their partners. For women who are at home it is they who have most contact with the neighbours, and indeed a lot of their informal social life may be with the neighbours.

Inside the home husbands and wives talk a lot to one another, or they do if they are middle-class; they discuss what they have done that day, and the day's news, and they may give each other sympathetic social support. This conversation takes place during meals, while watching TV or doing housework. Working-class couples do this less; Komarowsky (1964) found in his study of American blue-collar workers and their wives that they would like to talk to each other but did not have anything to say (Argyle, 1994b).

FRIENDS AND LEISURE

Leisure is one of the main sources of friends; Willmott (1987) found that churches and other leisure groups were the next most common source of friends after work and childhood or school. Leisure groups were particularly important for middle-class people; as we shall see later, there are strong class differences in belonging to such clubs. Since we make friends with others who share common interests, it follows that work and leisure will be important sources of friends.

And leisure is what *friends* do when they are together. Argyle and Furnham (1982) found that the most characteristic activities which people did with their friends rather than with those in other relationships were: dancing; tennis; sherry parties; going to the pub; intimate conversation; walks. This was a rather middle-class sample of Oxford adults, which explains the particular choice of leisure activities here.

Friends want to be together, but they have to *do* something. What they often do is talk, but this is usually accompanied by eating or drinking something; somehow just sitting and talking is not enough. We saw earlier that employed men spent, on average, twenty-four minutes a day visiting or entertaining friends or relatives; housewives spent forty-five minutes a day. Employed men spent another eighteen minutes a day at pubs or clubs, women rather less than this.

Friends talk about a lot of things, including: sheer sociability, chat, jokes, keeping up with one another's news; gossip about other friends and acquaintances; shared interests, experiences, politics, building a shared cognitive world; and self-disclosure, seeking information and advice, seeking and giving social support (Argyle, 1991).

Friends often do other things together. Some of this is done in leisure groups to which they belong; these will be discussed below. They may go to concerts, dances, parties, or to watch sport. They may play tennis or take part in other sport or indoor games like cards and Scrabble. These games and other joint activities cannot be done alone, they need a partner or an opponent, they depend on cooperation.

Alcohol is a common feature of social life with friends. Experiments have shown that alcohol produces enhanced feelings of happiness, sociability, excitement and freedom (Larson, Csikszentmihalyi & Freeman, 1984). It leads to enhanced sociability by the reduction of inhibitions, and increased intimacy (Iversen & Iversen, 1981), although alcohol is a source of serious social problems – crime, dangerous driving, quarrels in the home and cirrhosis of the liver. Thirty-four per cent of men drink over twenty-two units of alcohol a week, and 9 per cent over fifty-one units; women drink much less (GHS, 1988).

Kin spend quite a lot of time together in working-class circles, much less for the middle class, because they live further apart. However, they come together for family gatherings, on birthdays or other occasions; they may have less in common than friends by way of shared interests, but they do have a common interest in the welfare of family members. And they are more willing than friends to provide major help, financial or otherwise, when it is needed.

Neighbours meet often informally, over the fence, in the kitchen or in the street. They discuss the local news, matters of common interest, but there is little self-disclosure. They often provide minor help, for example with pets or plants, or shopping, but not the major items which kin help with (Argyle & Henderson, 1985).

The amount of leisure time spent with friends varies greatly with age, and with the stage in the life cycle. Friendship becomes very important to children from about the age of twelve, when they feel the need for a close friend. Children visit each other's homes, then they belong to youth and sports clubs organized by adults; these provide a safe and controlled setting for their early contacts with the opposite sex. But after sixteen or seventeen they find these too strict and prefer to go to discos, pubs, or hang around shopping centres or cafés, or wherever the local teenage crowd decides to spend their spare time. 'Fast-food cafés and bus shelters are not being used to buy food or await transport. They are theatres for self-display, observation points for assessing the roles of others and of oneself, meeting grounds for establishing and maintaining solidarity with one's group' (Hendry et al., 1993). They have a great deal of leisure, and an overriding interest in the opposite sex; for this purpose they like settings which are informal, and where there is loud music. All this conversation and companionship seems to be important in the development of the self-image, becoming independent of parents, solving common problems, such as how to deal with the other sex, and acquiring social skills.

With the advent of marriage, job and children, the hours which can be spent with friends drop dramatically. In middle life friends are seen much less often; they are replaced by time spent with family and work-mates. Friendship continues to be important for those who remain single. Friends made earlier often move away, so that middle-aged people may have few friends. But in later life, after retirement, and in widowhood, they need friends again, and seek them through leisure groups (Argyle & Henderson, 1985). Concern with kin is at a low ebb during early adult life, though links with siblings are kept up. When children have grown up, they continue to be part of an important relationship.

We have seen that *work relationships* are a major source of friends, and that they may be invited home. This is particularly the case with men in middle life, for whom these relationships are very important. Most of these contacts take place at work, however, in the rest periods and during the work itself. We found that there are two main kinds of social contact at work. There is help and cooperation over the work, discussion of the work, and keeping up the flow of more or less relevant gossip. But there is also a great deal of chat, jokes, games and personal conversation which has nothing to do with the work (Argyle & Henderson, 1985).

Men and women have different kinds of friendships. Pairs of women form closer friendships; they discuss more intimate matters and give each other a lot of social support. Men are more likely to do things together, such as joint leisure, and are cautious about too much intimacy.

A number of studies have shown that middle-class people have more friends than working-class, in Britain, but that the working classes see their friends more often: an average of about three are seen a week (Willmott, 1987). They enjoy the companionship of discussing common interests, may give advice, information or social support. Middle-class friends tend to come from work and from leisure groups, as well as from childhood, school and college, so they will often be seen at work or at clubs, churches, et cetera and they are also invited home – middle-class homes have space for entertainment. Friends who are made at work or in leisure groups will be invited home, where they spend a lot of time talking about their common interests. Working-class friends are more likely to be seen at pubs, social clubs and bingo, but invite each other home less.

The setting for this informal sociability, besides the home, for middle-class people, is in sport, music or other leisure groups. Many of the working class go to the pub or club once a week or more, some every day. Pubs have traditionally been havens of male, working-class culture, though they are now changing. They provide entertainment and games, the possibility of sexual adventures, and sometimes a meeting for the criminal sub-culture. They were said to have created a 'beer-sodden working class', but they also created 'fuddled joy' (Smith, 1983).

Working-class people see more of their kin, and call on them when they need help or advice. Part of the reason for this is that working-class folk are less geographically mobile, and have more relatives living quite near; some married women see their mothers daily, for example, and give each other a lot of help with shopping or babysitting. Similarly, working-class people have more frequent contact with neighbours: 21 per cent call round for a chat daily or more often (9 per cent for classes A and B, MORI, 1982). Again the reason is partly geographical – working-class houses and apartments are closer together, while middle-class ones are further apart and separated by high walls and fences.

In the next section we shall discuss leisure groups, where friends are often found and meet one another. However, not all friendships are like this, and it is useful to think also of 'networks' of friends. A network can be plotted by asking all the people in a neighbourhood or other community who their friends are or who they see regularly. On the second criterion the network will include neighbours, kin, work-mates and acquaintances, as well as friends. There may be 'dense' parts of the network, and these are much the same as groups. Networks are important for leisure, because they stretch a long way through the community, and may lead to individuals being invited to join a leisure group or to people finding out about a leisure group via the network. Networks are a great source of information, and may be the only way of finding out where, for example, it is possible to do Greek dancing, American football, or study early weighing machines (Argyle & Henderson, 1985). This is how most people come to join leisure groups.

LEISURE GROUPS

A great deal of leisure is carried out in, and made possible by, leisure groups, such as tennis clubs, churches and voluntary-work groups. These are rather different from the other groups which have been studied by psychologists, such as industrial work groups or committees. Some of the quite dramatic differences will become clear in the course of this section. The differences are so great that the 'social psychology of groups' needs considerable revision. For example, most leisure groups form close relationships and provide a lot of social support; there is also acceptance of members of different ages or social backgrounds; they are not hostile to out-groups, but often do good works for some out-group; they are often not democratically run, and the members do not object; perhaps the most interesting fact is that members are prepared to work, unpaid, for the group.

Turning to the ten kinds of leisure which we have been following in this book, leisure groups play a central part in sport, social life, religion, voluntary work and music. There are more temporary groups in tourism; more amorphous ones among sports spectators; groups which are important but meet less often for hobbies; imaginary groups for soap-opera watchers, and perhaps for readers of novels.

Many people belong to these clubs, and there are thousands of them, for example there are 110 in Banbury (pop. 19,000) and 300 in Kingswood, Bristol (pop. 85,000) (Bishop & Hoggett, 1986). Many of them are quite small, though some churches, for example, may

Table 5.1: Members of clubs

	Professional and managerial	Clerical	Skilled	Semi-skilled and unskilled
Active members of at least one club or association	69	51	49	36
Officers or committee members	28	16	13	4

Source: Young & Willmott, 1973

Table 5.2: Friends from clubs

	AB	C1	C2	DE
Know best				
1. members of a sporting club	15	7	6	4
2. members of a club associated with a hobby or interest	12	9	7	7
3. members of a voluntary organization	4	3	2	3
4. people you meet at a local pub or club	11	11	19	21
Speak to weekly				
1. members of a sporting club	25	19	15	8
2. members of a club associated with a hobby or interest	30	23	20	15
3. members of a voluntary organization	17	12	10	9
4. people you meet at a local pub or club	33	35	39	37

Source: MORI, 1982

have several hundred members; the average size in my survey was thirty-one. In this country about half the adult population belong to at least one club; about 16 per cent of the adult population are officers or committee members; more middle-class people belong to clubs, and they are much more likely to be officers, as is shown in Table 5.1 (Young & Willmott, 1973).

Goldthorpe, Llewellyn and Payne (1987) found that their class 1 men belonged, on average, to 3.6 clubs, compared with 1.7, 1.6 and 1.5 for the three lower classes which he used. A MORI survey (1982) found that many of the people known best and seen most frequently came from a club (see Table 5.2).

It can be seen from Table 5.2 that middle-class people were more likely to belong to sporting clubs or other groups which pursued some particular interest or activity, while working-class individuals were more likely to meet at pubs and clubs, where the main activity would be drinking and talking.

Some sections of the population join clubs more than others, notably middle-aged people, middle-class people, and men. There are a lot of clubs at universities and colleges; my own college has about thirty-seven clubs (total membership of the college 1,000). According to my findings, reported in Chapter 6, extraverts join more than introverts.

Recruitment of new members is often by invitation; indeed many groups are difficult to find except via the social network. It follows that those recruited will be similar to the existing members. Where there is more than one group in a social niche, for example wives' lunch clubs, there will be competition for members, and a kind of Darwinian battle for survival between groups (Liedka, 1991).

SOCIAL RELATIONSHIPS IN LEISURE GROUPS

One of the most striking features of many leisure groups is the closeness of the relationships formed. Table 5.3 shows some of the results of my survey of several hundred leisure groups in the Oxford area. Respondents were asked how their relationships with other club members compared with their other friendships. The overall result was that 11 per cent said that the leisure-group relationships were closer, 40 per cent that they were similar, but for churches and voluntary-work groups much higher percentages said that the relationships were closer.

It is a familiar finding in the psychology of religion that many close friends go to the same church; it is interesting that voluntary groups have the same property. It is also familiar that churches are a major source of social support. Our findings on social support received are given in Figure 5.1.

Churches and voluntary groups give the most support, closely followed by 'social' groups.

Why are some leisure groups so cohesive and supportive? The explanation is not yet known, but there are some possibilities.

Table 5.3: How close are leisure group friendships?

	%
Closer than other friendships	
Religious	37
Voluntary work	29
Total	11
Very similar	
Musical	78
Social	54
Sport	41
Dancing ·	40
Total	40
Different	
Political	60
Voluntary work	43
Evening classes	43
Total	22
Less close	
Sport	40
Evening classes	37
Hobbies	33
Total	27

There may be a high level of self-disclosure, and hence of intimacy, in these groups, which would produce close relationships. Church house groups, for example, involve discussion of personal problems and beliefs. (2) There may be norms of good behaviour of various kinds, so that there is a generally high level of helpful and sympathetic behaviour in the group. (3) These groups have shared ideals for higher standards of behaviour in some way, and such shared ideals may be a powerful source of friendship.

In Chapter 8 we shall discuss the curious problem of the popularity of TV, and especially of soap operas. We shall see that part of the explanation at least lies in the 'parasocial' belief that the viewer actually knows the people in the story; that he or she actually belongs to the group, so that they have a new, though imaginary, social group to belong to.

We have seen in Chapter 4 that leisure has important benefits for

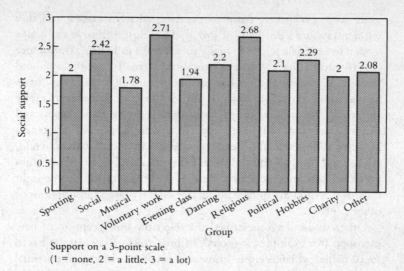

Support on a 3-point scale
(1 = none, 2 = a little, 3 = a lot)

Figure 5.1: Social support from different leisure groups

health and happiness, and that one of the main factors is the social support received during leisure. Religious individuals, for example, are on average in somewhat better health, mental and physical, and are a little happier than other people, but the main source of these benefits is to be found in the support of the religious group.

THE MEETING OF SOCIAL CLASSES IN LEISURE GROUPS

Sociologists say that one of the main 'functions' of churches and other leisure groups is to integrate different classes, races and other sections of society. How far does this happen? Every leisure group has its own niche: it attracts members with similar interests, beliefs or concerns, and usually those who live in the same neighbourhood; groups also have a certain degree of homogeneity, in that the members may be of similar age, race or class. If this homogeneity is too great, there cannot be much social integration. Warner (1963), in his studies of 'Yankee City', a small town in New England, found that many leisure groups spanned three to four of his six classes, though some were exclusively from one or two adjacent classes, and that women favoured this kind of group. The most exclusive clubs also tended to be single sex, as in many men's clubs in Britain. Bottomore (1954) studied the 125 leisure groups in a small English town and found that seventy of them had members from all three of the classes he was using, though in thirteen of these the class A members rarely appeared, thirty-one groups were drawn from two classes, and twenty-four from only one class. There were large class differences between different clubs, between Conservative and Labour clubs, cricket and football clubs, different churches and so on. Many clubs preferred new members who were of the 'right type', i.e. the right class, and would discourage unsuitable ones by large subscriptions or other expenses.

Other studies have described the selection and reception of new members (for example Hoggett & Bishop, 1985). Every group has its social niche, which is either known or becomes obvious to potential new members. Most clubs are officially open to all, except in the case of élite, exclusive ones, but not everyone is able to fit in equally well. Many members join as the result of invitation, especially in the case of voluntary groups. Churches make a point of being open, but not all succeed, and most have their social niche. After new members have joined they have to be socialized in the ways of the group, which may involve learning new skills, learning the social norms which govern life in the group, and sharing the group's values. These vary between clubs apparently doing the same thing, for example one tennis or dancing club may be more concerned with developing a high standard of performance, while another is more concerned with having a warm social atmosphere.

In an Australian study, Wilde (1974) studied the 108 associations in 'Bradstow' in New South Wales; he found that each club had its social niche, but that each had a certain spread. He distinguished six social classes, from the 'gentry' (mainly large sheep farmers) to the 'no-hopers' (see Figure 5.2). So there is quite a range of social classes in leisure groups, though there is also quite a lot of segregation. For example, only members of the top two classes in 'Bradstow' could play golf, and the only club which the no-hopers could join was for rugby league football. How much social integration is there within clubs? Do members from different classes really get to know and

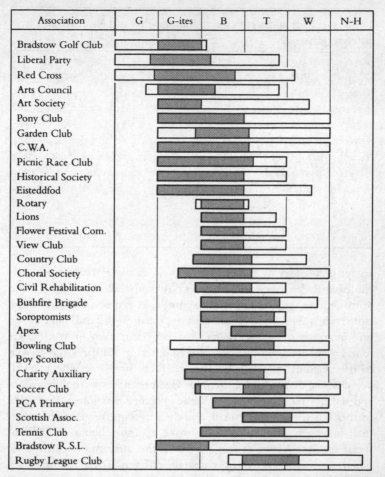

Key:
G = Gentry
G-ites = Grange-ites
B = Businessmen
T = Tradesmen
W = Workers
N-H = No-hopers

Source: Wilde, 1974

Note: The open bars show members
the shaded bars show offic

Figure 5.2: Leisure groups and social class

Table 5.4: Mutual acceptance and integration of people from different classes

	%
A lot	
Total sample	67
High	
Evening classes	84
Religious	69
Low	
Sporting	61
Social	61
None	
Social	15
Sporting	8

accept each other or do they keep their distance? Bottomore concluded that there was greater integration in clubs where there was some definite activity, like sport or music, as opposed to purely social clubs; when there is a definite activity, status in the club depends on skill at music or tennis, rather than on occupation or wealth. He found that friendship choices went to others of similar social class or to the adjacent class, but no further; there was a definite manual/non-manual divide, and sometimes vice-presidents were rather aloof and did not mix. He obtained some evidence that integration went further when clubs were small, and the meetings frequent and informal; in larger groups the clubs broke up into cliques of different social origins. Aversa (1990) described the difficulties which arose when two different yacht clubs of different social composition formed the same club.

Warner (1963) found that the majority of the clubs in Yankee ~~ty~~ were small: 54 per cent had under twenty members. In my ~~ey~~ the respondents were asked about the extent of social-class ~~tion~~, and the results are shown in Table 5.4. It can be seen ~~e~~ greatest integration was reported for churches and sport. A ~~which~~ may make for social integration is the wearing of similar ~~mes~~, as in sport, since this conceals class differences expressed by ~~erent~~ clothes.

These clubs can be the scene for a certain amount of social mobility, because membership of clubs and status in them are part of the basis of status in the broader community. Being president of the drama club does not affect your income, occupation or education, but people take account of other factors, such as who someone's friends are, or the circles in which they are accepted in the community, in deciding on their social standing. Warner (1963), in his Yankee City studies, used social reputation as the basic definition of social class. I have argued elsewhere that this is better than measures like occupation, as is the usual practice of social scientists, since this is how people actually place each other (Argyle, 1994b). Warner found a number of individuals who had been socially mobile in this way. In some cases it had been positively Machiavellian; some made friends with high-status members of a club, who were persuaded to sponsor them as members of another, higher-status club. It was particularly middle-class individuals, and members of clubs with a broad social membership, who did this. Bottomore found the same, and reported that the drama club was often used in this way, and also for finding boy- and girlfriends.

So much for the integration of social classes. Less is known about the integration of racial groups; a number of clubs are based on ethnicity, and while this would be a good source of social support, it would not make for any social integration. Age is another source of social divisions, and some leisure groups are for certain age groups, such as adolescents or old people. However, some do achieve a certain degree of mixture, which is most obvious in the case of churches, which cater for all ages and where children, adults and old people often appear to get on well together.

The 'contact hypothesis', which is used to predict how inter-racial prejudice can be reduced, holds that different groups will come to like each other and modify their prejudices, as the result of sheer contact, but only under the right conditions. These are contact where there is. equal status, while people are engaging in rewarding and cooper? activities, with some degree of intimacy, and where there is a c' of social support for this contact between the groups. These con are all to be found in leisure groups, perhaps more than in other of social contact; for this reason it would be expected that they w be one of the best settings for such a reduction of prejudice.

RELATIONS WITH OTHER GROUPS

Although there may be quite a lot of social integration *inside* clubs, do they do anything for relations with other clubs or other social groups outside the club? A traditional feature of social groups, often found, is that they have positive attitudes and beliefs about members of the in-group, but correspondingly negative attitudes and beliefs about out-groups. This is most clearly the case with different racial groups, different social classes and other groups which are in competition with one another (Hinkle & Brown, 1990). How far does this principle apply to leisure groups? To begin with, a number of groups are primarily concerned with the welfare of some out-group, as in the case of voluntary work and charity groups. Other leisure groups do a certain amount of this; churches collect money for charity and do some voluntary work. A number of other groups adopt charities, have raffles and so on, though this is quite unconnected with their main purpose, which may be sport, dancing, or social activities. In my survey I asked about attitudes to groups outside, and found that 75 per cent reported positive relations to relevant out-groups, and that there was very little evidence of negative attitudes.

We should not take these results at face value, since it is politically correct to say that you like members of other races, et cetera. In the case of churches, there is now some evidence from the USA that if indirect measures of racial attitudes are used, church members are often quite racially prejudiced (Batson, Schoenrade & Ventis, 1993). However, these measures are so indirect that there is doubt about their validity. Earlier studies had found that church members had negative attitudes to drug addicts, unmarried mothers, homosexuals and other 'sinners' (Adorno *et al.*, 1950), but this applies most to the more peripheral members. The explanation for this somewhat ironic finding is that despite the failings of church members, they may feel that they are at least trying to be good, while these outsiders obviously are not; in such cases, people are inclined to exaggerate the homogeneity of each group and exaggerate the differences between the groups (Tajfel, 1978). Indeed the great cohesion of church and voluntary-work groups, described earlier, may find its explanation in the shared confrontation with such out-groups, and the resulting generation of both self-esteem and derogation of the out-group.

Table 5.5: Is the club run democratically (i.e. elections, limited period of office, committees)?

		%
Yes		
	Voluntary work	86
	Political	80
	Music	78
	Total	42
No		
	Evening classes	81
	Dancing	56
	Sport	39
	Total	34

THE LEADERSHIP OF LEISURE GROUPS

Earlier American studies found that many voluntary organizations were not democratically run, i.e. there was not an elected committee or officers, but the club was often run by a small oligarchy, with passive followers (Sills, 1968). British studies have found that there is usually a committee, though the amount of democratic participation varies, and the leadership hierarchy often reflects the class system (Hoggett & Bishop, 1985). In the study in Australia by Wilde (1974) described earlier, the officers and committee members were usually of a higher class than the other members, as is shown in Figure 5.2. In my survey I asked about the degree of participation in leadership, with the results shown in Table 5.5.

It can be seen that 42 per cent of clubs had full democracy, and 34 per cent none at all. The least democratic were clubs engaged in evening classes, dancing and sport. We also asked, where there was little democracy, whether the members objected to this, and found that 72 per cent did not mind at all.

These are quite surprising findings. What is their explanation? There are several possibilities. (1) Being an officer, or even a committee member, takes quite a lot of time and work, which many members may not be able or prepared to put in, especially if they have full-time jobs. The central members are sometimes retired individuals or housewives, and thus able to spare the time. (2) If you don't like the way your club is run, it may be easier to join another one than to try to change things. Particularly in cities there may be a large choice of churches or tennis clubs, for example, though less choice of rarer activities, and there is much less choice in villages. (3) Clubs often have subgroups or cliques, which pursue special interests, or do things in a special way, which is another alternative to changing the whole club. (4) There is less concern with participation than at work, for example, since there are no material gains at stake; it's all for fun, and it is more fun getting on with the music or dancing than having meetings arguing about it. (5) The class system, even in Australia, is sufficiently pervasive and accepted to provide the leadership; as Lady X used to run Red Cross groups, social class suggests who should be the leaders (Argyle, 1994b). Professional people are likely to have some useful skills, rich people may help with finance, and business people may have useful social contacts. On the other hand, expertise at tennis or Scottish country dancing commands respect in these clubs, which may be the most important factor.

Leadership involves social skills. People at work often receive training in leadership skills, but this doesn't usually happen in leisure groups. Unless members have these skills already, they have to pick them up as they go somehow; indeed this has been regarded by sociologists as a useful function of leisure groups, that they provide the occasion for such skills acquisition, so that more people learn them and are able to play a fuller part in society (Sills, 1968).

The skills needed to lead leisure groups may be similar to the skills needed to lead any group, though most of the research has been done with working groups. Three basic components have repeatedly been found to be important: (1) *initiating structure*, i.e. telling people what to do, how to do it, and making sure that the group task is done; (2) *consideration*, or rewardingness, looking after the welfare of members and keeping good relations between them; (3) the *democratic-persuasive style*, leading by consulting and persuading, encouraging participation in decisions (Argyle, 1989).

However, leading leisure groups may be different from leading working groups, and may be more difficult. An obvious difference is that the leisure leader has much less power to reward or punish. He or she can deliver some rewards, but not material ones, by selecting individuals for teams or special roles, and by giving verbal approval and positive non-verbal reactions. The power to punish is almost zero, apart from leaving individuals out of the team or not giving them good parts or other roles. It is not usually possible to expel them from the club. Etzioni (1961) distinguished the kinds of leadership which can be used in different kinds of organization. In prisons and armies leaders can use punishment, in industry they can use financial rewards, and in 'moral' organizations, such as hospitals, and research and educational organizations, a leader can appeal to the followers' commitment to the goals of the organization. Leisure groups are most like this third type.

These problems have become most acute in voluntary-work groups, and in social service and medical organizations which have paid, as well as voluntary, workers. The voluntary workers are generous with their time, and motivated to help, but they treat the whole thing in a more relaxed way, indeed as a leisure activity; they have no interest in promotion, they can't be sacked, and may take little notice of the leadership hierarchy. There may be similar problems in other leisure groups who do some 'work', such as those engaged in restoring old canals or railway lines.

In some groups there can be a lot of friction between the members, as has been reported for amateur drama groups, where there is a lot of competition for good parts or to be in the centre of the stage (Stebbins, 1979). In other groups there may be rival cliques, who want to do things their way, which need to be held together. This all calls for social skills on the part of leaders.

GROUPS AND THE MOTIVATION FOR LEISURE

The study of leisure groups may help us to solve the problem of how leisure activities are motivated; why, for example, people will spend a lot of time and effort, unpaid, to do voluntary work or improve the environment.

Most leisure can't be done alone
Sport, music, dancing and many other leisure activities require the cooperation of others to do them at all. The group is needed in

several ways, not only providing the other players or performers, but also in providing coaching, standards of performance, leadership, and arranging the occasions and facilities when leisure can take place. We shall see later that for those kinds of leisure which can be done alone, like gardening, there are various kinds of social activity – such as mutual help, exhibitions or other meetings, and journals.

Social rewards

People enjoy the social interaction, as well as other aspects of leisure, such as the actual music making. As in other groups, the members spend quite a lot of time in conversation which has nothing to do with the club's activities. We saw earlier in Figure 5.1 that church and voluntary work groups provided more social support than any other kind of group, though this is certainly not the official purpose of voluntary work. In the same survey we asked about the emotional state of members at the end of a typical meeting, including the amount of joy; the results were shown in Figure 4.1. Although dancing produced the most joy, quite high levels were also reported for voluntary and charity work. This all suggests that the affiliative rewards of leisure groups may be a powerful source of motivation to do serious work. We shall see later that there are a number of different affiliative needs, including intimacy, sex, dominance and others, which may be important for different individuals.

In the study of industrial work groups it has been found that apparently irrelevant sociability has another important consequence. Those men who play games, gossip and joke during rest periods are later found to be cooperating and helping one another over the work (Homans, 1951). Affiliative motivation is operating here via the establishment and enjoyment of relationships: members turn up to work because they like the other members. In cohesive groups, people will work harder because the work is a way of enjoying interaction with the others (Argyle, 1989). Another aspect of commitment is to the other members; when strong affective bonds have been established there is enhanced motivation to the shared goals.

Social identity

We shall see later how group membership contributes to a sense of identity and self-esteem, and how this is particularly helped by public

performances and wearing special uniforms, as in musical performances. This contributes to identity via the perceptions of outsiders: an
example of the 'looking-glass self' theory of the self-image. Even
more important is being accepted by other group members as a
competent performer at whatever the group does. This will include
the required level of effective effort, for example at collecting money
or other good works, or physical effort in the case of environmental
activities. For those who are not at work, their leisure groups may be
their main source of identity, and for many who are at work, but
whose jobs are much like other jobs, leisure may be the more important source of identity and self-esteem.

People often become committed to groups or organizations; part
of this commitment is to the goals or values of the group. We quoted
Etzioni (1961) earlier, for his doctrine that in voluntary and other
groups the members can be controlled by leaders by appealing to
such shared values.

Social norms
Leisure groups, like all other kinds of group, form social norms – that
is, shared beliefs, attitudes or forms of behaviour; these are not only
shared but are also, to some extent, enforced, by the disapproval, or
eventually by the rejection, of members who fail to conform. Working
groups form norms about how the work should be done, and how
hard the members should work; sometimes groups are formed round
experienced members, who will create norms of high standards of
performance. Groups of research workers have such 'upward' norms
of numbers of publications, visits abroad, or other aspects of high
productivity. These norms are all maintained by the social pressures of
possible rejection or disapproval by other members. The same is found
in leisure groups; the more central or core members have been found
to be more motivated by the social rewards of approval by other group
members. For these central members, the group and its approval are of
greater importance than for more peripheral members (Pearce, 1993).

Social motivation

Why do people need social relationships at all? Argyle and Furnham (1983) found three main factors in satisfaction from friendship,

marriage and other relations. These were: (1) material and instrumental help; (2) emotional support; and (3) companionship. The second factor, emotional support, may be carried out in the setting of conversation, eating and drinking together. For the third factor, companionship, friends, especially same-sex friends, were a major source of satisfaction, nearly as high as spouse. Companionship is deeply rewarding because it makes possible a desired activity, such as tennis, because of the exchange of positive non-verbal signals, as was described earlier, and because cooperation as such is experienced as a basically rewarding relationship, probably for innate, evolutionary reasons (Argyle, 1991). The second factor, emotional support, may be obtained in the setting of conversation, eating and drinking together; however, Rook (1987) has found that companionship conveys greater benefits for mental health than social support does.

Is social leisure based on intrinsic motivation? As Table 8.1 will show, social life is reported to be low in challenge, though not so low as TV, low in concentration, quite low in perceived freedom, but quite high in positive affect, more than sport or eating. In terms of general challenge and activation, it is between sport and TV, though nearer to TV.

Can the pursuit and enjoyment of social leisure be accounted for in terms of 'affiliative motivation' – the need to be with people, and to establish and maintain positive affective relationships with them? Or can it be accounted for in terms of 'intimacy motivation' – the motivation to seek a warm, close and communicative exchange with others (Argyle, 1991)? I suggest that there is a whole spectrum of social motivations here, to seek a variety of different social relations, and that these may be found in different kinds of social setting. Some examples follow.

Intimate activities
A number of leisure groups engage in quite high levels of self-disclosure. T groups and encounter groups were once very popular, but disturbed some of their members, mainly because of the mutual criticism (Argyle, 1994d). Churches, and especially church house groups, are somewhat similar, in that the members often discuss quite personal problems. Counselling can be a leisure activity as in co-counselling, which goes further. Dancing, aerobics and some

kinds of sport involve removal of clothes or bodily contact. Encounter groups also used exercises involving a lot of bodily contact. All of these activities are likely to lead to close relationships.

Heterosexual activities
Some activities produce or encourage close relationships of a sexual character. Dancing is an obvious example, even when it is formalized, as in Scottish country or other kinds of folk dancing. We shall discuss the nature of this relationship in Chapter 8. Teenage party games, involving a lot of kissing or hiding in cupboards, are more overtly sexual. However, some contact between the sexes takes place in most kinds of leisure group.

Cooperation
This can occur in a number of activities. Ecological, voluntary work and charitable groups cooperate to work together for their respective goals. For example, nature conservation groups restore paths and ponds, railway groups restore bits of railway line. Choirs and orchestras cooperate to produce music, though there may also be an element of competing with other groups, or of public performances, to which we turn later. Folk-dance groups cooperate to perform dances, where there is often a heterosexual component as well. Children's games, like see-saw, are almost wholly cooperative, as are skipping games. Popular forms of individual exercise are often done in groups, though this is not strictly necessary, as with walking, swimming, cycling and jogging. All these purely cooperative activities will produce positive relationships with the other group members.

Public performances
This is the central activity for drama groups, for some choirs and orchestras, and can happen in sport and dancing. Some studies have found the great importance of public performances for amateur drama groups, and have described the high degree of excitement, together with some anxiety that is generated (Stebbins, 1979). A number of leisure groups dress up in special costumes, often very smart or impressive ones, especially for public occasions – for example, most kinds of sport, dancing, music and church.

Altruism

Helping others is a very satisfying activity, and several kinds of leisure offer opportunities to do this. It is the main purpose of voluntary and charitable work; it is often part of church life, and in many other groups there are opportunities to help new members – for example, beginners at sport or dancing. Ecological and similar groups are also doing good works. Being a loyal and helpful member of any club probably gives satisfaction of the same kind.

Competition

Tennis, chess and many other games are like this; without the other player the game is not possible and, furthermore, each player must to some extent try to win. But there is also a strong cooperative element, in that they must agree to keep to the same rules, and they must play in the same spirit, for example the same degree of seriousness or aggressiveness. There are strong social pressures to be generous to opponents and not to cheat. There is also a high degree of coordination, so that anyone observing a rally at tennis might be excused for thinking that this is a case of cooperation. We shall discuss in Chapter 8 the nature of the relationship so produced. Football, cricket and other games involve teams, where there is cooperation within the teams. Within the teams there is mutual help, division of labour and other forms of cooperation to beat the other team, producing close relations within the team, but hostile ones between the teams. Indeed, in rough games, such as football and ice hockey, there is some degree of violence between the opposing teams.

Aggression

Games such as boxing are very aggressive and yet, as in the case of tennis, the contestants have to play within the rules, and can also be observed to be coordinating their moves very closely. Rough-and-tumble play between boys may be an antecedent of such fighting games, and seems to be more cooperative than aggressive, in that it is done between friends. Fights between animals, and between young men in some subcultures, are common, and are usually interpreted as battles for status or over access to females. There is a great interest in such fights on the part of spectators too. In cock-fighting in Bali, fights are arranged between well-matched birds and large bets laid, so that pride, poise and masculinity are at stake and there is a high level of tension, a 'status bloodbath' (Geertz, 1973).

Power and dominance

We said above that most club members don't want to have to run the club, but there are those who do and who enjoy having positions of influence; they can have a career in which they may end up as influential trainers, examiners or on national committees, for example. For retired professional people this may be a matter of using their old skills. And some groups are concerned with power, as in the case of political groups and pressure groups, which want to influence other people.

An obvious objection to this emphasis on social motivation and relationships is that much leisure is carried out alone, apparently without the assistance of other people. However, I shall argue that all of these activities are partly social. Watching TV involves an imagined relationship with presenters and the characters of soap operas. Most books are about people, their personalities and relationships, and readers often identify with the characters of novels and biographies. Religious life is partly carried out in private, but here there is some kind of relationship with God. Hobbies, such as collecting things or gardening, are mostly done alone, but there are meetings with other hobbyists, exhibitions, organizations, and journals with news of members. These issues will be pursued in more detail in Chapter 8.

⍤

CHAPTER SIX

Personality and socialization

Why do some people, in their leisure time, watch TV, while others do voluntary work, or keep fit or pursue a religious life? Part of the explanation lies in their different personalities, part of it in the social influences to which they have been exposed.

PERSONALITY TRAITS

Social psychologists have been interested in how far an individual's behaviour is a function of his or her personality and how far it is due to the situation in which they find themselves. The general conclusion is that personality traits do affect behaviour, and can partly explain individual differences. We shall now look at studies which have correlated individual leisure activities with personality. And we shall be particularly interested to see exactly how strong any of these connections are. There has been a lot of research on the personalities of those individuals who take part in sport, or who engage in competitive sport or do particular kinds of sport, for example running, boxing, parachuting. There has been similar research, though less of it, on participants in other kinds of leisure.

To begin with, there is evidence that leisure activities are partly due to innate factors. Leisure interests and abilities are more strongly correlated for identical than for fraternal twins, though this effect is weaker than for inheritance of intelligence or major personality traits. In a study of 850 pairs of twins, which included reports of seventeen leisure interests, it was found that for identical twins these interests correlated .66, fraternal twins .50 (Loehlin & Nichols, 1976). In a similar study Waller et al. (1990), using 1,800 twins, found evidence for a stronger genetic factor in religious interests and attitudes. Furthermore, some major personality traits, as we shall see, are associated with participation in and ability at sports, so that there is at least a predisposition to choose these activities. The same applies to participation in sociable forms of leisure, since these correlate strongly with extraversion, which in turn is about 50 per cent innate. Musical abilities have also been found to have a partly innate basis, both from twin studies and from studies of the families of musicians (Shuter, 1968). It should be emphasized that these genetic effects are mostly quite weak; all they do is to make certain leisure activities more attractive and easier to do well.

It is possible to study personality dimensions using leisure activities as the measures of personality used. Kirkcaldy and Furnham (1991) asked 306 mature students to rate their interest in fifty leisure activities. This yielded four factors – combative (for example judo, boxing), creative/crafts (for example painting, drama), competitive (for example tennis) and board games (for example cards, Trivial Pursuit). It would be possible to describe people in terms of their scores on these four factors. There were very weak relations between these factors and established traits: for example the combative factor correlated with psychoticism, .14 for men, .11 for women, and the competitive factor correlated .18 with extraversion for men, and − .14 with neuroticism for women.

However, there are relationships between leisure and personality, though they are not very strong. A major study was carried out by Sack (1975); data on 15,000 people were analysed, comparing runners and non-runners. The runners were found to be dominant, aggressive and achievement-oriented, the non-runners to be more neurotic, anxious and introverted than the population mean. The effects of these personality variables were quite small and accounted for only 7 per cent of the variance, comparing sportsmen and non-sportsmen. Eysenck, Nias and Cox (1982) found stronger relations than this, using other personality measures, and a broader range of sports. The amount of variance in sport due to personality, however, is probably 10 per cent or less (Kirkcaldy, 1985).

It may be possible to find stronger effects by being more specific about leisure. For example, sports vary greatly: some require endurance, some special skills, others strength; some are in teams, others are done alone; some are competitive, others cooperative; some are

Table 6.1: Scores on extraversion, emotional lability and masculinity of runners, joggers and controls. From Fiegenbaum, 1981.

	Extraversion	Emotional liability	Masculinity
Runners	3.65 ± 2.06	1.40 ± 1.41	5.44 ± 1.17
Joggers	3.09 ± 2.03	1.86 ± 1.60	4.96 ± 1.34
Controls	2.46 ± 2.19	2.22 ± 2.25	4.67 ± 1.99

P (psychoticism), E (extraversion), N (neuroticism) and L (lie) scores of 500 controls and 192 Olympic athletes

	500 Controls	192 Olympians
Psychoticism	2.48 ± 2.08	3.77 ± 2.74
Extraversion	12.56 ± 4.76	14.60 ± 4.31
Neuroticism	8.40 ± 5.02	7.43 ± 4.68
Lie	7.93 ± 3.97	6.47 ± 3.83

Source: Eysenck, Nias & Cox, 1982

dangerous, others not (Furnham, 1992). Very different physiques are needed for different sports; perhaps they need different personalities too.

EXTRAVERSION

This dimension has been found to have stronger links with leisure than any other, and especially with sport. There have been many studies here, and they have all found a clear relationship between extroversion, or E, and being active in sport. For example, Feigenbaum (cited by Eysenck, Nias & Cox, 1982) found that runners scored 3.65, joggers 3.09 and controls 2.46, a difference of about half a standard deviation. The runners here were marathon runners with good times. Similar differences were found for a sample of Olympic athletes and others (see Table 6.1).

The effect of extraversion has been found in other studies and is very robust (Eysenck, Nias & Cox, 1982; Furnham, 1992). The difference is greater for team sports, and for top performers, and is greater for sports such as ice hockey, sprint running and bobsleigh, which require sudden bursts of energy. The explanation usually offered is that extraverts are at a lower level of cortical arousal, and seek higher levels of stimulation; they also have higher pain thresholds, and are less easily distracted (Howarth, 1969). Their sociability can explain their preference for team sports. The only form of intense physical activity where the performers have been found to be introverts is ballet (Bakker, 1988).

Extraversion also correlates with any leisure which is primarily sociable. Argyle and Lu (1990) carried out a factor analysis of thirty-nine leisure activities, and found five factors. Factor 3 consisted of items such as participation in team sports, social clubs and going to pubs; factor 4 consisted of activities such as going to parties, dances and debates. Extraverts enjoyed both groups of activities more, and participated in the factor-4 group more, with mean differences of .75 to .80 of a standard deviation, corresponding to a correlation of .50, or 25 per cent of the variance, rather more than the relation between E and sports (see Table 6.2).

What do introverts do in their spare time? We might expect that they would stay at home, read books and listen to music. There is some evidence for this: Nias (1977), in a study of 1,270 adults, found that interest in music correlated with introversion at .20 for males and .10 for females. Introverted men also read more crime and mystery books (.18). It was found that adolescents who spent fifteen hours a week at ballet school were more introverted than controls (Bakker, 1988). Another study found that music students were more introverted and more unsociable than controls (Marchant-Haycox & Wilson, 1992).

It is not clear what we would predict for religious activity, since this is partly a social, and partly an individual, activity. Francis (1985) carried out a number of large-scale surveys of young people and found small correlations with introversion, usually less than .15 – i.e. taking up a very small amount of variance, less than 3 per cent. We have seen that church membership gives benefits for happiness, and that these are mainly due to participation in the social side of church, and especially for those otherwise socially isolated, for example by being widowed or retired. Perhaps church is good for some individuals who can find acceptance in a community without the possession of the social skills of extraverts.

Table 6.2: Leisure factors

Items	1	2	3	4	5
28 gardening	0.75				
34 sleeping	− 0.72				
32 dressmaking/knitting	0.65				
7 card games	0.63				
1 chat with friend	− 0.62				
16 reading detective story	0.61				
4 country walk	0.56				
31 DIY	0.56				
22 pottering about the house	0.52				
21 exercise	0.51				
30 driving	0.30				
9 quiet family evening		0.56			
26 reading a newspaper		0.53			
35 walking by yourself		0.51			
29 travelling		0.51			
27 reading magazines		0.48			
17 reading non-fiction		0.47			
19 pop music		0.47			
18 music (classical/jazz)		0.47			
13 soap opera		0.30			
24 film and video			0.69		
36 social club			0.55		
3 pubs			0.52		
12 other sports			0.46		
11 team sports			0.44		
15 reading a novel				0.65	
14 TV				0.58	
2 noisy party				− 0.55	
37 long bath				0.48	
10 debates				− 0.47	
20 dancing				− 0.46	
5 meeting new people				− 0.40	
6 party games					0.68
8 jokes/funny stories					0.61
25 cinema					0.59
33 sunbathing					0.43
23 writing letters					0.31
Reliability χ	0.80	0.64	0.60	0.60	0.57
Variance explained	14.2	9.5	7.7	6.5	5.3

Source: Argyle & Lu, 1990

In Chapter 5 we argued that choice of leisure depends not only on overall sociability, as assessed by E, but also on finer divisions, such as the differences between those who prefer intimate relations and those who like to dominate, compete, or put on public performances. Later in this chapter we shall consider the social skills needed for the corresponding leisure activities.

NEUROTICISM

Here the findings are less clear. Again neuroticism (N) is a general trait, with a substantial innate basis, which correlates with many aspects of behaviour. In the Feigenbaum study cited earlier, the sportsmen were a little lower than controls, less than .25 of a standard deviation, but this has not always been found. The results are clearer for high-level performers such as members of Olympic teams, and these are nearly always found to score less on neuroticism. For example, Dowd and Innes (1981) found that highly rated squash and volleyball players in Australia were lower in neuroticism and higher in extraversion than regular but low-standard players. In different sports, low scores have been found for bobsleigh, fencing, volleyball and hang-gliding. The explanation of these findings may be that these are sports in which anxiety has to be kept under control. In a famous study of parachutists, Fenz and Epstein (1967) compared anxiety in experienced jumpers, who had done over 100 jumps, with those who had done less than five. The anxiety of the beginners increased up to the point of the jump to a heart rate of over 145 beats a minute, but that of the experienced jumpers did not get above 100; it did not increase after the point of entering the aircraft. There was a similar difference between experienced jumpers of different degrees of ability, which suggests that the difference in anxiety was at least partly due to personality rather than experience.

Anxiety, due to N, can prevent people from engaging in a variety of leisure activities. Those individuals who are high on N take much longer to learn to swim (Whiting, 1970). We saw earlier that N is lower for those who engage in frightening forms of sport. They are also likely to do badly at sports in which anxiety can disrupt performance, as is found in tennis, for example (Davies, 1989). When players are too anxious, their muscles are tight, they tremble, their attention is distracted by their worries, and their visual field contracts; when arousal rises past an optimal level, performance deteriorates for all these reasons (Gill, 1986).

Social anxiety has a similar effect on performance at sport and other kinds of leisure. For example, tennis is often played in front of large audiences, which some players find very stressful. We have seen that most forms of leisure are carried out with other people; social anxiety may make it difficult to meet strangers, to handle disagreements, or put on public performances. For example, anxiety can make it difficult for musicians to perform in public, and perhaps for this reason there is a small negative relation between N and interest in music in children (Nias, 1977).

We saw that musicians and ballet dancers were more introverted than average; they also score higher on neuroticism. The same has been found for actors and artists (Kirkcaldy, 1982; Marchant-Haycox & Wilson, 1992).

In the Francis (1985) studies of church members, small correlations with neuroticism have been found, usually as low as .10. But as we saw in Chapter 4, church membership has, on the whole, a good effect on the mental health of those who join, even for those who get caught up in very strange sects.

Argyle and Lu (1990), in a longitudinal study of causes of happiness, found that it was people higher in neuroticism who chose to do hobbies, though we also found that this benefited their happiness level. Plante and Schwartz (1990) found that hobbyists were *less* neurotic.

There is a relationship between active leisure and good mental health, partly because leisure is good for mental health. In fact the relation has such strong face validity that active participation in leisure is often taken as a criterion of mental health, and has been used to chart the recovery of patients (for example Khanna, Rajendra & Channabasavanna, 1988).

SENSATION SEEKING AND PSYCHOTICISM

In the Feigenbaum study (see Table 6.1) the Olympic performers had a high level of psychoticism, P. Male athletes are particularly high on the P dimension (Kirkcaldy, 1982). This does not mean that these people are partly mad, more that they have a kind of 'tough minded-ness' i.e. they have traits of aggressiveness, achievement motivation, assertiveness, masculinity, sensation seeking, manipulation, and insens-itivity and lack of concern for others (Kirkcaldy, 1982).

We said that extraverts seek stimulation in order to raise their level of arousal. Zuckerman (1979) located a type of personality – 'sensation seekers' – who seek very high levels of arousal, which they do by activities involving risk, high speed and sex. Comparison of those who choose different sports has found that there are high scores for parachute jumpers, white-water rafters, scuba-divers, rock-climbers, water-skiers and cavers compared with those who do hiking, running, cycling, tennis or gymnastics (Rowland, Franken & Harri-son, 1986; Zuckerman, 1979). It was found that bikers, especially those with a lot of infringements on their licences, were sensation seekers, and also aggressive, impulsive risk takers (Jackson, 1993). Individuals who preferred 'explosive', high-arousal sports to those involving endurance and planning have been found to be higher on impulsiveness and a paratelic dominance scale (Sveback & Kerr, 1989). Hehl et al. (cited by Eysenck, Nias & Cox, 1982) found, as predicted, that hang-gliders were more sexually promiscuous and self-indulgent than cyclists.

The sensation-seeking scale has been found to correlate with both E and P. Does psychoticism help in sport? It probably does: if it is extraversion which makes people interested in sport, it is the P factor which gives them the aggression and ruthlessness to win. They take bigger risks and are more likely to get injured (Wittig & Schurr, 1994). This may be because they underestimate the risks they are taking (Zuckerman, 1983).

There are some sports in which top performers say that they seek and enjoy the risks involved, as in motor racing, skiing and climbing. There are other sports in which violence is a route to success, as in ice-hockey and, of course, boxing. Some cricket bowlers have said that they enjoy injuring batsmen: 'I enjoy hitting a batsman more than getting him out. It doesn't worry me in the least to see a batsman hurt, rolling around screaming and blood on the pitch' (Eysenck, Nias & Cox, 1982).

This kind of person is found in particular positions in sports teams: Kirkcaldy (1985) found the most aggressive and tough-minded players in the offensive roles in American football; they were also more neurotic. It has been said that 'young talent have no option but to acquaint themselves with the entire repertoire of fouls which had transformed their predecessors into world-class athletes' (Kirkcaldy, 1985).

Gambling is another leisure activity which has often been found to be associated with psychoticism. There is no aggression here usually, but there is high arousal created by the high level of risk (Walker, 1992).

PHYSIQUE

There are clear relations between physique and sport. It does not need any research to realize that sumo wrestlers would not be likely to do well at pole-vaulting, or to appreciate the advantages of being over seven feet tall for basketball. Indeed there is an optimum physique for every kind of sport. It is found that high-jumpers are tall, hurdlers have long legs, sprinters are short and muscular, throwers are tall and heavy, and weightlifters and wrestlers more muscular than the rest of the population (Tanner, 1964). Furthermore, these are strong relationships, some of the strongest in the field of physique research. This may partly reflect personality since, for example, mesomorphs are more extroverted. However, it is more likely that these kinds of physique simply give an advantage for different sports.

CONCLUSION ON TRAITS

Most of the research has come from sport, and it is found that the three Eysenck dimensions correlate with interest and success in sports. The strength of this relationship is modest across the population, but is stronger for top performers, and for sports requiring intense effort or risk. Overall personality differences account for 10 per cent of the variance at most.

The extraversion dimension also correlates with taking part in and enjoying sociable forms of leisure though, as we saw earlier, social needs take a number of different forms, which predispose to different kinds of sociability. Here the contribution of personality is stronger than for sport.

Other leisure interests seem to have weaker connections with personality. Religious activity and music have both been found to have very small correlations with personality.

ABILITIES

Physical skills are needed for all sports. In some cases there is a basic minimum before you can participate at all, as in swimming and skating. In other cases it may be impossible to join a club or get a game unless you have some competence, as in tennis, squash and golf.

Ability affects success at sport in several ways. We have looked at the physique of sprinters, weightlifters and others above. It is not possible to do well with the wrong physique.

A number of separate factors of human skilled performance have been found. Fleishman and Quaintance (1984) found nineteen of them, consisting of several kinds of muscular strength, flexibility, rapid reaction time, coordination, especially of eye and hand, speed of movement and precise movement; there are tests for each of these. Most sports need strength in one part of the body or another, but weightlifting, followed by throwing the hammer and putting the shot, needs most; running needs the least (Dick, 1989). Some need great agility, as in gymnastics and diving. Some need very precise movements, as in snooker and shooting.

Some need a lot of stamina, as in marathon running or swimming long distances, while other sports need short bursts of energy, as in the 100 metres.

Similar considerations apply to some other forms of leisure, like dancing. Possessing the right skills is not in itself a feature of personality, but it does depend on capacities which are, such as coordination, strength and, in some cases, lack of anxiety.

Other kinds of leisure also require some ability in order to take part in them at all. Music is an obvious example, where again there are a number of ability factors. Several such factors have often been found, such as pitch discrimination, memory for rhythm and tunes, and perception of harmony (Shuter-Dyson, 1982).

Social skills are needed for many kinds of leisure, since they are so often done in clubs or in the company of others. These are the basic skills of being able to get on with people, which involves some capacity for conversation, to send non-verbal signals, to be rewarding, to see others' points of view and cooperate with them. For the many club members who take a turn on the committee or as an officer of the club, leadership skills are necessary, and when some performance in public is needed there are further skills of handling audiences. There are many who lack these social skills, with the result that they are likely to become isolated and lonely (Argyle, 1994d). As we shall show later, joining leisure groups may be a solution to their problems; not only are they likely to be warmly accepted, but also they may acquire some social skills through taking part in club activities, including such skills as leadership and public speaking. Social competence is associated with extraversion and assertiveness.

Social activities may involve some other skills, including some capacity to dance or play games, if this is what a group is going to do. Even appearance may be relevant. To go on the stage requires some degree of physical attractiveness, and being too fat may prevent women from going on the beach, for example.

Hobbies usually require some knowledge and manual skills, as in the cases of gardening, DIY, sewing and photography. Some gardeners seem to be very good at making things grow and are said to have 'green fingers'. These skills are learnt, in the home and later; some DIY and car-maintenance skills involving metal work may be acquired at work. Some hobbies need a lot of knowledge, such as gardening and photography. They often need a certain manual dexterity – for example, being able to pick up seedlings without killing them.

There are other leisure activities which seem to need no skills at all, such as watching TV and listening to the radio. Some require very little, like reading and walking. These forms of leisure also involve no risks and cost little or nothing. This may be part of the attraction of these activities.

SOCIALIZATION

We have seen that personality traits and abilities affect some of the leisure activities which people choose. Personality traits have a modest effect on choice of sports, a larger one on certain sports, a slightly larger effect on sociability and a very small effect on religion and music. Other areas of leisure are affected in a similar way, from no effect at all to a rather small effect. Abilities affect success, and therefore enjoyment, in sports, music and sociability. There are other kinds of leisure where abilities have no effect at all. So there are some constraints in the leisure pursuits which can be chosen, though these are small in most areas. The remaining variation in leisure choice must be due to either socialization or the choice of opportunities available – and most of the forms of leisure which we have discussed are fairly readily available. Can we explain the remaining variation in leisure choice in terms of social learning? Of course socialization is a major source of personality traits too; we are not thinking of this kind of socialization now but of more specific kinds of social influence, to become interested in tennis or archaeology, rather than becoming extraverted or assertive.

Social learning is clearly of some importance. It would be very unlikely, for example, that a person brought up in England would spend his spare time bull-fighting, chariot-racing, or sumo wrestling – these belong to other times and places; there are no facilities, training courses, or friends who will invite you along for a meeting of those clubs. At the heart of the motivation to pursue leisure interests is the question of how it becomes established, how a leisure activity becomes its own reward. This happens when the leisure interest is acquired.

First, when are leisure interests acquired? Kelly (1977) surveyed adults in a number of American towns and asked them this question. About half had started as a child and the other half when an adult. The results for all leisure interests and activities were as follows:

as a child with family	42%
as a child with friends	8%
at school	3%
as adult with family	27%
as adult with friends	10%
alone	14%

The origins of leisure varied with the activity: for example cultural interests were often started alone (29 per cent), and interpersonal activities often began with the family as an adult (39 per cent). Some sports came most from the family: swimming, walking and jogging; others, such as tennis and team sports, came more from school and friends. School was also a common source of arts and crafts, religion and interest in museums and theatre. Reading, music and hobbies mainly came from outside the family. In a British study, Nias (1985) found similarities between the leisure interests of parents and children; for example, between mother and daughter on playing a musical instrument (.40), or father and son on watching sport, but none between father and daughter on shopping and going to dances. It was found that parents encouraged children most in the interests they shared themselves. Families influence the development of leisure interests in their children in several ways. An interest in a sport may be produced by the parents playing themselves, providing models for their children, by taking them to watch matches, by giving them a football or tennis racquet, and by coaching, encouraging and rewarding their performance. It is found that support from someone in a close relationship is a common source of participation in sport. On the other hand, the over-involvement of parents applying too much pressure has been a common problem in the USA and Australia (McPherson et al., 1989).

Musical ability and interest have been found to be strongly affected by the amount of musical activity in the home. In a musical home there would be a piano and other instruments, music lessons would be arranged, and a lot of music would be played on the radio or records. Rainbow (1965) gave families points for different aspects of music in the home, of this kind; he found that the resulting score correlated .34 with a test of musical ability and .415 with interest in music. Some of this could be explained through inheritance of musical ability, but more of it would be due to social learning.

Research into the psychology of religion has found that parents are a major source of the religious attitudes and beliefs of their children. When they are of college age, there is still a correlation of the order of about .60 between the children's beliefs or attitudes and those of their parents. The relation is stronger with the views of the opposite-sex parent, those of the preferred parent, if there is a close relationship and if the children are still living at home. When a person is brought up in a household devoted to religion, or to a particular political party, he or she is very likely to come to share that outlook, for a time. They hear only one side of the question, see only certain newspapers, for example; issues are discussed in terms of certain words and concepts, so that it is almost inevitable that they will see things in the same way (Argyle & Beit-Hallahmi, 1975). They may break away later, as we shall find.

We have now seen that parents have a strong influence on the leisure activities of their children, and that a proportion of their adult leisure activities derives from early family influence. However, during adolescence a rival influence appears on the scene, the peer group, and young people often identify with, and accept, the influence of the peer group as part of the process of becoming independent of their parents. Where the two influences conflict, it has been found that the peer group most often wins in the field of leisure, especially in deviant forms of leisure such as drug taking, but parents have the greater effect on education and career. Kandel (1986), in a longitudinal study of 4,000 adolescents, found that the peer group had ten times the effect of parents on smoking marijuana, while parents had seven times as much influence as the peer group on the decision to go to college, for boys, and a smaller effect for girls.

Sport is an important part of youth culture. There are many opportunities, there are role models, and it is a sphere of achievement separate from school work. It is a world outside the family where adolescents can form close relationships, find social support and can learn leadership and other social skills (McPherson et al., 1989). Hoff and Ellis (1992) studied 400 pre-university students and found that the weighting of four sources for the internalization of leisure interests, in a statistical model, was as follows:

peers	.31
parents	.15
teachers	− .03
TV	.13

An example of peer-group influence during this period is religious conversion. A student who goes away to college and shares a house or staircase with a group who have a different set of beliefs may experience 'gradual conversion'; if he or she gets on well with the new neighbours, and spends hours talking to them, he or she will come to use their language and ideas, and by a process of gradual cognitive change will come to share their outlook, seeing the world in terms of sin and salvation, the sufferings of the proletariat and the overthrow of capitalism, or whatever. 'Sudden' conversion is different. It is a dramatic and sudden change of beliefs; it happens after a period of conflict, anxiety or guilt, when a powerful message is delivered by a preacher, offering a solution to these problems and supported by a group of peers. The peer-group influence is a most important part of the process and was said to have been the main reason for conversion in some surveys of the recently converted.

A less desirable kind of peer-group influence, from the point of view of parents, is taking drugs, which involves a special kind of social learning. People have to learn how to smoke marijuana. Becker (1963) showed that to learn to experience the desired highs, users had to learn to smoke it in the right way, to recognize the effects and connect them with the drug, and to learn to enjoy these sensations. Learning to drink alcohol is similar, but easier. Much the same may be true of other kinds of leisure too. Singing in choirs, Scottish country dancing, religion, all involve learning how to do it, and their joys cannot be appreciated until some competence has been acquired.

Peer-group influence continues throughout life. We shall see later that one of the main ways in which people become involved in voluntary work is through being invited to take part by a friend; this is probably the main way in which new members are recruited into many clubs, and hence into new leisure activities. Members of a group invite friends or acquaintances who, they think, would like it and would fit in – in other words, people like themselves. So new members already know one or more members of the group. We shall also see that keeping up the relations with friends is a continuing source of motivation to keep up the activity.

But how does peer-group influence work? It is familiar that groups have social norms, and that members who fail to conform to these are likely to be rejected. This is one of the oldest findings in social psychology (see Argyle, 1969). Very often this process goes further: when the norms become internalized, members want to conform, they really believe in the norms, and they now influence other members to conform. There are several ways in which this can happen.

Members may admire and take as models some other members of the group; they want to be like them. They have often been exposed not only to social pressure to conform, but also to various forms of argument and persuasion, so that they think about the situation differently from before. Their self-image depends in part on their membership of the group, so that it is important to them to be accepted and feel that they are members. Finally, intense shared experiences by group members can produce close attachment not only to the group, but also to its values. We shall see later that part of the motivation of voluntary workers probably comes from such experiences on training courses.

In Kelly's surveys (1977) school was said to be the origin of a number of leisure interests, from tennis to arts and crafts and theatre, for between 20 and 25 per cent of individuals, varying with the activity. At school there is educational input in the form of lessons and individual work, and support from the peer group, who are doing the same thing. Some subjects which start as education may end up as leisure, such as art and music. Pupils are introduced to several kinds of sport, singing in choirs or playing in orchestras, drama, debating, mountaineering and other activities. These interests may stick. However, it is mainly middle-class children and those who stay on after sixteen who do these things. Youth clubs, run by adults, for the local authority or voluntary organizations, are another source of leisure socialization. Hendry, Raymond and Stewart (1984) found that 60 per cent of a sample of unemployed British adolescents had kept up the school extra-curricular activities to some extent, and 75 per cent were members of youth clubs. However, after a time they move on to another stage in life, associated with conflict with parents, an increased desire for independence of adults, and an increased interest in the opposite sex. Youth clubs are now felt to be too constraining, and they prefer commercial leisure centres and amusement arcades in which to pursue other kinds of leisure, and a social life based on sex, drinking – sometimes drugs – and other near-delinquent activities (Hendry et al., 1993), while others join religious cults for a year or so.

Colleges and other places of higher education are important sources of leisure. They usually provide a great variety of leisure opportunities, so that students become aware of, and can try out, activities they have never had contact with before. Furthermore, some of these leisure possibilities may lead to later careers, as in the cases of acting and journalism, church and social work, while others are highly rewarded at college, as in the case of sports.

Kenyon and McPherson (1973) studied the socialization of sports interests in American male college athletes. The most influential sources were male friends, coaches and parents. However, this varied with different sports; teachers and coaches were more influential than peers for starting an interest in track and field, and family were important for traditional spectator sports. Peers were very important for team sports like baseball and football. Elite performers at a college, in Canada, usually had an 'idol', an admired star performer. The initial interest was often started by watching a game, or by a conversation with a committed player; TV had little effect. Something similar was found in a study of young adults by Brandenburg *et al.* (1982), who found that for social influence to occur, and a leisure interest to be adopted, certain pre-conditions were needed. These were: the opportunity to do it, in terms of access, time and money; knowledge of it – for example by seeing a display; family and peer group being favourable; and willingness to try something new, sometimes enhanced by divorce, moving house or just being bored. When such conditions were right, a key event could precipitate the new interest; this could be an invitation to take part, a gift of a piece of equipment, or accidents or mistakes leading to contact with the leisure activity. Very little 'learning' was needed. This is a kind of one-trial learning which bears fruit when people are in a receptive state. Invitation by friends, as we saw above, can work equally fast.

An important aspect of social learning, at all stages, is skill learning. This happens a lot at college, where there may be sports coaches ready to train beginners and improve performance; professional coaches are an important part of the American college scene. Sports training is directed primarily to improving skills, but is also concerned with increasing fitness, strength, speed and endurance (Dick, 1989). Where skills are important, facilities for learning them and people to teach them are needed, and these are often available at colleges, sports centres and, of course, the clubs which do the sport. We saw that there have been successful programmes in Britain to get unemployed youth interested in sport by the provision of facilities and training.

We shall see later that being good at a leisure activity results in more satisfaction from it and more participation. Bandura (1977) proposed a theory of 'self-efficacy', which says that when people think that they are good at performing a task, this acts as a kind of self-motivation to keep doing it. We shall discuss this theory later; the main evidence for it is that when individuals think that they are good at something, they enjoy it more, and are likely to participate in it more. However, this process can only work for sports, music, some hobbies or other leisure at which you can do well or badly. It is not important to watch TV well and, indeed, for many forms of leisure success or failure are not possible, which may be part of their attraction.

CONCLUSION ON SOCIALIZATION

We have seen how involvement in sports usually begins in childhood, when the main influences are parents and peers. Educational settings, especially college, provide more opportunities and coaching. There is a similar history for taking up music and, indeed, for all forms of leisure. Several forms of social influence are involved, acquiring the interest and acquiring the skills being the most important, which happen via several kinds of social influence and social learning. Two of these, recruitment by invitation and the effect of key events, are of great psychological interest, in that they work very fast and have not been noted in other areas of life. In addition, nearly half of adult leisure interests are acquired after childhood, some of them alone or by accidental contacts with the activity. Could anyone become interested in anything? Probably they could, but personality factors, and especially abilities, make some kinds of leisure both more attractive and easier to do. It seems that the power of socialization is considerably greater than that of personality.

CHAPTER SEVEN

Leisure motivation

This is an important aspect of the study of leisure because it can provide part of the explanation of why people engage in leisure activities, or particular leisure activities. Why do some people put such energy into running marathons or producing plays; why do they get so much satisfaction from it? It might be thought that this is the most important and central issue in the psychological explanation of leisure.

We saw in Chapter 5 that a great deal of leisure is connected with social motivation. However, this is not the only source of leisure, and we now turn to other motivations.

And in Chapter 6 we found that leisure activities are acquired in the course of socialization, and are partly due to personality traits. We saw how sport or other interests could become kinds of intrinsic motivation which give their own rewards.

The study of leisure motivation may contribute to the study of motivation, since most research by psychologists has been carried out in laboratory or work settings, and very little of it in connection with leisure. And leisure is an obvious field for the investigation of intrinsic motivation – people are not paid for engaging in leisure. It is possible that different kinds of motive not found in other spheres of behaviour may operate here. Knowledge of motivation may help with counselling individuals on which kinds of leisure they would enjoy most, and with the leisure needs which need to be provided by the community.

SELF-REPORTED MOTIVATION

One way to study motivation is to ask people to report what is motivating them. The trouble with this is that they may not know or may not be willing to tell. But we shall see what has been found. A number of investigators, building on each other's work, have produced gradually improved lists, based on ratings of the importance of different drives by samples of subjects, and factors analysing these ratings. Each factor consists of a number of motivation-related items which correlate together – that is, the same individuals would agree that all the items in the factor are of similar degrees of importance. Crandall (1980) produced a list of seventeen such factors, arising out of a series of previous investigations. These factors are shown in Table 7.1.

A later study was carried out in Australia by Kabanoff (1982), who was aware of Crandall's list, but also kept in mind possible comparisons with work motivation, so that all his items could apply to work as well. Table 7.2 shows his factors and the ratings of the importance of each given by a sample of adult Australians.

Both of these lists contain motives which are already familiar to psychologists. We can see that they include several forms of social motivation: seven of the seventeen factors on Crandall's list (numbers 6–12), and some others which are less familiar. Some of these motivational systems we know a lot about – that is, we know how to measure them, how they are acquired, how they are aroused and how they work. This is a great deal more than giving verbal labels to common patterns of behaviour. This is not to say that they are on any kind of official list of drives, but they are certainly on my list of motives needed to account for social behaviour (Argyle, 1994d). Other psychologists will have somewhat different lists, but they will be quite similar. However, there are several other needs which are familiar to psychologists but which do *not* appear in the lists of leisure motivations. Biological needs are never mentioned, though eating and drinking are central to many leisure activities. Sex is often not included, for example by Kabanoff, though we have seen that it is very important for adolescent leisure, and also for adult leisure groups. Concern for others is often not listed either, again not by Kabanoff, but we shall see it is of central importance for voluntary

Table 7.1: Crandall's list of motivations

1. ENJOYING NATURE, ESCAPING FROM CIVILIZATION
   To get away from civilization for a while
   To be close to nature
2. ESCAPE FROM ROUTINE AND RESPONSIBILITY
   Change from my daily routine
   To get away from the responsibilities of my everyday life
3. PHYSICAL EXERCISE
   For the exercise
   To keep me in shape
4. CREATIVITY
   To be creative
5. RELAXATION
   To relax physically
   So my mind can slow down for a while
6. SOCIAL CONTACT
   So I could do things with my companions
   To get away from other people
7. MEETING NEW PEOPLE
   To talk to new and varied people
   To build friendships with new people
8. HETEROSEXUAL CONTACT
   To be with people of the opposite sex
   To meet people of the opposite sex
9. FAMILY CONTACT
   To be away from the family for a while
   To help bring the family together more

10. RECOGNITION, STATUS
    To show others I could do it
    So others would think highly of me for doing it
11. SOCIAL POWER
    To have control over others
    To be in a position of authority
12. ALTRUISM
    To help others
13. STIMULUS SEEKING
    For the excitement
    Because of the risks involved
14. SELF-ACTUALIZATION (FEEDBACK, SELF-IMPROVEMENT, ABILITY UTILIZATION)
    Seeing the results of your efforts
    Using a variety of skills and talents
15. ACHIEVEMENT, CHALLENGE, COMPETITION
    To develop my skills and ability
    Because of the competition
    To learn what I am capable of
16. KILLING TIME, AVOIDING BOREDOM
    To keep busy
    To avoid boredom
17. INTELLECTUAL AESTHETICISM
    To use my mind
    To think about my personal values

I do this activity . . .
   (e.g.) to be creative

Never True	Slightly True	Somewhat True	Quite True	Always True

Source: Crandall, 1980

Table 7.2: Kabanoff's list of leisure needs

Leisure needs scale	Items comprising scales	Item means
1. Autonomy	Organize own projects and activities	2.78
	Do things you find personally meaningful	3.39
2. Relaxation	Relax and take it easy	3.20
	Give mind and body a rest	2.94
3. Family activity	Bring family closer together	2.81
	Enjoy family life	3.30
4. Escape from routine	Get away from responsibilities of every-day life	2.85
	Have a change from daily routine	3.12
5. Interaction	Make new friends	2.35
	Enjoy people's company	2.55
6. Stimulation	To have new and different experiences	2.66
	For excitement and stimulation	2.89
7. Skill utilization	Use skills and abilities	2.89
	Develop new skills and abilities	2.61
8. Health	Keep physically fit	2.47
	For health reasons	2.46
9. Esteem	Gain respect or admiration of others	2.11
	Show others what you're capable of	2.15
10. Challenge/competition	Be involved in a competition	1.87
	Test yourself in difficult or demanding situations	2.31
11. Leadership/social power	Organize activities of teams, groups, organizations	1.79
	To gain positions of leadership	1.48

Source: Kabanoff, 1982

and charity work. Achievement motivation is often left off, though related drives like competition or challenge can be found. Aggression is *never* mentioned; it may be wrong to classify it as a drive at all, since it is more a pattern of behaviour which is aroused by certain situations, but it may be relevant to the study of football fans, and indeed certain kinds of violent sport. So looking at motives which are already familiar to psychologists may help us to find the motivations for leisure, and suggests that we may need to add several which have not been included by leisure research workers so far. Probably these factors did not emerge from their studies because the relevant items were not included to be rated.

Should psychologists' lists of motives be revised to take account of the drives found in leisure research, but which are *not* familiar to psychologists? Two leisure needs which often come up are the need for relaxation, for example by watching TV, and the need for excitement, for example by dangerous sport. This is a little different from the specific needs listed above, and is about the desire for greater or lesser levels of arousal. Intrinsic leisure motivation, like intrinsic work motivation, covered by Kabanoff's skill utilization and Crandall's factor 14, self-actualization, et cetera, refers to the desire to carry out certain activities which are found satisfying in themselves and not because of any rewards they may provide; this will be discussed later in this chapter.

Leisure takes a lot of different forms, and we shall investigate whether further kinds of motivation need to be postulated to account for them. Research on sport motivation has come up with several factors; Dwyer (1992) found that for Canadian students the desires for fitness, fun and skill development were the strongest motives here. But Clough, Shepherd and Maughan (1989) found that for British marathon runners challenge and health/fitness were the main motives. Research on hiking, camping and American wilderness experiences produce Crandall's factor 1, enjoying nature, escaping civilization. Work on artistic forms of leisure leads to a creativity factor (Crandall's factor 4), and reading and study to Crandall's factor 17. These are far removed from familiar psychological motives, but they may be specific forms of intrinsic motivation, acquired during socialization, or they may be goals which serve other, more fundamental drives. For example, creativity may serve achievement, enjoying nature may produce relaxation. Later we shall look at the motivation for holidays, collecting, music, watching TV, and all the many forms of sport, and shall see what further goals are involved.

LEISURE AND WORK

We saw in Chapter 2 how leisure and work were not really separate for most people until the Industrial Revolution, when factory work made work a very distinctive activity and, in a sense, this created leisure as another part of life. Work was not a very pleasant part of life for most factory workers, and Engels was the first to suggest that leisure was a reaction to work, to compensate for its frustrations. At the same period most of the upper classes did very little work and devoted themselves to leisure, which presumably was not a reaction to work. Since then the hours of work have become much shorter, as has the working life, and working conditions have greatly improved. It has been shown by Kohn and Schooler (1983) how working conditions affect social relationships outside work; it seems very likely that work could affect, indeed motivate, leisure.

It has been proposed by Wilensky (1969) and Parker (1983) that this might take three possible forms, and this idea has generated much research on this topic. *Spillover* is where work activities and attitudes carry over into leisure. Parker gives the example of bingo, which 'has several features which are similar to the work experience of those who take part in it; it involves concentration and regulated patterns of physical movement, is supervised by someone else and allows breaks for refreshments'. *Compensation* is where people either do something in their leisure which is more creative and autonomous than their work, or where they react to the tensions and frustrations of work, as with the 'favoured leisure activities of pipelayers in the construction industry – fighting, drug-taking, stealing, and promiscuous sex', which 'show marked evidence of compensation for tough working conditions'. The third pattern is *neutrality*, where leisure is simply unrelated to work. Parker interviewed several hundred workers of different kinds, and found that those in banking and business were uninvolved with their work and showed the neutral pattern. Manual workers who became town councillors in their spare time showed the compensation pattern in their council work. And childcare and youth-employment officers, very involved with their work, showed the spillover pattern, though they also integrated their work and their leisure.

An important variable here, as in other studies, was that those with better jobs, or who are more educated, are more likely to show the spillover pattern, those with boring jobs the neutral one. The compensation pattern is more rare, and only applies to those with frustrating or dangerous jobs.

There have been many later studies, some with a longitudinal design which can show a causal effect of work on leisure. The spillover pattern is more common than compensation. Karasek (1979) found that over a six-year period workers whose work became more passive shifted to more passive forms of leisure. Positive correlations are usually found between the activities pursued at work and at leisure; Bishop and Ikeda (1970) found such a correlation for masculine and feminine types of work and leisure. Satisfaction with work correlates with satisfaction with leisure, though more for men than for women (Staines, 1980). However, this spillover may not be due to motivation but may be the result of similar skills or abilities, or personality traits affecting both, or social pressures about which kinds of leisure are appropriate (Staines, 1980). The kind of voluntary work that people do is an example of skill spillover: middle-class people tend to do committee work, teaching, and advice giving, while manual workers do transport, repairs and domestic work. Hobbies, which often involve the use of manual skills, look like another case of spillover; however, it turns out that it is not skilled manual workers but classes 1 and 2 who engage most in such hobbies.

Kirkcaldy and Cooper (1992) found that there was more spillover for women than men: those women who played competitive ball games were more competitive at work, and stronger in work ethic and achievement motivation; the same was true for men but the effect was weaker.

The main exception, and the main example of compensation, is for physical effort and for time, which are inversely related for work and leisure, and for work and family. And there are certain special occupations, such as those distant water fishermen (Tunstall, 1962), construction workers and, probably, miners, whose work is dangerous or stressful, and those whose work is unfulfilling and does not allow them to use their skills.

However, several studies have found that the relation between work and leisure is rather weak, so that the neutral pattern is actually the main one, and leisure is not derived from work at all. It is found particularly, as we saw, in bank clerks and similar clerical workers, whose work is neither fulfilling nor particularly frustrating. Work may be a factor in leisure but other factors are more important.

A further problem for the work–leisure hypothesis is that a lot of people are not working. For housewives leisure and work are not separated, and they have a lot of semi-leisure, like taking children swimming. As we saw before, their problem is not having enough real leisure time. The unemployed have a lot of free time but do not have much real leisure because they can't afford it, are under stress, or feel that leisure is only possible if there is also work.

Not everyone has a clear separation between work and leisure. We saw that, for different reasons, social workers and housewives do not; nor do writers and artists, musicians, academics and some businessmen, who may have no particular hours of work, a playful attitude to work and a serious attitude to leisure; many of their friends are drawn from work. They are very fortunate, but the working conditions of most workers do not allow this. However, ideal working conditions contain some of the features of leisure, such as autonomy and intrinsic motivation. The most satisfying forms of leisure have some of the features of work: they involve varied and meaningful activities, use of skills, serious commitment to goals and membership of cohesive working groups (Argyle, 1989).

INTRINSIC MOTIVATION

Intrinsic motivation and work

Work is nearly always paid or leads to other extrinsic rewards; indeed this is usually part of the definition of work. Leisure, also by definition, is not so rewarded, so that its motivation must take a different form. By intrinsic motivation is meant the motivation to engage in an activity for its own sake. This happens with animals: rats will run on activity wheels, monkeys will solve problems or manipulate equipment, for no reward. Children will play for hours for no external reward; they do not need to be rewarded with sweets for riding their tricycles. Indeed if they are given external rewards for playing at something, the motivation to do this for its own sake declines (Barnett, 1980).

There has been a lot of interest in intrinsic motivation at work. Some people carry on working, unpaid, after they have retired, others work at weekends. And some leisure looks very similar to work, indeed may consist of identical activities, as in the cases of

Table 7.3: The five job characteristics which motivate work performance

Job characteristics	Psychological states	Outcomes
1. Skill variety 2. Task variety 3. Task significance	Meaningfulness of work	High internal motivation, quality of work, satisfaction, reduced absenteeism and turnover
4. Autonomy	Responsibility for work outcomes	
5. Feedback	Knowledge of results	

gardening, voluntary work and the restoration of old railways and canals. An influential theory of such intrinsic motivation is due to Hackman and Oldham (1976), who proposed that there are five features of jobs which make them intrinsically rewarding. Work is more meaningful if it has the characteristics of skill and task variety and task significance; the other two features are autonomy and feedback, giving knowledge of results. When work has these features, there is increased motivation and more satisfaction (see Table 7.3).

There is some evidence that these job characteristics do lead to increased motivation, especially in those individuals who have 'growth need strength', people who want to accomplish something, learn and develop themselves. There is better evidence for the effect on job satisfaction, and this model has been used successfully to redesign jobs to make them more rewarding (Argyle, 1989).

Knowledge of results, i.e. information that one is doing well, has been found to be particularly effective. This may reflect the operation of the need for achievement. This motive system has been shown to be important at work, especially for entrepreneurs, scientists, sales personnel and junior managers. At higher levels of management the need for power is more important (McClelland & Boyatzis, 1982). Herzberg, Mauser and Snyderman (1959) found that the times when workers felt exceptionally good about their work were mainly connected to achievement and recognition.

However, if rewards such as recognition are involved this is not quite intrinsic motivation. And only a minority of workers value these non-economic rewards: managers and professional people may be like this, but most manual workers are not, and it has been estimated that only about 15 per cent of workers are so motivated (Hackman, 1977).

There are other ways in which intrinsic motivation may be created, apart from the nature of the work itself. One way is the setting of goals, especially where a whole group agrees to aim for some goal. Another is commitment to the organization, which may be due to a kind of affective attachment, after a long period of membership, especially a long period of participating in decisions and taking responsibility. Then there are many people who want to work for its own sake, who are imbued with the Protestant work ethic; such individuals value work and effort rather than relaxation and pleasure; they work hard, often unpaid; some become workaholics (Argyle, 1989).

Intrinsic motivation and leisure

There has been much experimental laboratory research on intrinsic motivation, often with children. A classic finding is that external rewards can weaken the motivation to do something which is enjoyed for its own sake, because this changes the perceived locus of causation – the subjects now think that they are doing it because they are paid to do it, not because they want to (Deci & Ryan, 1991). We showed earlier how certain kinds of socialization experience can produce new interests and intrinsic motivations. When this happens the new goal becomes part of the personality and is freely chosen. There is a sense in which all leisure is like this, except that we can account for some leisure motivation in terms of social or other familiar forms of motivation, which are not external rewards in the same way as food and money.

Intrinsic motivation has been used in leisure research to refer to people doing something simply for the immediate pleasure of doing so. Several methods have been used to assess the presence of intrinsic motivation during leisure. Neulinger (1981) used the 'What am I doing?' (WAID) scale, in which free responses to describe thirty-minute periods are scored for the amount of intrinsic motivation. Höltzman and Black (1989) analysed four studies, with a total of 480 subjects, using this scale and found that intrinsic motivation was somewhat higher for women, older and more educated people. Csik-szentmihalyi devised a similar procedure, in which subjects rate how strongly they want to do what they are doing and how much they would rather be doing something else. In later studies only the second question was asked, with a ten-point scale of response. Mannell, Zuzanek and Larson (1988) used a slightly different question: 'Did you choose this activity for your immediate enjoyment, or for its own sake, or for your long-term benefit?' In these studies subjects were given an electronic pager and contacted eight times a day for a week, providing a sample of fifty-six periods of work and leisure (Graef, Csikszentmihalyi & Gianinno, 1983).

The same authors investigated intrinsic motivation with time-sampled data from 107 male workers. It was found that intrinsic motivation was reported about 22 per cent of the time, but much more during leisure than work, while extrinsic motivation was more common at work (see Figure 7.1).

The main interest of this study is in showing that there can be intrinsic motivation at work and extrinsic motivation during leisure. Subjects with higher levels of intrinsic motivation were found to be happier, less tense and less bored.

Several studies have found a high correlation between reported intrinsic motivation and positive affect, and between both and parti-cipation. For example, Losier, Bourque and Vallerand (1993), with a sample of elderly Canadians, found correlations of about .50 between intrinsic motivation and both positive affect and participation. They found similar correlations with self-determined extrinsic motivation, such as doing something 'for my own good'.

Is intrinsic motivation produced by features of the activity in the same way that it is at work? One possible factor is competence at the activity. Spreitzer and Snyder (1976) found that perceived ability was the strongest predictor of leisure activities for adults. We shall pursue this topic further later.

Some of the leading leisure researchers, such as Neulinger (1981) and Iso-Ahola (1980), have emphasized the importance of perceived freedom from constraints as part of the meaning of leisure, and as a source of intrinsic motivation. Iso-Ahola carried out an experiment in which subjects rated a number of situations for whether they would be experienced as leisure, and perceived freedom was found

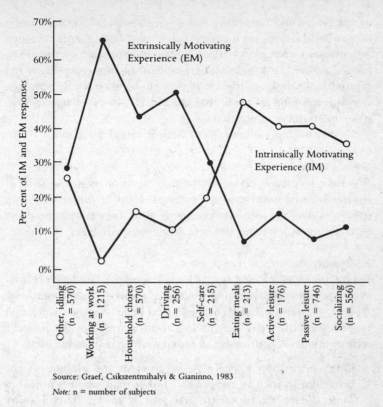

Source: Graef, Csikszentmihalyi & Gianinno, 1983

Note: n = number of subjects

Figure 7.1: Intrinsic motivation and leisure

to be an important variable. In the same way, we saw earlier that intrinsic work motivation was affected by autonomy. Kelly (1983) showed that the amount of free time which is perceived as free is as low as 45 per cent because of the many obligations to other people.

Csikszentmjhalyi (1975) tried to find out how leisure was motivated by interviewing 173 individuals engaged in serious forms of leisure – rock-climbers, composers, dancers, chess players and basketball players. The reasons which they gave for why they enjoyed this leisure were: enjoyment of the experience and use of skills; the activity itself – the pattern, the action, the world it provides; development of personal skills. These were the elements which Csikszentmihalyi came to believe were the main sources of intrinsic motivation, though other reasons were given – friendship and relaxation (high for climbers and dancers), risk and chance, problem solving, competition and creativity. If people are asked why they choose their leisure activities, the most common answer is, 'Because I like it', or a similar statement, reflecting intrinsic motivation.

So what are the sources of intrinsic motivation in leisure?

Social motivation

We have seen how pervasive social motivation is in the field of leisure. Is social motivation an 'external' form of motivation? In a sense it is, since the social motivation of sport, for example, produces behaviour which is rather different from basic sociability.

Basic bodily pleasures

Eating and drinking, and sex, as leisure activities, need no explanation. Sport may provide other bodily pleasures – take swimming. Apter (1982), from a different theoretical point of view, which will be presented later, gave swimming as an example of the paratelic state of mind, i.e. performing an activity which is an end in itself:

> One's orientation is likely to be towards the pleasure of the behaviour in itself in the present, rather than towards a goal in some distant future. What one asks is to be able to enjoy performing some particular skill or skills. Furthermore there is the pleasure that derives from the various sensations of diving and swimming: the feeling of release as one dives, the cool shock of hitting the water, the murky other-worldliness beneath the water, the sudden burst of noise and colour as one surfaces, and the sensation of being buoyed up. Then, as one swims, one experiences the feeling of surging movement, of water streaming over one's skin, and the impression of temporary escape from gravity and freedom to move in any direction. All these may be intense experiences of exactly the kind which are relished in the paratelic state (Apter, 1982, p. 99).

However, many people do not find swimming so rewarding, and may prefer horse riding or skiing. Competence is probably part of the answer – you won't enjoy swimming much unless you can swim, and will enjoy it more if you can do it reasonably well.

Social learning

We showed in Chapter 6 how many leisure interests are acquired in childhood, and others from school, college or peer groups. And we showed how new drives and interests are acquired. What is learnt is partly skills, partly knowledge and a new way of looking at things, and partly affective associations. The last may be the most important, and leads to people looking with pleasure at footballs, swimming pools, dance floors or whatever is associated with their leisure.

CSIKSZENTMIHALYI AND THE CONCEPT OF FLOW

From studying rock-climbers, serious chess players and others, Csikszentmihalyi (1975) found that when they were engaged in these activities they attained a deeply satisfying quality of subjective experience, an intense and highly agreeable state of 'absorption' and loss of self-awareness, a kind of peak experience. He called this 'flow' and believed that it was the reward they were seeking, that it was the basis for their intrinsic motivation. In some early studies subjects were asked how far they had the following kind of experience, a description of flow:

> When I stop to think about it I realize that an important part of this state of mind is enjoyment. I get so involved in what I am doing, I almost forget about time. When I experience this state of mind, I really feel free from boredom and worry. I feel like I am being challenged or that I am very much in control of my action and my world. I feel like I am growing and using my best talents and skills; I am master of my situation. (Allison & Duncan, 1988).

He theorized that flow is brought about by a balance between challenges and skills. It is argued that there are four possible combinations: if both challenges and skills are high, there is flow; if challenge is too high, there is anxiety; if too low, boredom; and if both are low, there is apathy (Csikszentmihalyi & Csikszentmihalyi, 1988). Flow was later measured by the combination of high reported

challenges and skills, each rated on ten-point scales, and it was predicted that a number of positive consequences would follow.

A number of studies have used the 'experience sampling' method
with an electronic pager. They found that, during periods of flow,
subjects reported higher levels of concentration, creativity, control
and activation. There were also differences in the amount of flow in
different activities. There was much more flow at work than at
leisure – three times as much. And the greatest flow for leisure
activities was for art and hobbies, socializing, sport and games, and
reading; the lowest was for TV watching, eating, resting and napping
(Massimi & Carli, 1988).

However, the relation between flow and positive affect is not so
clear. Happy individuals report being in flow more of the time, but
flow-giving situations are not all the most enjoyable. Carli, Delle
Fave and Massimi (1988) found that, for samples of American and
Italian teenagers, happiness and satisfaction were greatest for 'control',
i.e. when skills were rated as greater than challenges, and the same
was found with English YTS students (Haworth, 1993). This should
produce boredom, according to flow theory. Most people in their
leisure, when they can do what they like, choose less demanding
activities much of the time, such as watching TV, though the not
very challenging activities of reading, driving and socializing were
sources of flow for some.

Csikszentmihalyi thought that intrinsic motivation would be a
source of flow, intrinsic motivation being assessed by the reported
wish to be doing the current activity and not something different.

Mannell, Zuzanek and Larson (1988) studied ninety-two retired
adults to test the hypothesis that both the freedom to choose activity
and intrinsic motivation are causes of flow experience. Freedom did
function as predicted, but intrinsic motivation did not. It was extrinsic
motivation that produced more flow. It was suggested that work
provides greater challenges and that it is only serious leisure, where
commitment is important, that can produce comparable levels of
flow and satisfaction.

However, the artists, rock-climbers and others who Csikszentmihalyi first studied *were* engaging in demanding activities, where skills
are needed to cope with challenges. This produces intense positive
experiences of a special kind, but it does not motivate everyone, just

as challenging work only motivates workers with 'growth need strength'. Csikszentmihalyi found that the percentage of time spent in reported flow varied greatly between individuals. Some are able to find challenges and mobilize the skills to deal with them more of the time, thus avoiding both boredom and anxiety. He called these 'autotelic' personalities.

We carried out a study inspired by the theory, in which we compared those who did and did not have a seriously committed leisure activity. Those who did reported that their leisure was more stressful, challenging and absorbing; their leisure satisfaction was greater and they were happier (see Figure 7.2).

SEEKING HIGH AND LOW AROUSAL

We saw earlier that lists of self-reported motives included both relaxation and excitement, Crandall's numbers 5 and 13, for example. And we have just seen that, although people do seek challenging forms of leisure some of the time, they are more likely to seek relaxing, undemanding leisure activities.

A need for low arousal has usually been part of motivational theory, where it is assumed that people spend their time trying to satisfy drives and that this will result in a condition of satisfaction and low arousal. A need for high arousal on the other hand has been postulated because many people take part in exciting activities like dangerous sports, and listening to loud music, which seem to involve the pursuit of high arousal. The need for high arousal was incorporated into Zuckerman's Sensation Seeking Scale (1979). This has items about seeking new and varied experiences, including sex and high speeds. This scale was administered to a number of special groups, and it was found those who did parachuting or scuba-diving had higher scores than other people. High scorers also liked to gamble and, when they did so, took bigger risks and made larger bets. They also said they would be interested in travel to exotic places, even if this was risky.

Ewert and Hollenhurst (1989) studied people who engaged in risky outdoor sports, like white-water rafting, rock-climbing, caving and hang-gliding. They saw this kind of sport as an example of seeking for flow experiences, by matching increasing challenges and

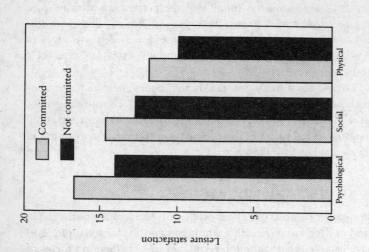

Figure 7.2a: Effects of having committed leisure on perception of leisure life

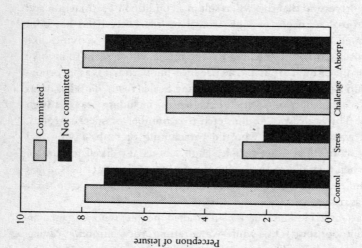

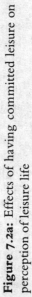

Figure 7.2b: Effects of having committed leisure on leisure satisfaction

danger with increasing skill. They predicted that, as participants became more experienced, higher levels of risk would be taken, levels of participation would increase, and participants would become more internally controlled and go solo more. All these predictions were confirmed, but there was no shift in motivation. However, McIntyre (1992), in a similar study of 148 climbers, did not find the expected increase in intrinsic motivation.

The quest for excitement has been given as the explanation for the behaviour of football hooligans, vandalism, racing stolen cars, and other aspects of juvenile delinquency. Boredom is common during leisure time and often leads to anti-social behaviour. People are often bored at work too, resulting in low job satisfaction, sometimes playing elaborate games and jokes (Argyle, 1989).

However, people often seek relaxation and rest during leisure, the very opposite of excitement. This is one explanation of the many hours most people spend watching TV. As many as 60 per cent say they watch for 'entertainment or relaxation' and 41 per cent 'because it is a pleasant way to spend an evening' (Comstock et al., 1978). Csikszentmihalyi and Kubey (1981) found that, while they were watching, people were relaxed and more drowsy, weak and passive than for any other activity, such as reading, eating, talking, other leisure or work. Holidays are another occasion for relaxing; in one large survey the most common reason given for going on holiday was the need to relax, though the women wanted also to indulge themselves; the workaholics wanted to get back to work (Rubenstein, 1980).

How can we reconcile this evidence that people want both to be excited and to relax? One solution is to suppose that there is an optimum degree of arousal, so that if arousal is too low, individuals seek to increase it, and if it is too high, to reduce it. Level of arousal varies from time to time, as Bryant and Zillman (1984) found in their study, in which subjects who had been given a stressful puzzle to solve chose a relaxing rather than an exciting TV film, while those subjects who had been doing a very boring task chose the exciting film. The preferred level of arousal is different for different people; an important theory of personality, for which there is a lot of empirical support, says that extraverts are normally at a low level of arousal and this is why they tend to choose physical activities and social events in their free time, while introverts are at a higher level of arousal and seek quieter activities (Eysenck, 1976).

However, there is more to be said about the 'reversals', whereby the same person can switch from seeking excitement to seeking relaxation. Apter (1982) has put forward a very interesting theory to account for this phenomenon. He supposes that there is not one homoeostatic equilibrium condition, but two, corresponding to high and low states of arousal, and to different motivations. When people are in a 'telic' state, they are oriented towards and pursuing serious goals, frequently plan ahead, and avoid high arousal; the end product of this state is attainment of the goal and a state of relaxation. When they are in a 'paratelic' condition, however, they are in a state which is playful, spontaneous, pursues goals only in so far as they add to immediate pleasure, and do things for their own sake, because they are fun or otherwise enjoyable; this corresponds to intrinsic motivation. The subjective experience of high and low arousal is quite different in the two states. High arousal is experienced as stress when in a telic state but as excitement when paratelic. Low arousal is experienced as relaxation for the telic but boredom for the paratelic mode. Apter thinks that his theory does better than optimum arousal theory, since the same state of arousal may lead to attempts to increase or reduce it, depending on which mode someone is in. There are often reversals where people shift from one state to the other, and this may happen because of changes in the environment, because of frustration or through satiation of the original state. So someone might become bored with watching TV and want to get on with some work, or vice versa. It is suggested that the enjoyment of dangerous sports can be accounted for by such a shift from high arousal being experienced as anxiety in the telic mode to excitement in the paratelic mode. But why is there such a shift, and can it be induced deliberately? When in the paratelic mode, more things are found funny, and presumably most leisure would be associated with this mode. According to reversal theory, leisure is a playful state of mind.

Individual differences on the telic–paratelic dimension can be measured by a questionnaire, the 'Telic Dominance Scale'. The paratelic end of the scale correlates with extraversion, as might be expected, and with a greater enjoyment of humour and of sex; it has some physiological correlates, such as lower heart and breathing rates under stress (Apter, Fontana & Murgatroyd, 1985). This theory has received a certain amount of support from laboratory experiments. However, I don't believe that people seek either high or low arousal as such, but that they seek particular kinds of arousal. Those who go to jazz festivals don't go just because of the loud music, but because of the particular kind of loud music, and many other features of the situation. Those who go to concerts in the Albert Hall don't go because the music is fairly loud, but because they like the states of mind produced by Beethoven, Mozart and other composers. Those who go to parties and dances where there is loud fun are seeking a particular form of sociable excitement. The same applies to relaxation. No one chooses to sit in a dark, locked room for their relaxing leisure, and they don't want to be asleep either. They seek forms of enjoyable, low-demand activities, like watching TV, looking at the sea and reading an easy book. A more general theory might be that people seek certain subjective states, including some high-arousal ones if they are young extraverts or sensation seekers, some low-arousal ones if they are another kind of person or need to rest after work, and probably some mid-arousal ones as well. Examples of popular mid-arousal leisure are going for a walk and talking to friends.

A further problem for the theory is that it can't account for the attraction of serious leisure, such as fairly serious sport, hobbies or voluntary work. These appear to be a combination of the telic and the paratelic modes.

SELF-IMAGE AND SELF-PRESENTATION

The development of a self-image, or identity, which is coherent, distinctive and positive, is regarded by psychologists as a major 'task' of adolescence; sustaining this identity is important later too. It is particularly important at certain periods of life: adolescence; middle age, when family commitments have diminished; and perhaps after retirement, when work identity has been lost. Maintaining this identity in the eyes of others leads to a certain amount of 'self-presentation', such as wearing special clothes. The self-image is often based primarily on work, especially for men, and for men with interesting jobs; for women it may be based more on their family (Kuhn & McPartland, 1954). However, for many people work is not their central life interest, because their work is boring or anonymous or because they are unemployed, young or retired. For all these people, identity may be sought more in leisure activities. Sociologists have argued that in modern mass society there is a need to form a self-image from more 'vivid and emotionally gripping attachments' than are readily available.

Leisure can certainly provide such identities. Haggard and Williams (1992) found that a number of distinctive attributes were thought to belong to guitarists, backpackers, chess players and others (see Table 7.4), and that students who belonged to such groups desired to possess those characteristics – based on ratings of 'it is important for me to become more . . .'

Identity formation through leisure is very clear in the case of serious amateurs. Stebbins (1979) studied devoted amateurs involved in theatricals, archaeology and baseball. For these people their leisure was a disciplined and demanding activity, with a high level of skill, which had become the centre of their lives; many could not imagine life without it. Their leisure led to 'the development and enrichment of self-concepts and actually becoming more of a person' (Kelly, 1983). Leisure creates an arena for developing the self-image by trying new identities and memberships, without commitment, by acquiring new skills or distinctive styles of performance.

Leisure is one of the most important sources of identity. Shamir (1992) asked 900 Israeli students to rate the relative importance of leisure as a source of identity compared to other sources. Leisure was particularly important for several kinds of serious leisure – politics, voluntary work, theatre and music, some sports, religion and education. The effect on identity was greater if there was social commitment, investment of time and money, if effort and skill were required and, above all, when it was enjoyed. However, students would not have become fully committed to a work identity yet.

Serious amateurs become very highly motivated, and capable of great efforts. Stebbins (1992) describes this process in connection with barbershop singing. Yair (1992) found that marathon runners who saw themselves as serious were more deeply committed, more determined to win and more willing to pay the necessary costs than

Table 7.4: Leisure identity images clustering with each of eight leisure activities

KAYAKER
  Adventurous
  Fun
  Fun loving
  Likes scenic beauty
  Loves fresh air
  Naturalist
  Outdoorsy
  Sociable
BACKPACKER
  Adventurous
  Carefree
  Casual
  Free
  Fun
  Fun loving
  Likes scenic beauty
  Loves fresh air
  Naturalist
  Nature lover
  Needs to get away from society
  Outdoorsy
  Relaxed
  Sociable
RACQUETBALL PLAYER
  Able to concentrate
  Competitive
  Concerned with physical
  appearance
  Ego motivated
  Proud
  Strategic
  Successful
VOLLEYBALL PLAYER
  Athletic
  Competitive
  Concerned with physical
  appearance
  Ego motivated
  Energetic
  Health conscious
  Physically fit

Proud
Sports minded
Team player
CHESS PLAYER
  Able to concentrate
  Analytical
  Cerebral
  Competitive
  Good problem solver
  Logical
  Math minded
  Quiet
  Strategic
OUTDOOR-COOKING ENTHUSIAST
  Adventurous
  Back to nature
  Conservationist
  Fun
  Fun loving
  Likes scenic beauty
  Nature lover
  Naturalist
  Needs to get away from society
  Outdoorsy
  Relaxed
  Sociable
GUITARIST
  At peace with themselves
  Creative
  Determined
  Introspective
  Intelligent
  Patient
  Quiet
WEIGHT TRAINER
  Athletic
  Competitive
  Concerned with physical appearance
  Ego motivated
  Health conscious
  Physically fit
  Proud
  Sports minded

those who did not perceive themselves so clearly as runners. This development of the self-image may be the basis of their motivation. Kelly (1983) studied some other devoted amateurs; one such group was involved in motocross – competitive off-road motor cycling in cross-country races, by working-class men. This example illustrates two aspects of identity formation in leisure, the development of special skills and wearing special costumes. Leisure can contribute to identity in a number of ways:

1. Belonging to a special group, which may become the centre of social life; some members play special roles as officers of the group and may become respected senior members. The group may confer some social prestige, as in the case of the Musica Viva (chamber music followers) group in Sydney, described by Kippax: They were a self-consciously élite group, proud of their musical sophistication (S. Kippax, lecture at Oxford).

2. Many forms of leisure require special skills. There may be competitions, prizes, training, but also the possibility of failure. We saw earlier that competence is a very good predictor of which sports people take up, and will see later that lack of competence is a major barrier to many forms of leisure. The explanation may be that competence is an important source of self-esteem.

3. Many forms of leisure lead to recognizable kit, clothes, badges or other aspects of appearance. The leather jackets of bikers, the sports club sweatshirts of students, club ties, 'country' clothing associated with outdoor sports, are all examples. Indeed many kinds of clothing acquired their meaning and popularity through such associations.

4. Many leisure activities include public performances, for example some sports, theatre, dancing and music. For these occasions the members dress up in special, and often impressive, ways and are publicly visible as members of the group and as displaying their skills.

5. Some forms of leisure create whole 'leisure worlds', in the sense that they become a way of life, with their own rules, beliefs, rituals, costumes and calendar of events, as well as their own social world. This is true of church, ballroom dancing, sailing, greyhound racing, indeed most serious forms of leisure.

BANDURA AND SELF-EFFICACY

We have seen that there is a strong relation between competence at a leisure activity, such as sport, and the amount of participation in it. Mobily *et al.* (1993) found correlations as high as .90 between time spent on different kinds of sport and assessment of ability at them, in a sample of elderly subjects. The same is found for social abilities; Sneegas (1986) found that perceived social competence correlated with participation in a lot of leisure activities, though the correlations here were quite small. However, these studies do not show that competence causes participation rather than vice versa, nor do they show why this should happen.

Bandura (1977) put forward a theory which has been very influential because of its practical applications. He proposed that the perception that one has the ability to perform a skill at a certain level acts as a motivator to do it. 'Self-efficacy' is a judgement of one's ability, a kind of self-confidence in relation to a specific task; it is assessed by self-ratings of confidence from 0 to 100 in being able to attain different levels of success, for example to run a mile in 8 minutes, 7 minutes. He proposed that self-efficacy has four sources, and there has been research on all of them. (1) Past success: many studies have shown that this affects self-efficacy both in sport and exercise. In sport this consists of winning games, in exercise it is successful performance of tasks, or objective measures of success. (2) Vicarious experience, for example watching someone else doing a back dive or learning to swim, has been found to increase self-efficacy. (3) Persuasion, for example by a coach, that 'you can do it', has sometimes worked, sometimes not. (4) Physiological state, such as being psyched up rather than anxious or depressed, has not worked as expected.

Many studies have shown that self-efficacy is correlated with performance, but does it have a causal effect? It has been found to work for gymnastics and diving. Feltz found that self-efficacy predicted success in the first attempt at back-diving, but that later trials were better predicted by success at the first one. Correlations over .50 have been found for success in gymnastic contests, and there have been similar results for ice-hockey teams (Feltz, 1992). It is possible, however, that the self-efficacy scores in sport are due to realistic appraisals of the prospects of success. Research on exercise has produced more convincing results, for predicting whether heart disease and other patients will adopt, and put effort into, a programme of exercise as prescribed. These are exercises like walking, jogging, using a cycling machine, sit-ups and stair-climbing. In one study sexual activity was included as one of the exercises. Self-efficacy has been successful in predicting whether these patients will take up, continue, and put effort into the exercises (McAuley, 1992). The value of the theory is in suggesting the factors which will increase self-efficacy.

This theory is obviously limited to sports, exercise and other forms of leisure where it is possible to do well, and in a way that is measurable to some extent. This applies to hobbies like gardening; the measure here is how well the plants do, and sometimes this is assessed at garden competitions. Similar considerations apply to music and dancing. In social clubs of all kinds there can be promotion to the committee or to be one of the officers. However, many members don't want to be promoted, and are happy for others to do the work. And in leisure like watching TV, listening to music, reading and walking, competence simply doesn't come into it.

Self-efficacy theory does not really explain how self-efficacy works. There are several possibilities. (1) Sport is all about competing with others, and it is rewarding to win, because it means you are better than they are. However, self-efficacy works for individual exercise too, which does not depend on beating others. (2) Successful performance of difficult moves, like back-diving, may give a sense of mastery, and this has often been proposed as a motive for sport. It could also be a factor in hobbies, as when a gardener succeeds in making things grow. (3) Successful performance may simply be more enjoyable; you could not enjoy swimming without being able to swim.

BARRIERS TO LEISURE

We have looked at a number of motivations for leisure; now we turn to the factors which prevent people from engaging in leisure. People can be asked why they don't take up activities, why they gave up or for their experience of barriers.

Kay and Jackson (1991), with 366 British adults, found that 53 per cent said that money was a constraint, 36 per cent that shortage of time was, while smaller numbers mentioned conflicts with family or with work, transport difficulties or their health. In a later study with 1,891 people in Alberta, Jackson (1993) asked them to name one desired activity, and then to rate fifteen possible barriers for it. Six dimensions of barriers were found, and the average barrier scores on a four-point scale were as follows:

social isolation (e.g. didn't know where to learn, didn't have partners)	1.73
accessibility	1.72
personal reasons (e.g. lack of skill or social confidence)	1.24
costs	2.30
time (v. family or work)	2.19
facilities	2.03

Raymore and colleagues (1993) proposed that constraints operate in a certain order. They found that intrapersonal ones come first (for example 'I'm too shy'); if this was passed, interpersonal ones had to be confronted (for example 'The people I know live too far away'), followed by structural ones, such as lack of money, time or transport. However, there is some doubt over how far these barriers actually prevent people engaging in leisure. Shaw, Bonen and McCabe (1991) surveyed 14,674 Canadians and found that out of eleven constraints listed only two were associated with a lower rate of participation in a range of physical pursuits – lack of energy and ill health. Discussion of this problem has led to the suggestion that people may not be aware of constraints until they take something up – for example how much it costs – and that barriers are in any case negotiable or soluble (Kay & Jackson, 1991).

Money came first in importance on the lists above, although Coalter (1993) found that money made very little difference to sporting activities, confirming Shaw, Bonen and McCabe's finding in a quasi-experimental design. They studied attendance at leisure centres which had put their prices up. Even when the increase in price was as much as 71 per cent, 85 per cent of members said it would make no difference, and only 12 per cent said they would go a little less often. Kay and Jackson also found that sport was very little affected, and that money was a greater barrier for going for drinks or meals out and entertainment. The reason may be that most sport is actually very cheap, even after a 71 per cent price increase. It may also be the case that engaging in sport becomes a part of life which it is very difficult to change. If we studied more expensive kinds of sport, like skiing or sailing, or very expensive kinds of sport, like polo, the effects of money might be more evident.

Time is another important restraint, which came second in the Jackson study and which can also be looked at as the effect of work and family on leisure. Those who work longer hours, have a long way to travel to work or who are exhausted when they get home, obviously have less time and energy for leisure, other than reading or watching TV. It is found by economists that the more people are paid, the shorter their working hours, though the strength of this relationship is now less than it was (Hunnicutt, 1985). This effect, together with the greater physical demands of manual work, could explain why working-class people have much less active leisure. Leisure is greatly reduced by the presence of children in the family; barriers are experienced as much greater during this period of life, as found by Witt and Goodale (1985) and shown in Figure 7.3. There is some joint leisure with the children, and this can be very enjoyable, but it is different from the leisure which is freely chosen when they are not there.

Resources and *accessibility* are needed for most forms of leisure; you can't go ice skating unless there is a rink or learn to ski unless there is a slope. And as Jackson found, there may be a problem with finding other people to do things with. It has been found that people are very sensitive to the proximity of such resources; it was found in a British study that they were three times as likely to use a park if it was within a quarter of a mile of where they lived than if it was between a half and three-quarters of a mile (Burton, 1971). However, this result may be largely due to mothers and children going to the park on foot; those with cars may be prepared to travel further than a quarter of a mile. Veal (1987) studied 'distance decay' for attending pools and sports or leisure centres, with the results shown in Figure 7.4. This shows that attendance at the pool was over fifteen times higher if it was within half a mile than when it was over two miles away. This may be partly because many of those who swim are children, who have to walk or cycle to get there. The distance decay is much less for leisure centres, often visited by adults with cars.

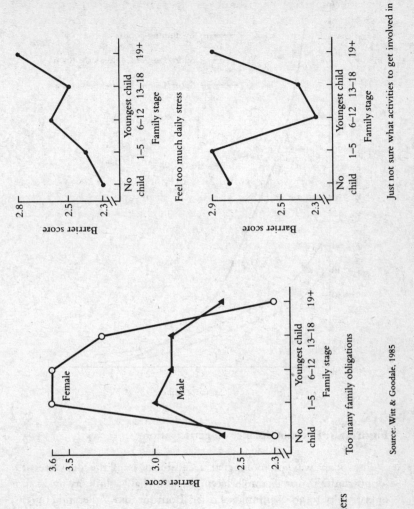

Figure 7.3: Barriers to leisure at different stages of the family

Too many family obligations

Feel too much daily stress

Just not sure what activities to get involved in

Source: Witt & Goodale, 1985

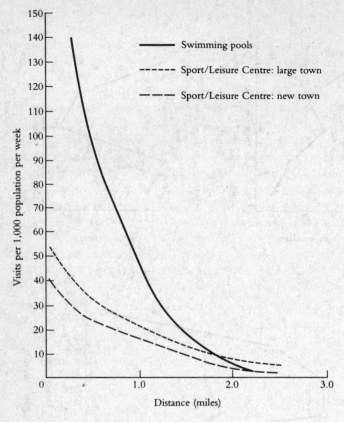

Source: Veal, 1979a, 1987

Figure 7.4: Effect of distance on participation

The other way of looking at accessibility is as the opposite of 'opportunities', for example having a pool half a mile away is an opportunity to go swimming. Losier, Bourque and Vallerand (1993) found that perceived opportunities correlated .37 with intrinsic motivation to do something, while perceived constraints correlated −.24.

Ability we discussed above, as one of the factors which predicts taking up different sports. Lack of ability is a major factor for giving up a sport or not trying it. Individuals may decide they are no good as a result of actually failing, or being labelled as no good by others, for example, being laughed at for their hopeless performance at tennis or golf (Mannell & Iso-Ahola, 1985). This particularly applies to sport and other spheres of leisure where you can be successful, but not to many others. Jackson found that lack of social skills was a barrier too.

Norms of various kinds prescribe which forms of leisure it is thought proper for different kinds of individuals to perform. In Britain it is thought okay for women to engage in cooking, crafts, dance, keep fit, gossiping and netball, but not the male preserves of going to the pub, sailing, mountaineering or home maintenance (Stockdale, 1987). There are similar stereotyped beliefs and social pressures to prescribe the leisure pursuits of different social classes. A working-class person who took up or tried to take up grouse shooting, or following the events at Ascot or Henley, would be as unacceptable as an upper-class one who went to greyhound races or spent his holidays at Blackpool. There are also norms connected with age, but there are also biological reasons why, for example, the elderly are less keen on playing rugger or marathon running.

CHAPTER EIGHT

Ten kinds of leisure

In this chapter I shall try to pull together research findings of different kinds about each of the main kinds of leisure which we have been bearing in mind in the course of this book. Actually only nine of them will appear here, since social life was dealt with in Chapter 6. The intention is to see how far each of these main kinds of leisure can be explained and understood. We shall find that they are each entirely different, and need different psychological stories to explain them, confirming our initial hunch that leisure is not a unitary affair, but a series of very different ones.

WATCHING TV

The rise of TV watching to what may be the third biggest use of time in the western world after sleeping and working is a most remarkable change in leisure. The consequence is that a lot less time is spent on other kinds of leisure.

Basic statistics

In Britain in 1992 people said that they watched an average of 26 hours 44 minutes a week, or 3 hours 49 minutes a day. However, this is not all 'primary viewing', that is, watching TV was not always the main activity. Collett (1987) installed video cameras in domestic TV sets which were activated when the set was turned on: an amazing variety of activities was observed, including sleeping and not being there at all. The Gershuny and Jones (1987) time-budget study found that employed men watched for 129 minutes a day, employed women 101 and housewives 147. In America Kubey and Csikszentmihalyi (1990) found that for TV watching as the main activity the figure was about one and a half hours a day. In the average American home, a TV set is turned on for 7 hours 5 minutes a day, including use of more than one set, but the sets are not looked at for 40 per cent of the time. Out of this time individuals watch on average 2.9 hours a day, and for 60 per cent of this time they are doing something else – mainly eating, talking and reading – as the primary activity. Nevertheless, as we shall see shortly, the introduction of TV has had massive effects on other activities.

There are considerable class differences. Classes A and B in Britain say they watch for 2.8 hours a day; classes D and E watch for 4.5 hours. This is a consistent finding in other countries, and in the USA blacks watch more than whites at the same income level. Women watch more than men: 3.92 hours a day compared with 3.27 for men; but Kubey and Csikszentmihalyi found that men watched more as the primary activity, while women had the set on more while they were doing housework or looking after the children. And men watch for a greater proportion of their spare time, 54 per cent, versus 40 per cent for women. Women over fifty watch a great deal.

There are also large age differences: children and old people watch the most. American figures are a little different in showing a much bigger drop for teenagers; they prefer being out with their friends to being at home with the family. There is a steady increase with age after thirty-five to forty-four. Those of different ages watch different programmes: for example the elderly look at more news and non-fiction material (BBC, 1989).

In most families the original TV set is in the living room, and family gather round. In 75 per cent of American homes there are now two or more sets, the second being most often in the parents' bedroom, with the result that more people are watching TV alone. However, when the VCR is used, often with a hired video, an average of 3.4 watch, compared with 1.7 at peak viewing time. Most households now have a remote control, and this has led to 'grazing' between channels, as if the activity is 'watching TV' as opposed to any particular programme. When watching recorded programmes, people often 'zap' to miss the commercials.

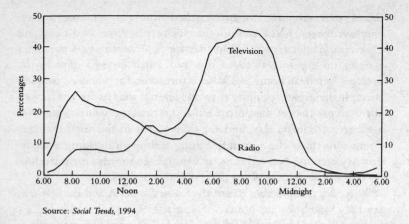

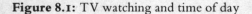

Source: *Social Trends*, 1994

Figure 8.1: TV watching and time of day

viewing time about 50 per cent of the adult population are watching TV, though they are watching several different programmes.

What has TV watching replaced? Robinson (1990) surveyed 25,000 people in twelve countries in 1965–6 to compare the use of time of those who did and did not have television at that time. Those who did slept for 12.5 minutes less, read for ten minutes a day less, and spent two to four hours a week less with friends and the social network outside the home, but they spent more time with the family – watching TV of course. They went much less to the cinema; in Britain in 1965 there were 327 million cinema admissions. This fell to 54 million by 1984 (a sixth), but since then increased to 114 million by 1993. In a British study, Belson (1967) found that acquiring a TV led to a 15 to 20 per cent fall in all other leisure activities.

History

Many of the population of the developed world now watch for one and a half to two hours a day or more, and this came about in a very few years. TV first became widely available in 1948; over half the American population had it by 1954, and 90 per cent by 1960. Most had colour receivers by 1980. The numbers watching continued to rise until quite recently, though they seem to have reached a plateau now. American sets were on for 4 hours 35 minutes a day in 1950, and are on for about seven hours today. The rise of TV watching in Britain has lagged about five years behind that in the USA, though the gap is now closing. There are several reasons for this increase. The first was the growth in the number of families with more than one set – 63 per cent of American homes by 1980. The next was the rise of video recorders – 64 per cent by 1989 – so that people could record programmes and also hire them. Remote control made viewing easier, and was available to 75 per cent by 1988. Finally there was cable TV, giving access to many more channels; 57 per cent of American homes had it by 1989.

In Britain 36 per cent have VCRs, and hire 6 million videos a year; 13 per cent of homes have cable or satellite now. Meanwhile the programmes have become much more professionally produced and have perhaps become more appealing to audiences. There has been the rise in soap operas, which are now by far the most popular programmes (Andreasen, 1990). British TV is different from American in that the BBC has a strong public service component, of providing educational and informative programmes, while American TV is mainly commercial. This difference is responsible for differences in soap opera: American soaps are romantic, wish-fulfilling fantasies in the Hollywood tradition, while British are strong in social realism, everyday problems and working-class life (Liebes & Livingstone, 1992).

The most recent move in the history of TV watching is that there has been a steady fall since 1986, of over half an hour a week. Perhaps people have discovered some other leisure activities.

Social relationships

The family

TV sets are usually in the living room and are often watched by the family together. The activities most often engaged in while watching are eating, talking and (more surprisingly) reading. We found that watching TV was one of the most characteristic marital activities (Argyle & Furnham, 1982). It is evident that TV harmonizes with family life, and has indeed become a central part of it. Heavy watchers spend more time at home, and many of the hours spent watching are also being spent with the family. While watching they talk for about 20 per cent of the time, though this is less than the 33 per cent they talk while together doing other things. Lull (1990) observed ninety-seven families while watching TV and concluded that it gave them something to talk about and in several ways made a positive contribution to family social life.

Interviews with families have shown in more detail how TV affects family life. Has it killed conversation or disrupted family life? In some ways it has, but it has also provided a new focus, perhaps replacing conversation round the dining table, a new timetable, new kinds of family interaction. TV is used to prevent conversation, when tired, or to avoid conflict, to reward or punish children or act as a babysitter, as an occasion for close physical contact, for heart-to-heart talks with the sound turned down, and it can create family solidarity through shared experiences and emotions. 'Television is being used for something which is more than entertainment. It is used as a focus, as a method for enjoying social interaction with others' (Morley, 1986). Family TV watching is particularly important on occasions like Christmas and New Year.

I have given some space to these findings, although they are not based on very extensive statistical evidence, since they provide a very good example of one of the themes of this book, that leisure activities are often chosen in order to bring about desired social relationships or forms of social interaction.

Nevertheless conflicts over which channel to watch are very common, though in the USA more than in Britain these are being reduced by owning more than one set; the growth in multiple-set ownership may reduce the central role of TV in family life. When there is a conflict, the parents usually win, and it is mother who monitors disagreements between children, but father who has most say.

Relationships with friends and others outside the family

The Robinson study of 25,000 people with and without TV showed that acquiring TV resulted in two to four hours a week less with social contacts outside the home. The socially isolated are found to be heavy viewers; they are those living alone, the widowed, divorced or unemployed, who lack other social contacts. The direction of causation may be from isolation to TV watching rather than the reverse. There is a positive side to the effect of TV and relations with friends, that it gives them a common interest to talk about, since they have often seen the same programmes. Some people ask their friends round, and they watch TV together, providing a shared topic of interest and of conversation. More widely than this, TV gives the whole nation a shared set of experiences, by participating live in major political or historical events, major sporting events, and sharing the day's news. TV sets a 'national agenda' of current concerns, and it reinforces traditional values.

Relations with TV characters

Levy (1978) found that 38 per cent of people agreed that 'The newscasters are almost like friends you see every day'. This was especially the case for older viewers and the early evening news. Livingstone (1988) found that 62 per cent of regular watchers of soap operas agreed that 'after a while the characters do become real people and we are concerned for their well-being just as we are for our friends and colleagues'. These viewers seem to have acquired an extra social network, one whose activities are more exciting than their own. Horton and Wohl (1956) called this 'parasocial interaction', which they saw as watching the interaction as if interacting with one or more characters, as if playing opposite them.

Some people believe that the soap opera characters are real, and send them wedding and other presents. A number of studies of the effect of violence on TV on aggression in boys show that this is more likely to happen when boys identify with the characters, and believe that they and their aggression are real (Huesmann, Lagerspetz & Eron, 1984).

Motivation

If people are asked why they watch TV about 60 per cent say for 'entertainment or relaxation', 20 per cent for 'killing time' and 12 per cent for information or to learn (Comstock et al., 1978).

In the 'uses and gratifications' tradition of TV research a number of motivational factors have been located. McQuail, Blumler and Brown (1972) interviewed people, drew up a list of items, these were factor analysed, and the following factors found: diversion, personal relationships, personal identity and surveillance (these terms will be explained below). In a later study of 1,000 subjects Blumler (1985) found a slightly different set of four factors: diversion, surveillance, curiosity and personal identity. This illustrates a problem with this kind of research, that the factors extracted depend on the items included, and these may vary with the initial questions put to subjects and the pool of subjects used. Nevertheless there is some degree of consistency about the main motivational factors found to be behind TV watching.

'Diversion' or 'entertainment' is always the main factor, and includes items about escaping the constraints of routine, escaping the burden of problems, and emotional release (McQuail, Blumler & Brown, 1972). Overall 55 per cent of people say that the programmes they watch help them to relax and only 10 per cent made them think (Barwise & Ehrenberg, 1988). The most popular programmes on TV are soap opera, sitcoms, game shows and the like, which induce a pleasant and relaxed mood and, it has been argued, replace a boring or stressful real life with a more interesting and low-cost life at second hand (Fowles, 1992). Most TV programmes present a cheerful, usually amusing story, with attractive people; they are pleasant and undemanding, and intended to attract an audience and put it in a good mood.

Experimental studies have shown how TV can affect mood states. Bryant and Zillman (1984) induced moods of boredom in some subjects, mild stress in others; the subjects were then offered a choice of TV tapes to watch. The experimentally bored subjects looked much more at exciting films, while the stressed ones looked much less at these and looked instead at comedies. In both cases the heart rate of subjects fell more than that of controls who saw no TV. In another study it was found that women feeling ill with their menstrual cycle chose more comedy than other women. Why do people enjoy suspense, where the hero is in danger, for example? It may be because they enjoy the arousal or the enjoy the resolution of the problem (Zillman, 1985).

However, light entertainment such as soap operas may meet a greater variety of needs than this. Livingstone (1988) used a different method of uses and gratifications research. She asked a varied group of fifty-two regular soap-opera watchers, 'Why is soap opera so popular?', and did a content analysis of the replies. This produced seven types of answer:

1. Entertainment and escapism. ('You can have a little romance, glamour, passion, love and hate in your life') (92 per cent).
2. Realism ('It [*EastEnders*] is very much a "soap of the 80's" dealing with the problems that occur in everyday life, such as unemployment, racism, adultery, rape, alcoholism and drugs') (89 per cent).
3. Characters as extensions of real-world networks. ('I know that after a while the characters do become real people and we are concerned for their well-being just as we are for our friends and colleagues') (62 per cent).
4. As an educational medium. ('We can relate to the situation and sometimes sort our own problems out through listening and doing what the character portrayed has done') (42 per cent).
5. As part of daily life. ('After a while you watch it so much it becomes a regular thing to do. On Wednesdays you come home, have dinner, do your jobs, watch *Coronation Street*, wash up and then it's time for *Dallas*') (40 per cent).
6. Emotional experience. ('When you're watching soap operas you can experience a full range of emotions from anger and despair to sheer joy, excitement and relief') (37 per cent).
7. Keeping a critical distance. ('Many people like to watch them to laugh because we all know that life is not really like that. However, even so, we like to get involved in their plots') (52 per cent).

We did a study of the relation between watching TV and happiness. The heavier watchers were less happy than others, but the heavy soap watchers were more happy. They reported more satisfaction of several kinds, especially 'educational' satisfaction (Lu & Argyle, 1993) (see Figures 8.2a and b).

This leads us to some of the other uses and gratifications originally found by McQuail, Blumler and Brown. 'Surveillance' refers to watching news, current affairs and similar non-fiction. It also includes

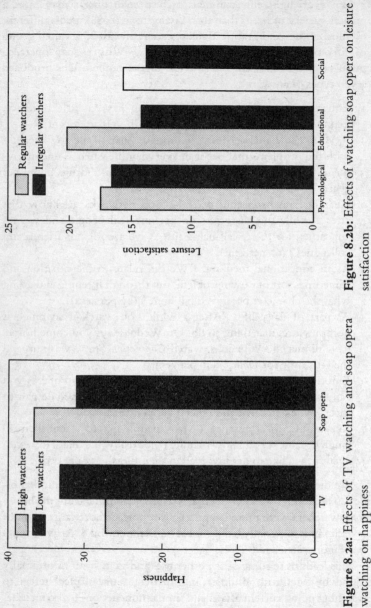

Figure 8.2a: Effects of TV watching and soap opera watching on happiness

Figure 8.2b: Effects of watching soap opera on leisure satisfaction

'reassurance' that things are all right, especially when there is bad news. The people who watch these programmes most are more educated, more middle-class and older than other watchers.

'Personal identity' means seeing people like ourselves on TV, giving salience to things important in our own lives, seeing people cope with problems like our own and getting help with solving them, and reinforcing our values. In the study cited above we found that subjects reported great educational satisfaction from watching soap opera; this sounds absurd, but it probably means they can learn how to cope with everyday situations. 'Personal relationships' refers to both parasocial relations and the benefits of TV in providing a common topic of conversation and social bonds, as we described earlier.

Although different programmes seem to provide different benefits – news, comedy, sport, et cetera – we have seen that people carry on watching a variety of different programmes, that the basic activity is 'watching TV'. In which case, is there not a common motivational theme which applies to all programmes? Kubey and Csikszentmihalyi (1990) paged subjects electronically and obtained self-reports at random points during the week, including times of watching and not watching TV. They found that, while watching, their sample of 107 subjects felt less active and alert than in any other activity, with less challenge, skill and concentration. They felt more relaxed than in any other activity. When comparisons were made between moods before, during and after watching, it was found that watching induced less activation, a less positive mood and greater relaxation than before (see Figure 8.3).

In other studies by members of this group it was found that, while watching TV, people were at a high level of apathy and boredom, and low intrinsic motivation, i.e. they wished they were doing something else (Massimi & Carli, 1988). Kubey and Csikszentmihalyi suggest that the state which viewers are in is most similar to idling and daydreaming, other altered states of consciousness of low cortical activity which help to pass the time. We saw earlier that sleep is one of the activities which TV replaces. In an interesting critique of this work, Livingstone (1995) argues that TV watching is more active than these results suggest, as is shown by the evidence of positive choice of programmes, especially soap operas and the news, and that

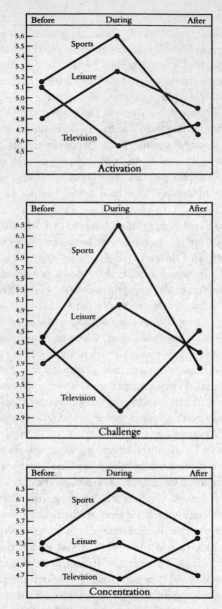

Source: Kubey & Csikszentmihalyi, 1990

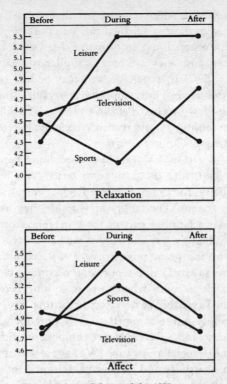

Source: Kubey & Csikszentmihalyi, 1990

Figure 8.3: Effects of TV watching and other leisure on moods

viewers are active in interpreting what they see on the screen. A number of studies have confirmed this selection of programmes – because they are entertaining, informative, aggressive, useful for conversation, or because they are seen as similar to the viewer's self-image (Preston & Clair, 1994). Viewers may be half asleep but they rate programmes as very interesting and enjoyable: on a scale from 0 to 100, British viewers rated *Pot Black* 88, *Colditz* 84, *Crossroads* 80, the news 76, wrestling 75, and romance/comedy, et cetera 70 (Goodhardt, Ahrenberg & Collins, 1987).

An important part of TV watching is becoming familiar with and attached to a particular programme or series. This may start with previous publicity, for example in the *Radio Times*, or from recommendation by friends. The family may decide they like it and very soon it becomes a familiar part of the timetable; from much other research in psychology it is known that we like what is familiar. The explanation for the great popularity of TV, combined with the rather low level of satisfaction reported, is becoming clearer. This is a 'filler' or 'default' activity when there is nothing better to do, but which is readily available at no effort or further cost, and which is enjoyable, familiar and relaxing (Barwise & Ehrenberg, 1988).

I would like to add a second major component in the motivation of TV watching – social motivation. We have seen that TV watching is often a family activity and now plays an important part in family life. But one of the main activities which TV replaces is social life with the social network outside the home; the lonely and isolated watch the most TV. What is seen on TV is social behaviour, or presenters who seem to address the viewer personally. We saw that many people think they know the TV people personally, that they are 'like friends'. It follows that watching TV is a kind of social interaction in fantasy, with a lot of very nice people, which needs no social skills and carries no risks. And as we said, families often watch TV together, and it is a characteristic marital activity; friends often discuss soaps or other programmes they have been watching, creating a further common interest.

Finally, as Kubey and Csikszentmihalyi say, although other activities may be more enjoyable and invigorating, there are no constraints to TV watching, there are no costs, no other people are needed and you can watch as long as you like. This could explain why those with lower incomes watch more TV, about 80 per cent more in Britain comparing the different classes; richer people can afford to do other and more interesting things in their leisure. Alternatively, more educated individuals have acquired more leisure interests and skills in the course of education.

So what is the overall effect of spending so much of our time in front of the TV set? We pass at least an hour and half a day on average, in a form of mildly pleasant, low-key relaxation. We are prevented from seeing our friends, reading or engaging in other leisure for the same period, though we have something else to talk to them about if we do see them. Those who watch informative programmes may become a little better informed. Does watching aggressive programmes make people more aggressive, or is it that aggressive people like to watch these programmes? This issue has been much debated, but the conclusion of a number of longitudinal studies is that violent TV can make people more aggressive (Berkowitz, 1993). It has long been suspected that TV adverts increase desires for material possessions. It has also been found that TV can have positive effects, if the contents emphasize generosity, helping, cooperation, friendliness, rule-keeping, delaying gratification, or lack of fear (Rushton, 1979). Counts of kind and helpful acts per hour of TV show that these are about as common as aggressive ones; they are most frequent in sitcoms; and there is evidence that TV watching has more effect on the prosocial behaviour of children than on their aggressiveness (Cumberbatch & Howitt, 1989).

There may be other widespread social consequences. There has been concern that TV presents an inaccurate view of the world, particularly under-representing and stereotyping women and minority groups. Soap powder commercials usually show dominant, manly and professionally expert men in white coats telling feeble and passive women what to do with their dirty washing; the effects of soap commercials have been somewhat offset by soap operas, which usually have strong and assertive women in central roles. There are few blacks in central parts, though there has been some counter-stereotyping, as in *Till Death Us Do Part*. The old are shown little, but are shown positively (Cumberbatch & Howitt, 1989).

Postman (1985) argues that TV reduces every topic to light entertainment, and thinks that we are 'amusing ourselves to death', that we are laughing instead of thinking. However, audience appreciation of TV programmes is high if they are either enjoyable or interesting; programmes with small audiences, like *Panorama*, receive high ratings from those who do watch them (Goodhardt, Ahrenberg & Collins, 1987). Sixty per cent of viewers of programmes like this say that it makes them think, only 15 per cent that it helps them relax (Barwise & Ehrenberg, 1988). It is true that some other activities have to compete with TV – evening lectures, for example – and they now have to be entertaining too. What may apply to education may also apply to politics, religion and other spheres of life – all have to be amusing and, as a result, trivial. Or we could say they have to be much better presented than before in order to compete with the professional competence of TV.

MUSIC AND RADIO

I have grouped these two categories together because of the large overlap between them – 57 per cent of radio listening is to music, and a great deal of music listening is via the radio. Listening to music is a major leisure activity in the modern world, though a lot of listening is done while doing something else, such as driving, housework or eating. Much of it is from the radio, though there is an increasing amount of listening to cassettes, particularly on personal stereos, and to compact discs, as well as attending concerts. A smaller proportion of the population play or sing themselves.

Statistics

Most people in Britain (about 90 per cent) listen to the radio and, as we said, 57 per cent of this is to music – on Radios 1, 2 and 3, and independent stations – for an average of one and a half hours a day. About 76 per cent listen to tapes or records; sales of cassettes peaked at 82 million in Britain in 1989, but have now been overtaken by discs, which sold 70 million in 1992. Radio listening has increased from one and a quarter hours a day in 1986 to one and half now (TV watching fell during this period). In an Australian survey of teenagers it was found that the most common amount of radio listening was one to two hours per day, but for lower-class children at weekends three to four hours per day was nearly as common (Kippax, Koenig & Dowsett, 1984).

A rather smaller number attend concerts; 12 per cent say they go sometimes to classical concerts, 5 per cent to jazz, and 5 per cent to opera (Reid, 1989). Some sing in choirs, others in church; some play instruments in orchestras, brass bands or just at home or with friends. We are mainly concerned with amateurs here since the book is about leisure, but in the case of music there is a lot of mixture between the two. The conductor and soloists, or the orchestra or part of the choir may be professionals and the rest amateurs, for example. We know that about 3 per cent engage in amateur music or drama. About 16 per cent of adults go dancing, once a week overall, but 65 per cent for seventeen to twenty year olds (Hendry et al., 1993). We shall see that singing and dancing have been regarded by some as the origins of music.

There are extensive class differences in listening to and making music. Middle-class people in Britain listen to far more classical music than working-class; classes A and B spend twenty-eight minutes a day listening to the classical station Radio 3, compared with an average of four minutes for classes C2, D and E; for the popular music on Radio 1 it is the other way round. Surveys of American students find that middle-class ones listen to more serious music – classical and jazz – and to folk music, working-class ones to hard rock and blues (Hargreaves, 1986). Black Americans listen to much less music of most kinds, except that they listen to more jazz, soul and rock (DiMaggio & Ostrower, 1990). More middle-class people listen to records or tapes, 90 as against 64 per cent. More middle-class people in Britain go to classical concerts (28 as against 5 per cent), jazz concerts (14 as against 5 per cent) and opera (13 as against 2 per cent). The most active dancers are in class D (semi-skilled manual workers and their families): 22 per cent of the females in this class went dancing compared with 13 per cent in A and B. Amateur music and drama are pursued by 6 per cent of professional people, and 1 per cent of unskilled (Reid, 1989). There are special class differences in the adolescent age group; it has been found that middle-class children who rebelled and rejected school became interested in heavy rock and reggae music, seen as anti-establishment at the time of the study, while the working-class rebels engaged in delinquent street culture (Murdoch & Phelps, 1973).

Gender differences are less marked. The main difference is that women are more interested in music in general, particularly in classical music and ballet, but also in pop music, while males are more interested in jazz and rock music. And women go dancing more often.

There are extensive age differences in musical activity. Mothers sing to babies and at twelve months babies respond to music and produce 'babbling songs'. One theory about music is that it originates in the communication between mother and infant. Children listen to music a great deal, and some are taught to play an instrument, but their first love is usually pop music, the Top Ten. Music plays an important part in the life of teenagers, since pop music is connected with dancing and love, and other kinds of youth music are linked with protests of various kinds. During adolescence children spend less time at home watching TV with their parents, more time with the peer group listening to music and dancing. Every phase of youth culture has been linked to a style of music, so the music plays a part in expressing an ideology and proclaiming an identity as member of a group. Interest in classical music increases with age, and older people do not like new forms of music, such as new forms favoured by youth cultures (Hargreaves, 1986).

History

The origins of music are unknown. However, it is found in all preliterate societies and, often with singing and dancing, it is used to accompany feasts, funerals, initiation ceremonies, work, religious worship, protest and to prepare for war (Blacking, 1987). Music may play a more important part in primitive than in modern society. 'Singing and dancing serve to draw groups together, direct the emotions of the people, and prepare them for joint action' (Wilson, 1975). Music plays a central part in group rituals which motivate cooperative action. Baumann (1987) described a very cooperative primitive society, the Miri in Sudan; he concluded that the very high degree of cooperation and mutual help is motivated by the frequent festivals of song and dance in which the whole village takes part and shares an intense emotional experience, almost to a state of trance, generating strong feelings of group unity. It has been suggested that in these societies music, combined with singing, dancing and ceremony, expresses both knowledge and social relations (Storr, 1992).

We described in Chapter 2 how music developed in the ancient world and in the Middle Ages in Europe. From 1600 the baroque, and from the late eighteenth century the classical period, showed a dramatic increase in musical activity. Most of the current concert repertoire comes from the period between 1600 and 1939. It was mainly secular and there were symphonies, operas, chamber music and other styles. Modern music, from about 1945 onwards, has made much less impact and appears relatively little on concert programmes.

Round about 1900 saw the birth of the blues and other jazz forms. This came from black Americans, and expressed the deprivations of the former slaves and the consolations of religion. It also led to a whole stream of jazz-derived styles. There were Broadway musicals, and there was pop music. The latter was produced for a mass market, which had been created by the growth in radio, and in the commercial record industry. Much of this consisted of songs about love, unrequited or otherwise, and was associated with dancing. Country and Western music has been found to appeal mostly to older and better-educated Americans, where folk and rock appeal more to the alienated (Fox & Williams, 1974).

Since 1960 there have been several waves of protest music, which have had a strong appeal to the young in the West. Bob Dylan, Joan Baez and others became spokesmen for the younger generation, with songs which were critical of nuclear weapons, racial discrimination, the war in Vietnam and the unethical nature of the society of their parents. The Beatles continued the rebellion against the supposedly unthinking and insensitive older generation, the Rolling Stones proclaimed the counter-culture and the joys of drugs, Pete Seeger took up the ecology movement, and there were religious musicals by Andrew Lloyd Webber and others. Meanwhile, in addition to all these messages, popular music continued to deal with the traditional problems of broken romance and unrequited love (Perris, 1985). Dancing has also gone through a series of fashions. Ballroom dancing was displaced, for the younger generation at least, by rock and roll in 1956, disco dancing from the 1970s, and by a number of lesser styles. There has been a considerable revival of folk dancing, such as Scottish country dancing.

Listening to music over the radio was even more popular before the sudden rise of TV, which caused a drop in listening (Daniel, 1989).

Social behaviour and relationships

Relations with the audience

Music consists basically of one or a group of performers playing to an audience. The players are communicating a mood via the music, or the beauty of the piece played, or an attitude, such as protest or worship, or a rhythm for dancing. In classical concerts there is separation between players and audience, the performers dress up, come to the stage by a different door, behave with great formality; the audience likewise have to sit very quiet, and are not able to talk to the performers. It may take an effort not to tap the feet or otherwise beat time; the only action allowed by the listeners is clapping at the end (Small, 1987). At dances they respond by dancing, of course. At jazz concerts there is much more interaction between performers and audience, who clap intermittently, buy the performers drinks and talk to them during intervals (White, 1987). Performers, especially at classical concerts, often suffer from audience anxiety or stage fright, which causes their performance to deteriorate, and they may have to take tranquillizers (Sloboda, 1987).

The group who make up the audience come to share an emotional experience; they may know some of the other members, or recognize them as members of the same social group, who share a set of attitudes, an identity. Opera-goers may wear dinner jackets and show that they belong to a social as well as a musical élite. Young people who go to pop festivals recognize each other as fellow members of anti-bourgeois and radical youth. Church-goers, of various persuasions, share a musical experience, as do those who go to folk concerts, and music of other specialized kinds.

Relations between performers

The performers may consist of a conductor, soloists and a hierarchy of other performers. The conductor is at the top of the pecking order, and has total power to control what happens, including perhaps who will play and what will be played. He makes a lot of use of non-verbal signals, including eye-contact, gestures and facial expressions of approval or disapproval. Within the other players there is a clear hierarchy, with soloists at the top, followed by the first violin in an orchestra, the other string players, and then the wind instrumentalists.

Players often perform, in private, for themselves, in string quartets, sonatas, songs and the rest. This was a more common activity in previous years before the advent of TV. The same players will play in a variety of groups and settings, and see a lot of other members of the local musical community. For every kind of musician there are national organizations, which arrange training and examining, conferences and concerts, and occasions to meet each other. For many people music is the basis for the whole of their leisure and social life: 'Railroading, like music and thieving ... is a world by itself' (Caplow, 1954).

Dancing

Music usually has rhythm, and if it has a strong rhythm, it is difficult not to move in time with it; a number of studies have found that subjects made involuntary movements to beat time with hands or feet while hearing music (Valentine, 1962). When people move in time together they are dancing. If it is the rhythm which makes them want to dance, it is the loudness which generates excitement; in primitive dancing this may take the form of ecstasy or 'possession'. The mood created by the music may be aggression – as in primitive war dances – romance or just sex.

There is a lot of dancing in primitive societies, often in connection with religion, and it is common for some or all of those involved to go into trance states, 'possessed' by spirits. We saw earlier how dancing can lead to high levels of cooperation and mutual help. Blacking (1987) describes dances among the Venda, where the Tshikoma dance produces a shared state of ecstasy, which is said to make the sick better, brings peace between groups and enables old men to throw away their sticks and dance, and there is a powerful feeling of group solidarity. This kind of dancing is said to generate a lot of social levelling. Dancing is important in black American culture, accompanied by loud jazz music, or versions of it such as rap or reggae; this is said to produce not only pleasure but also feelings of power and self-confidence (Kuwahara, 1992). Ballroom and disco dancing have a different purpose, an opportunity for mating and enjoying heterosexual contacts, though the sex is largely suppressed in the case of ballroom dancing. However, this may be an occasion for sexual competition and display. The music may be romantic rather than exciting. In Scottish and other folk dancing the emphasis is on co-operation, enjoying the joint and coordinated activities of the group, including some bodily contact and other positive non-verbal signals, the very agreeable music and, of course, the exercise. It is probably this combination which produces the high level of joy which has been found. The effect of all these forms of dancing is to generate arousal and pleasure, and also strong interpersonal bonds, both heterosexual and between group members. There are national and in some cases international organizations for every kind of dancing, with examinations, competitions and the rest.

Solitary listening

As Storr (1992) points out, 'Music began as a way of enhancing and co-ordinating group feelings' but now many people listen to music by themselves, which he regards as a modern phenomenon. This has been brought about by radio, and the growth of the record industry, giving between them an immense choice of music. Listening to music when alone can be used to produce whatever mood is desired or to remove an undesired one. It also provides company for the lonely, and Storr thinks that there is some contact with the mind of the composer; even more perhaps with the performers. Some play an instrument alone, and many others sing, hum, whistle, or inwardly produce tunes which they know, or variations on these, for an hour or two a day according to a study by Sagi and Vitanyi (1988). Some listen to music when out and about on their Walkman, and this effectively cuts them off from contact with others.

THE MOTIVATIONAL ROOTS OF MUSIC

Music as a source of pleasure

Music clearly does give a great deal of pleasure; it also produces states of arousal, followed by feelings of tranquillity and peace in which the cares of the world are forgotten, sometimes of 'oceanic' ecstasy. So music produces a number of enjoyable states of consciousness; the question is why? Psychologists have been trying to find out when a series of notes is heard as a tune. Berlyne (1971) thought that a crucial feature was possessing an intermediate degree of complexity, and that pleasure was derived both from moderate increases in arousal and in return to a lower level. Konecni (1982) found some support for this by finding that subjects chose a sequence of pieces of music which kept arousal at a moderate level.

Another feature of music is its power to express and arouse different emotions. Langer (1942) argued that music does not arouse emotions but expresses them, so that the listener contemplates them at a distance. However, one of the best laboratory methods of 'mood induction' is to use music, and this can actually produce joy or depression, for example (Pignatiello, Camp & Rasar, 1986). It does this partly through the similarity of musical sounds to the human voice, which can readily express a range of emotions. Scherer and Oshinsky (1977) generated 188 sounds, which were varied along eight aspects of sound on a Moog synthesizer, and these were then rated for their emotional tone. The investigators were able to isolate the cues for each emotion, so that sadness, for example, was produced by low and falling pitch, and slow tempo; such sounds on the synthesizer were recognized as sad. There are other ways in which music produces emotions; for example major keys are heard as happy and pleasant. An emotion which is evoked by most popular music is romantic love, expressed by both words and music. Langer (1942) also suggested that there are two kinds of communication, one based on logic and language, the other on emotion and non-verbal symbols. Nevertheless people are able to put words to their experience of music: Valentine (1962) found that Beethoven's Pastoral Sonata was described by one person as, 'The joyful uplifting of an oppressed soul that feels released from depths of anguish through faith in a kind, heavenly "Father".'

Something else which music communicates that is certainly non-verbal is the impulse to make bodily movements, as in dancing.

Do people choose to listen to music which will control their mood as they do with TV watching? Konechi (1982) found that subjects who had been insulted preferred to listen to simple rather than complex tunes, presumably to keep down their arousal level. Subjects who listened to simple melodies at low volume were less aggressive if later insulted – the music was soothing. It is through the calming effects of such music that music therapy is successful in relaxing patients (Thaut, 1989). Music can also increase arousal, and this is done by the sheer volume of music, as at pop concerts, or the speed, as at some dances.

Music as a group activity

We have seen that music probably started in groups, singing and dancing, engaging in religious ritual, preparing for battle, and that this joint musical activity produced cooperation and mutual help in the group. This suggests that there may be an evolutionary origin to music, and we have seen that music is found in all human societies. There is not much evidence of musical activity on the part of non-human primates; there is in birds, but we are not descended from birds. And this would be a case of evolution via group selection, and there is some doubt over whether this works (Argyle, 1991). Making music together, including singing and dancing, may be routes to emotional closeness, which would satisfy the affiliative drive.

We have seen that some audiences take their music very seriously because it helps them define themselves, provides a self-image, as with punks, skinheads and other adolescent groups. The same is true of ethnic groups, such as the Scottish, Irish, or blacks. National anthems are another example, together with other nationalistic music, regimental march pasts and the rest, often played by brass bands. These all induce feelings of pride in the members as they play, sing, march or just listen.

Expressing attitudes and ideology

We have seen the importance of music in expressing social protest, such as jazz and rock for blacks, 1960s' pop for rebellious youth. The meaning of the message here was partly conveyed by the words, but these were supported by a powerful emotional message in the music, with its roots in American slavery and black poverty. All religions use music, and in the West we have a clear idea of the religious sound, deriving from a much earlier period of church music. In terms of the emotional message this corresponds to a kind of 'serious joy'. There are other religious sounds that are widely used, such as the ringing of bells and intoning texts, as in plainsong, as there are other religious, non-verbal signals, like candles and dim lighting. However, it is doubtful whether there is a universal religious sound (Perris, 1985).

READING AND STUDY

Statistics

A time-budget study of 25,000 people in twelve countries (not including Britain) in 1965–6 found that, after they had TV, the time spent on all kinds of reading and study fell as follows:

	before TV	after TV
	[minutes per day]	
reading books	14.1	8.3
newspapers	15.3	15.2
magazines	5.4	3.9
study	18.1	15.7

Total reading time fell from 34.8 minutes per day to 27.4, but newspaper reading was not affected (Robinson, 1990). The British time-budget study by Gershuny and Jones (1987) found that employed men read books and papers or engaged in study for 23.7 minutes a day, and non-employed women for 21.7 minutes (averaging the findings for three different years).

The General Household Survey asked if respondents had read a book in the last four weeks, and in 1990 62 per cent said they had. The Euromonitor survey of 27,000 people in 1980 asked if they were reading a book now, and 45 per cent said they were; this is a better index of the number of regular readers of books. Public libraries had been visited by 26 per cent in the last four weeks, 34 per cent had bought a hardback book in the last year and 49 per cent a paperback book in the last year (Reid, 1989). Average weekly expenditure on books, et cetera was £3.84. The books read, bought or borrowed were about 65 per cent fiction (75 per cent for women), the rest being mainly education or study (10 per cent), biography (7 per cent) and history (5 per cent) (Mann, 1982).

We have seen that people read the papers for about a quarter of an hour a day. In Britain 68 per cent of adults read a national daily paper, 31 per cent an evening paper, and 74 per cent a national Sunday paper. The most widely read papers are the *Sun* (25 per cent) and the *Daily Mirror* (20 per cent). The serious papers, as I will call them, were read by much smaller sections of the public: the *Daily Telegraph* by 6 per cent, *The Times* and the *Guardian* by 3 per cent each, and the *Independent* by 2 per cent in 1987 (National Readership Survey, 1987).

Then there is the four minutes a day spent reading magazines. Reading a general weekly is reported by 38 per cent, but this is mainly the *Radio Times*, followed by the 26 per cent – mainly women – who read women's weekly magazines, and the 33 per cent who read women's monthly magazines. Next comes the monthly *Reader's Digest*, read by 15 per cent, and a lot of more specialized magazines about gardening, cars, sport and hobbies and leisure interests of all kinds. We shall see later that these are important in maintaining the cohesion of groups of gardeners, bird-watchers and followers of many leisure pursuits.

A proportion of the population is illiterate; exactly how large a proportion is hard to say since literacy is a matter of degree. In 1900 97 per cent could sign the marriage register, but this is a very weak criterion of literacy. In 1948 5.7 per cent were found to have a reading age of only nine, in 1994 21 per cent had a reading age of thirteen, and a survey in 1987 found that 13 per cent admitted to reading, writing or numeracy difficulties in daily life (Hamilton & Stasinopoulos, 1987); since this depended on confession of difficulty it is probably an underestimate. We have seen that many people do not read books at all, and while 74 per cent read a Sunday paper, most of them are reading papers which use short words and short sentences. It looks as if about half the population read books, and another 25 per cent read books and papers if they are not too demanding.

About 5 million (14 per cent of adults) attend adult classes of some kind, with 2 million working for degrees, and others attending courses for no particular qualification, organized by local authorities, the WEA or other bodies. The courses for degrees and various technical qualifications are mainly to get a better job or promotion, but there are also many 'leisure' classes in art, literature, music and social studies. While these courses involve attending lectures, most of the work is done at home, with a book – which is why I have included them here rather than under leisure groups. Other people do correspondence courses, including Open University degree courses, and this is mostly done at home.

Class, gender and age differences

There are quite large class differences here. Middle-class people read, borrow and buy more books. The percentages of those who have read a book in the last four weeks were 81 per cent for professional-class people, 38.5 per cent for unskilled, in 1986 (GHS, 1986). Public libraries were visited by 43 per cent of those with degrees or equivalent, 18 per cent of those with no qualifications. There are greater differences in buying books, and most of those in classes C to E buy no books at all. The most important variable here is probably education, which encourages reading.

Newspapers are read by all social classes, but the number of readers falls in class E, unskilled workers, from about 70 to 52 per cent. However, there are very big differences in which papers are read. What I called the serious papers are really only read by classes A and B, professional and managerial; there is a large drop to C1, white-collar; and the *Sun* and the *Daily Mirror* are read mainly by classes C to E. The *Daily Mail* and the *Daily Express* have a broad coverage, with more readers at the middle-class end (Euromonitor, 1987). Women's magazines have their social niches too. *Good Housekeeping* and *Homes and Gardens*, for example, are read mainly by middle-class women, and *True Romances* by C1, white-collar-class women (Reid, 1989).

Adult education was originally intended to help working-class individuals who had missed out on education. However, the middle classes are very over-represented at these classes, the working classes under-represented, while clerical and skilled workers turned up in the expected proportions. It has been found that many of those at adult classes had already been upwardly mobile; they planned to take more classes in the future, perhaps in the hope of further mobility (Woodley *et al.*, 1987).

Women read more books than men: 68 per cent read a book in the last four weeks in 1990, compared with 56 per cent for men. The books which women read are different too: they read a higher proportion of fiction, 75 per cent, and a lot of these are romances, followed by historical fiction, while men read more crime, thrillers, war and adventure stories. A survey of Mills and Boon readers, all women, found that two-thirds of them borrowed these books from the public library; the rest bought them, typically ten to nineteen volumes a year, some of them buying over sixty volumes (Mann, 1969).

In adult classes organized by local authorities, mainly for leisure purposes, there are three times as many women as men (Legge, 1982).

People read at all ages. Older people, over fifty-five, use the public library more, those over sixty-five read the papers a little less, and women over fifty-five read Mills and Boon books less. Children read a lot, and we shall see later how certain kinds of stories have a great appeal for them. Different magazines are read by women at different ages. Children read comics; adolescents read about romance and fashion. Young women read about grooming, the presentation of self at work and conforming to the peer group. Young mothers seek practical advice and escapism. When the children are older or have left home, women no longer need advice or escapism but develop other interests and read more specialist journals. Local authority classes contain a lot of people between thirty and fifty-five and also a lot of older ones; young people doing more vocational courses do them at colleges of various kinds (Legge, 1982).

The history of reading and study

We traced in Chapter 2 how reading and literacy expanded in the nineteenth century. By the end of the century many of the working class could and did read; but many commentators then and now consider that what they were reading was mainly rubbish. 'Women wore their eyes out following the scandalous doings of fictional lords and ladies, or the spicy peccadilloes of real ones. Men and boys in the factories devoured tons of hack-written adventure stories, composed of hair-breadth escapes, desperate villainy and superhuman heroism' (Altick, 1957). Typical of this reading material were the 'penny dreadfuls'.

Throughout the nineteenth century the Religious Tract Society tried to improve working-class reading by the publication of religious tracts and bibles. There were many improving publications, including journals such as the *Boy's Own Paper*. The numbers sold ran overall into millions of copies, but the company finally collapsed in 1951. In the twentieth century other publishers combined commercial acumen with the intention to improve what people read. Mills and Boon started publishing popular romantic novels for women in 1908, but were careful to avoid premarital sex and to keep the books 'wholesome'. Penguin Books started in 1935 and made a wide range of good novels and serious non-fiction available, originally at the price of 6d (McAleer, 1992).

In the late twentieth century the scope for reading a good book is far greater than before. To begin with there are simply many more books, both good and bad, to read. There are many 'good' novels, of the Booker Prize type, and there are many more popular books, usually sold in paperback, by Agatha Christie, Ian Fleming and many others, which are at a much higher level than the penny dreadfuls and other popular writings of the last century.

Adult education could be found in the eighteenth century in connection with clubs, debating societies, circulating libraries and scientific societies. In the first half of the nineteenth century there were the Mechanics' Institutes, intended to introduce science to the working class; later there were many classes put on by radical working-class organizations and their middle-class sympathizers. In the twentieth century there was a great expansion of adult education – the WEA, university extension and voluntary bodies, but above all by the local authorities, who were required to provide it by Acts of 1944 and 1945. Some of this was intended as a second chance at education, some as a kind of radical enlightenment for the working class but, in the end, a lot of it was simply for leisure and self-development (Kelly, 1962).

Social relationships

Most books are about social behaviour: this applies to novels, biographies and history. It is widely believed that when reading a novel many people identify with one or more of the characters, that is they imagine themselves having the romantic affairs or adventures described. They may come to feel that they know the characters, liking some, disliking others. We shall see that the heroes and heroines of Enid Blyton stories are designed with such identification in mind. James Bond and other adventurers are more successful with women and with defeating wicked enemies than most men are. To read a novel is to take part vicariously, in imagination, in some very enjoyable social life. The same may be true of reading the papers, which are mostly about the activities of politicians, famous sports players, pop stars and others. These are real people whom readers may feel they have come to know and may admire, hate or identify with.

Readers of books and newspapers may feel aware of being addressed by the authors, of getting to know them. This is perhaps strongest in the case of newspaper columnists who write regularly, in a characteristic way, rather like a real 'correspondent' with whom readers have a personal relationship (Consterdine, 1988).

Readers may be aware of other readers of the same materials. In the case of magazines they may be members of the same club, social class, church, age group, or pursue the same hobby, and are glad to have news of members, meetings and activities of the group, and publications; the group is partly held together by the journal. Readers of a newspaper may feel a similar identification with other readers, since they will be people of the same political outlook, social class, et cetera. Reading a national paper keeps one in touch with the affairs of the nation's news, from whether it won a test match or the Eurovision Song Contest to the state of unemployment and foreign affairs.

Reading leads to various kinds of real social behaviour with librarians and book shop sales staff, with whom there may be regular interaction. Readers often discuss books with friends and colleagues, novels with friends, non-fiction books with academic colleagues, for example.

Adult classes have the same properties, such as providing social support, as other leisure groups. They are also easier to join than many; in a MORI survey (1982) respondents were asked what they did when they felt lonely; evening classes were the only kind of leisure group mentioned as a solution.

The motivation of reading

People may read for fewer minutes per day than they watch TV, but it is nevertheless rated as a greater source of satisfaction. An American national survey found that 32 per cent found reading a source of 'great satisfaction', compared with only 17 per cent for TV; reading scored about the same as 'being with friends' (see p. 81). Why is reading so satisfying?

Newspapers
We saw that on average people read the papers for a quarter of an hour a day, and this was unaffected by the advent of TV. The newspapers have discovered what sells papers, and it is violence, sex, famous people, especially royalty in Britain, and unexpected or bizarre events. The tabloids have a lot of this, and the actual news is put in terms of human interest stories, while the serious papers have more impersonal reports and commentary. In both cases the readers are being informed about what is going on in the world and their neighbourhood.

Magazines
These provide more specialized information and, as we said above, enable their readers to keep in touch with other members of a social group.

Light fiction
The majority of books which are read fall into this category: romances for women, thrillers and adventure stories for men. How can we find out what makes them so satisfying? One way is to ask readers, though it is quite possible that they don't really know. Mann

(1969) did this to a large sample of Mills and Boon readers. They thought that these books were popular for the following reasons:

well-written, interesting, good stories and plots	33%
pleasant light reading	25%
relaxing, easy to read	14%
clean, wholesome, not sordid	12%
can identify with characters, true to life	11%
escapist, helps one to forget troubles and cheer up	8%

Another way is to examine the special features of very popular writing. This has been done for the books of Enid Blyton, a very popular writer of books for the eight-to-twelve age group. Enid Blyton scholars think that the secret of her appeal is that the heroes and heroines are easy to identify with, having a similar background to that of most of the readers, except that they are a little older and more prosperous. The children in the stories are happy, successful, consume nice food and drink, have pets, and the boys face up to dangerous adventures and protect the girls (Ray, 1982). This looks clearly like wish fulfilment. But there are many very popular stories where such identification with the characters seems unlikely. How many readers could identify with Miss Marple or Hercule Poirot, for example? And many people enjoy *Alice in Wonderland* who are not small girls.

For any novel, play or story there has to be a plot, and this may be an essential ingredient, to maintain interest and make readers want to read on. There are a limited number of basic plots: in a detective story we want to know who did it and how; in a romance whether love will triumph, together with the lurid details of how it triumphs; in a thriller how the villains will be defeated, together with the lurid details of how they come to a sticky end; in a 'quest' how the hero or heroine will triumph over a series of obstacles. Once the reader becomes involved in the story, and to some degree suspends disbelief, he or she has become involved in a fantasy social world, which may be more interesting or more gratifying than his or her real social world. This process is sometimes interpreted as escapism, sometimes as relaxation. The relaxation theory is supported by surveys of readers; and Alan Boon, of Mills and Boon, said his books 'could take the place of Valium'. But while some books may be relaxing – Jane

Austen, for example – others are exciting and will have the opposite effect; a slightly smaller percentage of readers say they read to be stimulated, mainly men, who of course read a lot of thrillers and adventure stories.

There are several other ingredients of literature. Humour is certainly important in light reading and may be so in serious fiction too; it is certainly important in journalism. And it is important not only because it makes reading more rewarding, but also because the nature of humour is often to juxtapose two points of view of a person or situation, and this may add to understanding it.

Serious literature

What is the motivation for reading 'good' or serious literature, which does not consist just of romantic or aggressive adventures or murders? This is a minority taste; Mann (1982) found that only 3 per cent of his sample were reading a modern novel. These are books in which the characters and the relationships between them are more complex, involve moral conflicts, or provide some commentary on social issues or the meaning of life. So one of the gratifications of reading may be better understanding of the self. This can be obtained from novels and plays, but also from popular psychology books, and other 'self-improvement' literature. The large number of books on assertiveness, feminism, relaxation and the rest fall into this category. Solomon (1986) argues that literature educates the emotions, by re-creating and articulating with words and metaphors what it is like to experience romantic love, the terror of war or the emotional experiences of another culture. The reader, by identifying with the characters, acts out the drama in personal terms, he experiences and understands these emotions, and literary masterpieces are able to teach the collective culture and the spirit of the age, and he is able to understand himself better.

Study and non-fiction

Many people, as we have seen, engage in some study at home, in connection with their jobs or further education, while others read serious non-fiction books related to hobbies or other interests, such as gardening, travel, history or religion. In a survey of 5,600 taking adult education classes, it was found that the main aims for those

213

taking courses for qualifications and for other courses were rather different:

	qualifying (%)	non-qualifying (%)
for career or promotion	67	20
self-development	16	42
social	2	13
interest in subject	14	22

Source: Woodley *et al.*, 1987

Clearly the main motivation of those taking degree, technical or similar courses is vocational, but for the other courses, such as those arranged by the WEA and LEA, the aims were mainly self-development and interest in the subject. By self-development here was meant improving health and well-being, keeping the mind active or wanting to do something creative. There was much more interest in the subject itself in this group and also in the social aspects of education. The author once taught an extramural class which tackled totally different subjects each year, though the group stayed intact.

HOBBIES

I mean by hobbies a variety of activities which are carried out mainly alone and at home. These include gardening, DIY, needlework, arts and crafts, photography, looking after pets, bird-watching, geology, collecting things, making or operating radios or computers, most gambling and playing computer games. Nearly all of them involve some skilled activity, often using manual skills, and are therefore similar to some kind of skilled work, except that they are not done in a group or under supervision and there is no pay, though there may be some material benefit, as in vegetable gardening, needlework, DIY and, for some, gambling.

Statistics

In Britain in 1990 48 per cent of the population over sixteen did some gardening in the four weeks before the interview, 43 per cent did some DIY, and 41 per cent of women and almost no men did some dressmaking, needlework or knitting (General Household

Survey, 1990). In 1983 7 per cent reported engaging in hobbies, arts or crafts in the previous four weeks, typically on ten occasions in the four weeks, i.e. about two and a half times a week for those who did it. Murray and Kippax (1977) in Australia found that in a city with established TV men spent three and a half hours, and women four and a half hours a week on their hobbies.

Adolescents, especially boys, spend a lot of time on computer games, 30 per cent of them every day at the moment. They eventually get bored with any particular game, but the manufacturers keep up a stream of increasingly more sophisticated new models, now including interaction with film material, and of an increasingly violent nature.

Age

The proportion of the population who report hobbies rises to a peak at twenty to twenty-four and stays at a high level to age sixty to sixty-nine, after which it falls. The total number reporting either hobbies, gardening, DIY or needlework stays at over 80 per cent for most of the life span, well above any leisure activity (Birch, 1979). However, hobbies seem to be most important for the elderly and retired. Van Loon and Dooghe (1978) in Holland found that hobbies were more important than social life for predicting life satisfaction among the elderly. Luszki and Luszki (1985) found that increasing time for hobbies and other leisure activities was rated as one of the main advantages of growing older. Older people go out less and more of their leisure is in the home, which is where hobbies are carried out.

Children also take up hobbies; most of them collect things, such as stamps, engine numbers, dolls or model soldiers, but this falls off with adolescence (Olmsted, 1991). Girls in particular are very interested in pets, and boys have an early interest in scientifically related hobbies, like radio and photography (Johnson, 1987), though as we saw, computer games are at present their main preoccupation.

Gender

Hobbies are quite strongly sex-linked. Women do needlework, for example making clothes, and preserve food, men do DIY, as well as repairing cars or motor bikes, and doing things with radios and computers; both do gardening but men do a bit more. Both boys and girls collect things, but it is mainly men who collect things in adult life. And it is mainly boys who play computer games. We have just seen that gender differences in leisure appear in childhood.

Class
In the 1980 General Household Survey 21 per cent of those in social class 1 (professional) reported hobbies, arts or crafts, compared with 2 per cent in class 6 (unskilled). There are similar differences for gardening (61 as against 38 per cent), and for DIY (67 as against 23 per cent), though for dressmaking there is a reversal, plus a peak for class 3.

History

Gardens have been tended since the ancient world: decorative pleasure gardens for the rich, vegetable gardens for others. However, small domestic gardens with lawns, flowers and vegetables have grown in popularity since the early nineteenth century. Growing food and looking after animals hark back to the days before work and leisure became divided, and are a kind of forerunner of leisure as we know it. DIY, looking after and building houses, are very similar; this was a central part of life for centuries. But it is only since the end of the Second World War that DIY has become a leisure activity; the provision of the tools and equipment has become a major commercial activity. While men mended or built houses, women made and mended clothes and preserved food. These activities too can be traced to the days before leisure had been discovered. Those who could afford it have always collected things, such as books, pictures and furniture. We have seen that children like to collect stamps or dolls, and it is now possible for most people to make collections, even if it is only engine numbers or match boxes.

Other hobbies reflect developments in technology, as with photography and computing; others reflect a general increase of interest, for example, in ecology or bird-watching. We saw earlier that there is evidence that exposure to TV actually increases interests in hobbies. The hobbies people do vary with the culture. In China the most popular ones are shadow boxing and cultivating flowers (Hu, 1990).

Social relations

We have just seen that gardening, DIY, dressmaking and preserving food are traditional domestic activities. They were carried out at home, for the family, and usually by or with the help of the family. They were part of family life. Nowadays, however, they are usually carried out by individuals, working alone, and are much more solitary, though the family will benefit from the results.

Other hobbies, like collecting, arts and crafts, photography, et cetera are also basically solitary, although it is usual for the results to be shown, exhibited, or put into competitions. Very often people belong to a club, which has regular meetings, where there are talks, displays of work and sheer socializing with fellow enthusiasts. Gardeners meet over the garden fence or at allotments, give each other seedlings and may exhibit their prize marrows. There may be a journal with news of other members, developments in the field of interest and announcements of events. Collectors of pewter spoons or ancient weighing machines (these are real examples) have societies and journals, may have worldwide links with other collectors, and have regular meetings with others who share these interests. They join a social world, with leaders and committees, where it is possible to be esteemed. Small boys who collect engine numbers have less formal organizations, but they too go on outings together, watch trains at the same time and place, and compare notes on the engines which have been seen.

Other hobbies are social in a quite different sense. It is familiar that people talk to their pets, and dogs and cats have been found to provide a lot of companionship. People also talk to computers and treat them as people; boys have been heard saying, 'You dumb machine', or 'He's trying to get me' – the machine being seen as male (Griffiths, 1993). However, computer games are also social in a more familiar sense, since boys compete with one another to get the highest scores or compete directly in war games, some of them of a very aggressive and bloodthirsty character (G. Singh, personal communication).

Motivation

Social motivation is clearly relevant here; we have just seen how some hobbies are part of family life, and others link people into groups and organizations of those with the same interests. Stebbins (1979) interviewed amateur archaeologists; three-quarters of them thought the social rewards were important. Many of them took the family along on expeditions so, although the hobby was pursued outside the home, it was still a family affair. They also enjoyed the social interaction with the other archaeologists, talking shop, as well as singing and storytelling at meetings, and the group fieldwork expeditions. He found that for many of them about a third of their friends were also archaeologists. However, they thought that these social rewards were less important than the activity itself.

Hobbies are important sources of identity and self-esteem. Shamir (1992) assessed the importance of leisure identities compared to student and family identities. He found that leisure activities were salient in defining the self under certain conditions – when a lot of effort and skill was involved, time and money were put into it, and when there was also some social commitment. This applied most to involvement with politics, voluntary work and some artistic activities, but not to dancing, bridge or cinema. These conditions clearly apply to the kinds of hobby we have been describing. Stebbins (1979), in his studies of various kinds of amateurs, investigated several ways in which these might contribute to the self. His interviews found evidence for: self-actualization, such as development of skills and knowledge; self-esteem, via enhanced reputation; self-expression, by showing how well one can perform; and self-enrichment, as when an amateur archaeologist finds an ancient remain, and imagines the way of life of its original user 4,000 years earlier. Serious hobbies, as with other kinds of leisure, can create a kind of new inner world, a way of looking at things – as a calendar of events – what people think about much of the time, their hopes, preoccupations and fantasies, which are supported by a social network of those with similar concerns.

Hobbies look like cases of intrinsic motivation, since there is no external pressure to pursue them, once the interest has been established, and there is great satisfaction when its goals are attained, whether these be growing marrows, finding ancient remains, or spotting railway engines. Kleiber, Larson and Csikszentmihalyi (1986) tested seventy-five adolescents, and some of their results are shown in Table 8.1.

Table 8.1: Hobbies and intrinsic motivation

			Subjective experience		
Activities	IM	PF	Aff	Conc	Chall
Socializing	.26	.11	.36	− .16	− .24
Sports and games	.48	.29	.22	.38	.77
TV watching	.08	.40	− .09	− .19	− .72
Music listening	.53	.36	.10	.07	.48
Art and hobbies	.66	.57	− .01	.61	.98
Reading	.16	.58	− .25	− .11	− .17
Thinking	− .46	− .16	− .27	.06	− .12
Rest and napping	.57	.03	− .59	− 1.00	− .70
Eating	.45	.04	.30	− .29	− .51
Studying	− .44	− .37	− .27	.48	.73

Note IM = Intrinsic motivation, PF = Perceived freedom, Aff = Positive affect, Conc = Concentration, Chall = Challenge.

Source: Kleiber, Larson & Csikszentmihalyi, 1986

It can be seen that hobbies and arts scored higher on intrinsic motivation than any other activity (measured by not wishing to be doing something else); hobbies also scored very high on challenge and concentration, but quite low on positive affect. This gives a very good picture of engaging in a typical hobby – it is a serious and challenging kind of activity, done entirely for its own sake, it does not produce much immediate joy, but rather longer-term satisfaction.

Argyle and Lu (1990), with a sample of 114 adults, found that those who reported a 'committed' leisure activity reported more challenge, but also more leisure satisfaction and happiness than those who did not (see p. 168). McGoldrick (1982) studied 1,800 men who had retired early and their wives, most of whom were very satisfied with their early retirement and who were well off and in good health. They were very active, including taking part in hobbies like music, DIY, bird-watching, fishing and stamp collecting. Perhaps all this was a satisfactory replacement for work. Indeed, the key to understanding hobbies may be in terms of intrinsic job satisfaction; people enjoy their work when it has certain features, especially autonomy, use of a variety of skills, completing a meaningful piece of work, impact on the lives of others, and feedback on effectiveness (Hackman, 1980). Hobbies meet these conditions more than any other kind of leisure, and this is probably when they can be successful replacements for work. We discussed the spillover hypothesis in Chapter 7; we decided that this is a rather weak effect but does happen for some groups; there are workers who take up leisure which is related to their work. Gerstl and Hutton (1966) found that 23 per cent of a group of professional engineers did this, and 73 per cent did work-related reading. If hobbies are, as we suggested, like skilled work it might be expected that skilled manual workers would do them more, such as more DIY and gardening, since they have the skills to do it and because this saves money. In fact, only 7 per cent of skilled and semi-skilled workers and their families report hobbies, arts or crafts. The explanation for the much greater hobby activity of social class 1 may be that most hobbies require space in the home, or a garden or special equipment, so that richer people and those with larger houses are in a better position to engage in them.

There has been a lot of interest in the hobby of collecting; Freud thought it was a sublimation of anal motivation but there has been no support for this. Others have seen it as an irrational obsession in which non-utilitarian objects become 'sacred', as an obsession or addiction, as an economic activity, as an extension of the self, or to emphasize the new social world that is entered (Formanek, 1991). I think that collecting is a pure case of a new interest being acquired – through socialization, for example – with the result that pursuing and finding new specimens for the collection is rewarding in itself.

We return to computer games, which, as we saw, are the main leisure activity for many teenagers. These are not exactly 'hobbies', but they are mainly done at home, though not always alone, so we put them here. There is a variety of these games but all involve a TV screen and a computer. Examples are Nintendo, Street Fighter and Batman. About 30 per cent of teenage boys play daily, another 34 per cent more than once a week, and of those that play, 36 per cent do so for over two hours, 10 per cent for over four hours, and 20 per cent are 'addicted' in the sense that they gave affirmative answers to questions like 'Do you become restless if you cannot play?' This is sometimes a social activity, though the games are often played alone, and are usually taken up as a result of the influence of friends. There is social motivation when boys compete or 'fight' each other, and the main motivation reported is 'for fun', and play produces a good mood and excitement, but particularly in the addicts. This suggests that seeking arousal is part of the motivation here.

There has been some concern about the effects of this game playing. Most of the games are aggressive and several studies have found that children become more aggressive after playing, though nothing is known of the long-term effects. However, most adolescents discover other interests, such as the opposite sex or football, and it is unlikely that much damage is done (Griffiths, 1993). Furthermore, this may be a temporary craze and may pass, like the hula hoop.

About 8 per cent of adolescents play fruit machines in arcades; this is a form of gambling and costs money, which may come from lunch money or stealing, in some cases. These young people may meet at the arcade, and there is a group, but they usually play alone, though there may be competition here too. The risk produces a mood of excitement but also anger after losing, which is what usually happens (Griffiths, 1991).

Hobbies are evidently good for people, in being important sources of satisfaction, especially for the old and retired. They have less effect on immediate joy, though this certainly happens, for example when a collector finds something or a gardener grows something. Hobbies are often used with young people, both psychiatric cases and delinquents, as part of therapy. And research has found that hobbies can be therapeutic; Rasanen and Arajarvi (1985) found that they contributed to the recovery of children in a psychiatric hospital. Teiremaa (1981) found that people who developed asthma were less likely to have had hobbies.

SPORT AND EXERCISE

Sport is one of the main forms of leisure, and one that produces the most benefits. It is also theoretically interesting, in that it is one of the few forms of leisure which is both challenging and enjoyable. It contains a strong social component.

Statistics

American epidemiologists think that only about 20 per cent of the adult population takes enough exercise for their health, another 40 per cent takes some exercise but not enough, and the remaining 40 per cent has a sedentary life style (McAuley, 1992). What is the situation in Britain? As we saw in earlier chapters, walking is the main form of exercise; 41 per cent did it in the four weeks before the GHS survey, on average twice a week, and other studies show that it took them about fifteen minutes. The next most popular were swimming (15 per cent had done it, once a week), keep fit or yoga (12 per cent, but 16 per cent of women, 2.25 times per week), and cycling (9 per cent, 2.5 times per week). At least one activity was reported in the last four weeks by 64.5 per cent – 47.8 per cent excluding walking. Sport was rarer, the most popular being football (5 per cent, but 10 per cent of males, 1.25 times per week), and golf (5 per cent, once a week). Health research shows that to ward off heart attacks about twenty-eight minutes of exercise a day is desirable; it looks as if over half the population takes no exercise at all.

Men take part more in every kind of sport or exercise, except keep fit and yoga, which women do much more. Professional and middle-class people do much more sport and exercise; 60 per cent of professionals do at least one sport, apart from walking, compared to 28 per cent of unskilled. The only reversal is for the 'sports' of snooker and darts.

Sport and exercise fall off with age, and do so faster for women, who do very little after sixty, apart from walking. The main forms of exercise for the elderly are walking and gardening.

History

In preliterate societies and throughout the ancient world there were races, wrestling and ball games, sometimes with sticks. Most of these were individual contests, but there is also evidence of primitive team games, defending territory. In Egypt there was hunting, archery, fighting with clubs, and primitive bowling and territorial team games. In Greece sport was connected with military training; success carried honour and financial rewards. The Olympic Games, which started in 776 BC, were ahead of their time in being rule-governed and well organized. The Romans often used Greeks as sports performers to entertain them, and slaves and prisoners in gladiatorial displays, on their numerous festival days. Sport was again part of military training. However, there was also a love of fitness, and the baths, where there was swimming, were very popular.

In the Middle Ages there was a lot of individual exercise; many swam, skated and engaged in archery and hunting. There was some primitive football and tennis. From 1400 onwards there was a lot of 'folk football' in England, where whole villages would have a violent and uncontrolled contest (Elias & Dunning, 1986).

From the 1500s onwards, the social élite preferred dancing to sport, though there was a more elegant version of football, and the aristocrats also took part in tournaments. The middle class engaged in archery, the lower class in running, jumping and wrestling, but also in bull-baiting, dog-fighting and cudgelling. Gradually these violent and disorganized sports became displaced by more controlled and less violent ones. Cricket's rules were laid down in 1774. Meanwhile physical education was being developed in Germany and Scandinavia.

The nineteenth century showed a complete transformation of organized sport, much of it taking place in Britain. 'Sports that originally began elsewhere, such as tennis (which derives from Renaissance France), were modernized and exported as if they too were raw materials imported for British industry to transform and then ship out as finished goods' (Guttman, 1986). Organized sport became a worldwide leisure activity. Furthermore, this development of sport was very much a British middle-class phenomenon; football came from the public schools, perhaps as part of muscular Christianity; the rules for football were first laid down at Cambridge in 1862; rugby came from Rugby school. Golf, squash, badminton, hockey, rowing, athletics, croquet, horse racing, fox hunting, even skiing, were such British products, though ice hockey and lacrosse came from Canada, and basketball from the USA. Not since ancient Greece had athletic and other contests been so well regulated, but they were now less violent and the rules were written down in detail. Elias and Dunning (1986) argue that there has been a continuous development of rules, fairness and removal of violence from sport. This is true of the history of football, though American football is still violent. Ice hockey is even more violent and there are frequent rule infractions, often in the form of 'professional fouls'. Boxing is very violent, but the rules are enforced; it is doubtful whether the same can be said of wrestling. It must be admitted that there are still infringements of the rules, and the press gives far greater coverage to, and presumably the public gets more enjoyment from, such events as the Grand National failing to start, cricketers illicitly scratching the ball, ice skaters being hit with iron bars, runners barging each other off the track and athletes taking drugs, than to the actual outcomes (Barnard, 1994). For most sports there is a further expectation that players should not only play with courage, skill and self-control, they should also be courteous, kind and generous to their opponents, should try to win, but not ruthlessly, be good losers, and should play for the team, not for individual glory. Cricket and football were long regarded as sources of moral education (Winnifrith, 1989).

As we saw in Chapter 2, during the late twentieth century there have been two further developments: many more people now engage in exercise than in sport, and there has been the growing popularity of dangerous sports.

Since 1971 there has been a remarkable increase in indoor sports: the number doing at least one has increased by no less than 60 per cent, probably due to the building of new sports halls and pools; there has been an increase of 13 per cent in those doing outdoor sports. In addition the average frequency of participation has increased, and the increases have been most among the elderly and retired and women, suggesting that age and sex have ceased to be barriers (Gratton & Tice, 1994).

Social relationships

A number of social relationships are found in connection with sport.

Individual competition

This is one of the classic sporting relations; the non-aggressive games here are tennis, squash, golf and the like. These games are basically competitive, and the game depends on the players trying to defeat one another. But at the same time they have to cooperate, especially in keeping to and interpreting the same rules. They must play it in the same spirit, for example with the same degree of seriousness or competitiveness. There is also a high degree of coordination, where each anticipates and responds to the other, so that an observer of a long rally at tennis might be excused for thinking this was a co-operative enterprise.

Individual aggressive contests

These, like boxing and wrestling, constitute another classic relation. These look less cooperative, but again there is cooperation to keep to the rules, and in boxing there is split-second timing to anticipate and usually avoid the other's punches, while in wrestling there is close bodily contact. Rough and tumble play among boys doesn't look very cooperative either, yet they do it with their friends, and it is clearly a form of sociable activity. There may still be a positive bond among men engaged in more violent fights.

Sports teams

Here cooperation is needed within the teams, especially in games where there is a lot of coordinated play, as in football and basketball, as opposed to cricket and baseball. It has often been found that successful teams are more cohesive, that is they are attracted to the team and the other members. However, this is often not found if cohesiveness is measured by how much the team members like one another. But 'task cohesion', that is commitment to the team and its goals, has consistently been found to be related to team success and also to members staying with the team and to (low) absenteeism (Widmeyer, Brawley & Carron, 1992). But does cohesiveness cause success, or vice versa? Longitudinal studies have found both relationships. Cohesion is also found to be associated with satisfaction, in sports teams as in groups of other kinds. In some other kinds of groups there has been evidence of 'social loafing', that is the larger the group the less effort each member makes. This is not found in sports teams, like relay races, especially when individual effort is identifiable (Gill, 1986).

Leaders and followers

Research on some other kinds of groups has found that there are often separate task and social leaders. However, this is not found in sports groups – the same individuals do both jobs (Rees, 1983). Research on the skills of appointed leaders in other social settings has found widespread support for the importance of three dimensions of leadership: initiating structure (i.e. assigning tasks, deciding what will be done and how, et cetera), consideration (i.e. looking after the welfare of members, treating them as equals, et cetera); and the participant or democratic style. The combination of these skills has been found necessary both for effectiveness and satisfaction, though the balance of the dimensions varies with the situation (Argyle, 1989). These leadership skills have been found to be important for sports teams too, though there is strongest support for initiating structure, and not much for participation. The balance of these dimensions varies with the situation, for example a greater need for initiating structure rather than consideration at lower levels of skill (Bird, 1977), and a greater need for initiating structure with highly interdependent teams, as in basketball and football compared with swimming or tennis (Fry, Kerr & Lee, 1986). There is need for consideration in teams where there is rivalry between players, and all need recognition.

Chelladurai (1984) proposed a theory of sports leadership, which has been applied to sports coaches rather than to captains of teams. The central hypothesis is that performance and satisfaction will be greater if the leader's actual behaviour is consistent with the group's preferences and also with the requirements of the situation, along the five dimensions he distinguished. Support has been obtained for athletics and basketball, and it was found that these preferences vary: basketball players wanted positive feedback, track and field athletes liked a lot of training and instruction.

Another idea about sports leadership came from Grusky (1963), who suggested that players in central positions would interact more and have to coordinate more with other players, and thus develop leadership skills; they would therefore be likely to become captains or managers, and there has been some support for this.

Audience effects

There is often an audience for sport, sometimes a very large one. It is found that teams are more likely to win when playing at home; this may be partly due to familiarity with the territory or defence of it, but is more likely due to support from the crowd. The effect is greater for American football and basketball than for baseball and seems to be due to better offensive play (Edwards, 1979). Audiences are probably more effective when larger, physically closer and vocally enthusiastic. They can reward good performance, encourage aggression and energy, and intimidate the opposition; laboratory research on audience effects shows that it is more effective at motivating dominant, well-learned responses and when the audience is able to evaluate performance (Gill, 1986). It is doubtful whether an audience could evaluate the performance of rowing crews, for example.

Sports clubs

These are a special kind of leisure group, and there are several varieties, each with their special features. British rugger clubs, for example, are well known for their noisy, drunken, male atmosphere. Golf clubs are well known for their social exclusiveness, keeping out Jews and blacks in the past. Tennis clubs have been found to be exclusive both socially and in terms of standard of play (Waser, 1989). Many clubs have formal procedures for admission of new members, who have to be proposed and seconded.

Exercise

Some people do their exercises alone, at home on an Exercycle, for example, but many do it in groups, as in aerobics classes, at certain hours in swimming pools, or on particular jogging routes. As a result they become familiar with the others, and this gives them social support to carry on exercising, and also 'social facilitation', which encourages them to work harder. Little is known about the social relations in connection with dangerous sports. In some sports like rafting and rock-climbing, those concerned are closely dependent on each other; in some cases of parachuting they have saved each other's lives; this would certainly be expected to produce strong bonds between those concerned.

The motivation of sport

Some people put more effort into sport than into any other activity, including work and sex. Professionals get paid for it, but the great

227

majority of players are amateurs, and many of these also show signs of very high motivation, as in the cases of marathon runners, top athletes and, indeed, keen and successful performers at any sport. There have been a number of surveys, with tens of thousands of subjects, who were asked why they participated in sport. Markland and Hardy (1993) asked 400 English students why they took part in sport or exercise, and their answers were as follows:

fitness	56.6%
enjoy physical activity	51.3%
social and affiliative	35.3%
health related	30.3%
stress management or relaxation	29.0%
weight control	22.4%
develop personal skills	17.1%
competition	7.9%

American studies have found more evidence of motivation by 'fun' or 'challenge'. However, people may not be fully aware of their motivation; for example, what is the motivation for dangerous sports?

Social motivation may be more important than the above survey suggests, because all sport and most exercise is done with other people, indeed cannot be done without them, and in a close relationship with them. The rather general concept of affiliative motivation, coined by psychologists, is not very helpful here, since sports relationships take a variety of forms; perhaps we choose the sports which fit our particular form of social motivation. Some of the main ones are:

cooperation, for example rowing, team games and, in a more intense form, climbing and rafting;

competition, for example tennis and squash, but also competition between teams;

parallel performance is found in some cooperative sports like rowing, and also in non-competitive exercise like aerobics;

dominance applies to the motivation of sports leaders and coaches, and perhaps also to individuals and teams which 'dominate' the other side;

sociability, in the sense of enjoying each other's company and engaging in conversation, applies to membership of sports clubs, where the members are drawn together by their intense shared interest;

achievement motivation, which is predictive of an interest in competitive sport, and how long people stay.

Intrinsic motivation

Is sports behaviour due to intrinsic motivation? Many respondents to surveys say they take part in sport because they enjoy it. Those who swim or run find the sheer activity very pleasant. If they put some effort into it they start to feel euphoric through the release of endorphins, and this may explain why many become 'addicted' to exercise, that is they feel off colour if they have to miss it. Research by the Csikszentmihalyi group finds that sport is rated high on intrinsic motivation, and also on challenge and concentration (Kleiber, Larson & Csikszentmihalyi, 1990). It shares this pattern with hobbies, but sport produces more positive affect.

Sports motivation is increased, however, by the experience of success, and there is a clear relation between engaging in sport and being good at it. Intrinsic motivation is increased by freedom of choice, for example over the exercises used in a fitness class (Gill, 1986). A lot of research in this area has been inspired by Bandura's theory of 'self-efficacy' (1977). A number of studies have found that self-efficacy does correlate with sports performance, for example at basketball and back-diving, though it has some further causes (Feltz, 1992). It also predicts whether individuals will take up some form of exercise, whether they will stick to it and how much effort they will put in (McAuley, 1992).

Socialization

How is sports motivation acquired? Socialization research shows that about two-thirds of sporting interests are acquired in childhood. They come about equally from home and from school, though the balance varies between different sports. Schools often give massive reinforcement to sporting success, often more than to academic success. Parents, however, may pass on their own enthusiasms, teach their children to swim, climb mountains, et cetera. Studies of those who are later very successful in sport find that they were 'winners' the first time they played, showing a high degree of ability at an early age.

Aggression

Aggression plays a part in many sports. It plays a central part in boxing and wrestling; in the past there were more aggressive sports than these, such as cudgelling or boxing with iron bands round the hand, so that it was common for the performers to be killed. The most aggressive team game today is ice hockey. In Holland it is reported that there are 1.2 million sports injuries a year, mainly from this and from football. The aggression is instrumental, that is it seems necessary to the play, though there is no evidence that the more aggressive team wins (Gill, 1986). The reason for this aggression is thought to be reinforcement by coaches and the media, and imitation of professional players (Smith, 1979). Some have argued that aggression is present in all competitive sport, though the aggression is only indirectly to the other players, and directly to the ball, for instance; in the case of volleyball, however, the ball is likely to hit players on the other side.

Dangerous sports

Why do so many people risk their lives at hang-gliding, parachuting or mountaineering, at which many lose their lives every year? The simplest explanation, and it may be correct, is in terms of a need for excitement, that they are 'arousal seekers', just as others enjoy football crowds and loud music. However, the level of arousal in some of these sports is so high as to be terrifying, and scarcely rewarding in any ordinary sense. Another explanation has been offered. It is found that dogs, in experiments in which they received electric shocks, shifted rapidly from a state of terror to one of ecstasy when released. During their first parachute jump many participants are terrified, and stunned when they land. But in later jumps the terror is less and they experience a state of ecstasy afterwards which may last for some hours. Solomon put forward his 'opponent processes' theory that, when a period of stress ends, the central nervous system rebounds in some way to produce a strong positive affective state, and this sequence increases with further periods of stress; this is the reward

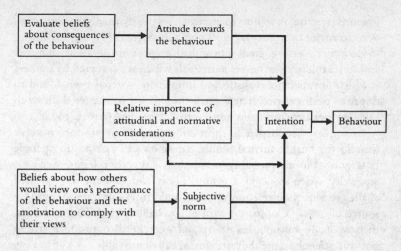

Source: Fishbein & Ajzen, 1980

Figure 8.4: The Fishbein and Ajzen model

which motivates further adventures (Solomon & Corbit, 1973). Yet another possible explanation is that participants enjoy the feeling of competence when they are able to perform a difficult task and to control their own anxiety; this is mentioned by climbers and racing drivers (Piet, 1987).

Health beliefs
Many say they engage in sport or exercise for their health, to keep fit, lose weight or improve their appearance, and this appears to be an important factor in jogging and aerobics. But the drop-out rate from such forms of exercise is very high, and we have seen that most people take too little exercise, from a health point of view. The most influential theory has been Fishbein and Ajzen's (1975), which said that behaviour is due to intentions, and these are due to expecting valuable outcomes and to the desire to comply with social norms (see Figure 8.4).

Studies of perseverance with regular exercise have found that intentions do not predict behaviour very well: people 'intend' to do it but they don't. Outcome expectancies have a moderate effect on intentions, social norms very little, and another factor is positive affect towards exercise. Attempts to increase exercise by manipulating intentions have not been successful (Roberts, 1989).

However, setting goals can enhance sport motivation. For example, if athletics coaches set joint goals which are accepted by trainees – which are specific, realistic and immediate – it has been found to improve performance. These goals should aim to master skills or to improve performance, and not just to 'try harder' (Ames, 1992).

As we saw in Chapter 4, sport and exercise can produce massive benefits for health, mental health, happiness and just putting people in a good mood, probably more than any other leisure activity, especially when done in a group. Sport and exercise also present challenge and require concentration and effort, and are a common source of 'flow'. Compared with other challenging leisure activities, such as study or hobbies, sport and exercise also produce strong positive affect because they are intrinsically enjoyable.

WATCHING SPORT

Introduction

Watching sport is a very widespread leisure activity, for example about 11 per cent of men in Britain do it about once a week. It has been a widespread leisure activity for a long time, from the Roman empire onwards. Today it is not chariot races but soccer which is worldwide the most watched sport; for example, 200 million watched the World Cup on TV in 1986. Soccer spectators have been the most studied, and we shall focus on them here, though Wimbledon and the Olympics also attract very large audiences, on the spot and via TV. And spectators include different kinds of people, with different kinds of behaviour. However, for all of them there is more to being a spectator than simply watching the game; they demonstrate their enthusiasm in a variety of ways, and they appear to be participating in an intense emotional and social drama.

Statistics

According to the 1983 General Household Survey, which interviewed 19,000 people, 11 per cent of males and 5 per cent of females had watched some sport during the previous four weeks, and they had done so about three times during this period. Six per cent of men and 1 per cent of women had been to a football match, a considerable decline since 1977. Far more people watched football than any other sport. Nearly as many had played football during this period – 6 per cent of men but no women – and they had done so five times during the four weeks. Other studies have found that the majority of spectators also play the game they go to watch.

There are few women at football matches, and they are mainly girlfriends or otherwise related to male fans. Women watch sport much less, and they watch different sports, such as tennis, gymnastics, swimming and skiing, though some of this is watching their children. However, it is reported that women too can take a keen interest in some violent games such as bull fights and boxing, or may be more interested in the male spectators or in providing a fashion show, as at the races.

The peak age for watching sport is sixteen to twenty-four, when 8 per cent of men watch football; this falls to 2 per cent for those over seventy. All social classes in Britain go to football games, though the rate is a little higher for class 3, i.e. skilled manual and routine non-manual. However, football hooligans are drawn almost entirely from the lowest social class. The social class of spectators varies a lot with the sport. Those who watch boxing or wrestling are nearly all working-class, those who go to golf, point to points or tennis much more middle-class. This may explain the differences in the amount of violence found.

History

In Chapter 2 we traced the development of watching sport from Greece and Rome to the Middle Ages.

In the seventeenth and eighteenth centuries the popular sports in England were cock-fighting, dog-fights, boxing and wrestling, and horse-racing. Some of these sports attracted very large crowds, for example 100,000 at Epsom, and 10,000 at major wrestling matches. The crowds enjoyed the more aggressive sports, relished in the blood, and there was drinking, gambling and violence. The horse races were also occasions for colourful displays of fashion, and other activities (Guttmann, 1986).

Elias and Dunning (1986) argue that there has been a long-term trend to civilize sport, making it more controlled by rules and less violent. Games have been made fair and equal, unlike some of the Roman spectacles with very uneven fights involving lions, dwarfs, women and such like. Guttmann (1986) thinks that this applied to spectators too, and that a 'culture' of spectators has developed, with more orderly behaviour and respect for opponents.

By the early nineteenth century cricket and football became the most popular sports. Cricket crowds, who were mainly middle-class, were well behaved, though not in Australia, where they were more working-class and often rioted and invaded the pitch. Soccer soon emerged as the proletarian sport; there were audiences of up to 50,000 by the 1890s, of mostly working-class men, who were often badly behaved, for example by invading the pitch. In America the popular sports were baseball and American football, and here too mass spectators appeared towards the end of the century, but were relatively well behaved. There were several reasons for this increase in spectatorship: the growth of leisure, the building of railways – making it possible to go to away matches – the increase in sports news and magazines, and the general commercialization of sport by its promoters.

The spectators at some other sports, like tennis, were much better behaved, with an atmosphere of afternoon tea and strawberries; many of them are women, and middle-class ones at that. Some other sports were more disorderly than football: boxing has always been for working-class males and involves a lot of drinking and gambling (Robins, 1982).

The social behaviour of spectators

Spectators don't just watch. We shall discuss what else they do, in the case of football. They certainly do watch, very intently, and they respond loudly and emotionally to what happens on the field, by jumping up and down and shouting, especially at the scoring of goals, at skilful play by star players, fouls and what are thought to be wrong decisions by the referee. The greatest excitement is shown by the supporters on the terraces, who are younger and of a lower social class than those seated behind them in the stands. Fans on the terraces arrive long before the match, sometimes in a procession; with their hats, scarves, flags, banners and whatever is the current 'uniform' they look like a medieval army (Morris, 1981). Anyone on the terraces not correctly attired would be looked at with disfavour, and anyone in the colours of the opposite side would be in trouble. There is constant noise from the shouting of chants – of which a supporters' group has a large repertoire – giving encouragement to their own team and shouting insults and obscenities at opposing fans, blowing bugles and whistles, and synchronized clapping. The insults typically suggest that the opposing supporters are weak, non-masculine 'wankers'. There are often racist slogans. Several forms of violence are common, such as invading the pitch, attacking players or referees, but usually trying to attack rival fans. This is restrained by a large police presence, usually of over 100 but of more than 300 for matches between some teams. Violent episodes are often precipitated by events on the field, such as fouls by the other side, violence on the field, or referee decisions.

Some of the fans drink a lot before the match, with their friends in the pub, and there is often trouble outside the ground and on the way to the game. The overall atmosphere is one of powerful drama, a mock battle, a quasi-religious spectacle, a serious and male-dominated display of team loyalty and identification with the group (Morris, 1981).

Varieties of spectators
Not all fans behave in the same way. Canter, Comber and Uzzell (1989) found that those who were standing were of a lower class, that they were less critical of physical violence and thought it was all right to humiliate the other side's supporters. There are informal leaders, some leading any violence, others leading the chants or clapping, or organizing travel and transport. Sometimes the behaviour of fans is planned beforehand by the leaders. The hooligans form a definite subgroup, of the more aggressive fans. A few fans, the 'nutters', who are probably emotionally disturbed, engage in extraordinary violence, such as trying to take on 500 of the other side.

There are different age groups. Younger boys, not yet old enough to be accepted as proper hooligans, look on admiringly, while the older members, now ex-hooligans, also stand apart, wearing more normal clothes, and look on at the antics of the hooligans (Marsh, Rosser & Harré, 1978).

The motivations of spectators

Football supporters may stand in the rain and freezing weather for long periods and evidently enjoy it. What is the source of their motivation? A number have often been suggested. They are interested in the game – most play themselves – and they enjoy the excitement of a game played by highly skilled players, with its unpredictable dramas, the satisfaction when their team does well, and watching the skill of admired heroes.

Zillman, Sapolsky and Bryant (1979) showed groups of students experimentally contrasted videos of televised sports to see which ones they enjoyed most. They liked most: in American football, successful runs and passes by the home team, especially if they were keen on the team or it was their college team; in basketball, scores by American rather than foreign players, especially by famous players; in tennis, when the liked Borg beat the disliked Nastase, and when the commentator suggested that there was bitter rivalry between players; in American football, when the game was very rough, or where this was emphasized by the commentator; when viewing the game in a small group; and in football, when high-risk plays were seen.

In a later study, Bryant, Comisky and Zillman (1981) found that spectators liked not only to see violence, but they also liked to see performers risking life and limb, as in motor racing. Although sport has become far more civilized since the days of Roman gladiators or medieval cock-fighting and bear-baiting, we still have boxing and wrestling; American football and ice hockey are violent, and football involves a lot of bodily confrontation, and often injury. The civilizing process has evidently not reached some sections of society.

Spectators have a strong sense of identification with the star players, the team, the club, the other fans and, sometimes, the city or country which the team represents. This identification is enhanced by the wearing of scarves, flags and other badges; the number of followers who have their ashes scattered on the ground has been causing damage to the grass. Leicester fans would attack fans from other clubs if they appeared in Leicester (Murphy, Williams & Dunning, 1990). Inter-group psychology has shown how individual self-esteem depends partly on the success of groups to which the individual belongs. The worst violence has occurred at international matches, in Europe and South America, where national pride has been at stake.

It has been suggested that it is the quest for excitement – for people who do dull, routine jobs – which is the attraction. We have seen how, at football and other sporting events, there is a great deal of emotional drama, excitement and entertainment, apart from the actual game being watched. One fan said, 'I get so much pleasure when I'm having aggro that I nearly wet my pants . . . I go all over the country looking for it' (Elias & Dunning, 1986). The excitement may arise from the supported team winning, and celebratory riots can cause a lot of trouble. The excitement may be partly sexual, from the sight of strong, healthy and partly clothed young bodies in action.

Attending sport is a social event in that spectators go with friends or family, join other members of a well-known group and take part in a variety of joint activities, which are closely coordinated. Social motivation is certainly part of the story.

Violence on the part of spectators is a major social problem and is not confined to football. It also happens with boxing, wrestling, American football, baseball (though this is not a violent game), basket-ball and ice hockey, but not with tennis, cricket, golf, swimming, athletics or gymnastics. This suggests that violence between players has something to do with it. Van der Brug and colleagues analysed Dutch football matches to find out when crowd violence happened. It was most common: by supporters of the losing side, towards the end of the game, when the outcome was fairly clear; and when there was more instrumental violence in the game. They also found that the most violent spectators were boys aged sixteen to eighteen, who were aggressive and delinquent outside the ground, and who had not received effective parental control (Bakker, Whiting & van der Brug, 1990).

Other studies of trouble at matches have found that this is more likely when crowds are large or dense, partly because this leads to more violence on the field, and also when spectators are frustrated by being unable to get in or out, and when the referee is thought to have been unfair (Mann, 1979).

Another way of doing research on spectator violence is by showing videos in the lab and obtaining measures of aggressiveness, such as the willingness of subjects to give electric shocks to others, or TAT (Thematic Apperception Test) scores. With these methods it has been found that watching violent sport usually makes subjects more aggressive, though the opposite happened with wrestling, and watching gymnastics does not increase aggression (Bakker, Whiting & van der Brug, 1990).

British social scientists have been very interested in our famous 'football hooligans'. They are, of course, all male and are mostly between seventeen and twenty. Sociobiologists think that there is an innate tendency for males to engage in inter-group or tribal wars, in defence of territory, for the survival of the group, as our pre-human ancestors did; young males become bonded through this joint action, and have to prove their worth through fighting (Tiger, 1970). Marsh, Rosser and Harré (1978) took this argument further, and argued that the apparent aggression of football fans is only symbolic, and is restrained by rules, so that actual aggression is avoided. They obtained evidence for the existence of such rules from interviews; fans thought it was all right to humiliate rival fans or make them look stupid but not to injure them. The only ones who were really aggressive, it was claimed, were the 'nutters', who don't keep to the rules. This theory is supported by the ritualistic aspects of fan behaviour described above. The main objection to all this is that at the more important matches, especially international ones, there have been really violent episodes and deaths.

An alternative view was put forward by the Leicester group (Elias & Dunning, 1986). They observed that the hooligans came from very poor social backgrounds and did unskilled manual jobs or were unemployed. They came from housing estates, like one studied in Leicester (Murphy, Williams & Dunning, 1990), where failure in education and occupation was normal and status was gained instead by a reputation for toughness and fighting, and feuds between families and physical punishment were normal.

It has been asked why there is no real equivalent to football hooliganism in the USA. Part of the reason may be that sports clubs are not so attached to local communities, but are liable to be moved about by their owners, who come from outside. Tickets are expensive, which keeps out the lower working class, and distances to away matches are greater, with the result that rival lower-class groups have not adopted sport as an arena to express their conflicts (Murphy, Williams & Dunning, 1990).

What of the effects of watching sport? We have seen that playing sport is good for us; but what about watching it? Experiments have found that watching aggressive sports, like boxing, makes people more aggressive, not less. We have seen that going to football makes people very excited, and the same is probably true of many other sports. We have seen that spectators are very partisan and vigorous supporters of their own side. This would be expected to increase not only identification with the group – to strengthen this part of the self-image – but also self-esteem if the right team wins or if the opposing fans are defeated; it would also be expected to increase hostility to the other side.

We have included watching sports on TV in this section since this is one of the main ways of watching. However, it has been argued that TV has added to the 'corruption' of sport, caused by the need to appeal to large audiences. Crowds may stimulate the players to greater efforts, but they also lead to more aggression by players, and sometimes to their putting on a performance which is irrelevant to the game, as happens with some tennis stars and professional wrestlers. TV commentators emphasize the violence, because this is what people want to see; cameras focus on spectacle and sensation, and little understanding of the game is conveyed (Calhoun, 1987).

Marsh and colleagues (1978) suggested that there is 'media amplification', i.e. that the media exaggerate how dangerous the fans are, with the result that the latter revel in and live up to this image.

RELIGION

Statistics

In Britain about 12 per cent of the population say that they go to church once a week or more, another 8 per cent monthly, and 13 per cent regard themselves as 'core members'. Many people watch services on TV, especially the elderly, and many also engage in private religious activities; 11 per cent say they read the bible every day, and a surprising 44 per cent say they pray every day, though we don't know how long they spend on these activities. There are considerable differences between countries in such statistics; Britain is rather low; in other countries of Western Europe 29 per cent go once a week, and in the USA about 40 per cent (Ashford & Timms, 1992, and other sources).

In Britain, as elsewhere, there are large class differences. British middle-class people go to church much more: about 17 per cent go weekly, compared with 9 per cent for semi- and unskilled manual workers and their families. This may be misleading, however: Gerard (1985) constructed an index of religious commitment based on questions about the acceptance of traditional Christian beliefs, perceiving oneself as a religious person, needing prayer and contemplation, and drawing comfort and strength from religion. On this index working-class individuals scored much higher. Previous research had found that working-class people hold more traditional, fundamentalist beliefs, but this index goes well beyond beliefs, with an emphasis on commitment and devotional activities. Working-class people favour more evangelical, fundamentalist churches. A better interpretation of the data may be that it is the working classes who are more religious, but the middle classes who go to church because they feel at home in churches, which have the ambience of middle-class clubs (Argyle, 1994b).

One of the best established findings in the psychology of religion is that women are more active in religion than men. The difference is greatest for saying prayers, followed by church attendance and beliefs. The difference is greater for some churches than others: it is greatest for small Protestant sects, least for Roman Catholics and Greek Orthodox. Many explanations have been offered but none as yet agreed (Argyle & Beit-Hallahmi, 1975).

Religion takes a different form at every age. Children accept parental beliefs, and pray for dolls or bicycles. Adolescence is a period of heightened interest in religion, both emotional and intellectual; they are worried about the meaning of life, the problem of evil, the existence of God; they may be converted, deconverted or converted back again, ending up with a less simple faith or lack of one. There is a decline in religious activity to the age of thirty, perhaps because of the pressures of worldly concerns, though a few have a second or 'mystical' conversion at this time. And there has been a lot of interest on the part of people in their twenties in new sects and cults. After thirty there is a continuous increase to old age in attendance and organizational activity; basic beliefs, for example in the afterlife, increase to 100 per cent of old people, though church attendance falls off when they become infirm.

The history of religion

It is, of course, absurd to write about the history of religion in one paragraph, but it would be more absurd to say nothing. An individual's religious beliefs and practices would be totally different if he or she were brought up in Tibet, Saudi Arabia or Oxford, and if their family happened to belong to one church or another, or none. Their religious outlook would also have been quite different if they had been brought up in the Middle Ages. The practices and beliefs of every church have been developed over the course of a long history.

Religion is universal to mankind and is found in the most primitive societies. Here there is typically a priest, who wears special clothes, and is esteemed for his religious powers, such as being able to heal people. He may be a shaman and go into trances at ecstatic group meetings. Such meetings are believed by anthropologists to strengthen group cohesion, and are found in tribes where this is important in order to be able to deal with dangerous deep-sea fishing or the hunting of wild animals (Hayden, 1987).

With the development of the world religions more complex religious themes emerged with more universal appeal, together with more elaborate forms of worship, a hierarchy of priests and more extensive theologies. At different times and places during the last two thousand years these churches have been very powerful; they have been state religions and able to enforce their practices, if not their beliefs. The long period of the Middle Ages was such a time in Europe.

There have been many divisions within these churches, as splinter groups have formed: large ones, like Protestantism, and many small ones, like some of the Protestant sects. These churches, like the originals from which they split off, have had a standard form: they were led by a charismatic leader, whose ideas had a strong appeal for a group of followers, and who possessed the ability to conduct emotional group meetings. John Wesley is an example of this very successful kind of leader. The sects so formed started in a very informal way but later underwent changes towards more formality of worship, often ending up not very different from the parent church (Pope, 1942).

During the nineteenth century in the West there was a lot of conflict between science and religion, starting with the theory of evolution. This is one factor leading to a decline in church attendance in the current century from a high point in the 1890s, though there has been less of a decline in the USA. There has been a further decline in Britain and the rest of Europe in church attendance, though not in beliefs, since 1980 (Ashford & Timms, 1992). Meanwhile there has been rapid growth, especially since the 1960s, in another kind of religion: sects and cults, some Christian, some derived from Indian religions, some based on psychology, many emanating from California. A number of these sects became popular during the 1960s, and were targeted at alienated young people, many of them on drugs. The established churches have also been changing during the past few years, with a growth of charismatic services, the ordination of women, and the rewriting of hymns and prayers in a modern idiom.

Social relationships

There are reasons for thinking that a religion is basically a social phenomenon – it is conducted in groups, its benefits, as we saw earlier, are derived mainly from social attachment to churches; social influence and learning are very important.

Solitary religious activity

Some aspects of religion seem to be solitary activities, such as prayer and bible reading. And of those who report mystical religious experiences, 61 per cent say that these occurred when they were alone (Hay, 1982). However, the majority of all these people belong to churches or similar religious groups and have received a great deal of religious instruction. Furthermore, the contents of prayers and of religious experiences are themselves social in character – praying for the well-being of others and experiencing a 'desire for more harmonious relations with others, renouncing self-seeking, an empathetic, self-forgetting, mystical outlook' (Wulff, 1991). The power of the group on mystical experiences is shown by experiments on the effects of drugs; psilocybin and other hallucinogenic drugs produce what is described as a religious experience under certain conditions, i.e. having a religious background and being in a religious setting, such as the 'good Friday miracle' by Pahnke (1966), where a group of theology students were given the drug in connection with a group meditation on Good Friday.

Religious people feel that they have a relationship with God, Jesus, the Virgin Mary, or various saints, in different branches of the Christian religion. They may experience God as a kind of person, feel that they are not alone, or take part in a kind of 'religious coping' where God helps in joint problem-solving (Pargament et al., 1988).

Kirkpatrick (1992) applied Bowlby's theory of infant attachment to parents to the relation with God. In both cases there is resort to a 'secure base' when danger threatens, and this gives protection and comfort. This idea is supported by the finding that people turn to prayer on the battlefield, when dangerously ill and when bereaved; God is thought of as like the real parents, and he is resorted to more when the relation with them is difficult, or following separation from parents. However, this is an example of a 'deficit theory' of religion, although Kirkpatrick says that the need for this kind of attachment is normal; many religious folk don't appear to have many deficits – many more middle-class people go to church, for example. An alternative model is that of G. H. Mead, that we are concerned with the opinions and reactions of our real social circle and also an imagined one. Social support from God may give us direction and satisfaction as much as that from friends and relations. Pollner (1989) found that those who felt closest to God had greater happiness, and other kinds of well-being, especially if they thought of God as omnipotent. Imagining God's reactions to our behaviour may lead to hearing his voice.

Relations with other church members

We saw earlier that the benefits of religion are mainly due to going to church and that these benefits are greatest for those otherwise isolated. We also saw that the amount of social support reported from this source was greater than for any other kind of leisure group, and that over a third of church members said that their church friendships were closer than other friendships. The social contacts with other church members consist of taking part in services together, chatting before or after services, belonging to church groups, and taking part in other church events during the week. Why are these relationships so close and supportive? There are a number of possibilities: it could be the confidence of total acceptance in this community, the social support given for unverifiable beliefs, or the high level of intimacy and self-disclosure common in church groups. A high proportion of people who are converted say that this was mainly as a result of social influence; it looks as if the social bonds often come first, the beliefs second. The Moonies developed the technique of 'love bombing' in which potential converts are loved so intensely that they crack.

The services themselves are the focus of church life, like the actual singing in choirs and the dancing in dance groups. In religious services there is joint participation in singing hymns, prayers and rituals, with a very serious purpose and often with a high degree of emotional arousal; this may all lead to the formation of emotional bonds. Religious rituals, as with dancing, singing and sport, involve a lot of coordinated non-verbal activity; however, religious rituals are full of symbolism with emotive meanings, wine for blood, water for purification, and also include some bodily contact, as in the kiss of peace and laying on of hands. Spickard (1991) argues that religious experiences aroused in services are shared ones, being created by the same rituals, in the same way that feelings are aroused together by music. Csikszentmihalyi (1975) suggested that religious practices produce a state of tense absorption or flow through the concentration on structured rituals, though he has not produced any data. Rituals may be intended to influence the deity; whether they do or not, they certainly influence those taking part, producing powerful emotions, group cohesion, and sometimes healing, at least of psychosomatic complaints. If members help one another with advice, sympathy or other support, this would further strengthen the bonds. It is common in churches for the members to take a sympathetic interest in each other; it may go a lot further than this and take the form of informal or formal counselling. Sometimes lay members of the congregation do this regularly, while others may go to church in the hope of receiving it. Some of the new sects of the 1960s placed special emphasis on therapy for their members.

Priests – or the clergy – have a special role in churches and are the focus of more interest and emotions than other kinds of leaders. Often new religions or new sects start with a charismatic leader and his followers, for whom his message has special appeal. Part of the role of the clergy is to proclaim the beliefs of their church, as well as to perform the rituals and conduct the services. They are also expected to provide help, advice, counselling or other support to their congregation, some of whom may be very demanding. In some sects the members have been obedient to the point of agreeing to mass suicide, as happened in Jonesville and Waco.

The motivation of religion

Religion probably meets a number of needs, some of which apply more to a particular kind of church, or section of the population, or aspect of religion. Several psychological theories are primarily about religious beliefs. For example, it has been proposed that people believe in the afterlife to reduce fear of death. This is supported by the fact that the older people are, the more likely they are to believe in an afterlife, and the majority of church members over fifty give 'reassurance of immortality' as a reason for going. This belief works in that believers are less afraid of what is to come, and religious individuals who are terminally ill have been found to be positively looking forward to it. However, the theory does not explain why so many people should believe in hell. Religion can help with other problems – why there is unfairness, evil and suffering in the world – and with cosmic problems about how the world started and how it will end, and the meaning and purpose of life. Religious beliefs can be seen as what sociologists call social constructions, since they are group solutions to such problems and need social support to maintain them (Berger & Luckman, 1967). However, social constructions may reflect some underlying reality, as in the case of mathematics. Karl Marx and others thought that religious beliefs were compensations for deprivation in this world, the hope for better things in the next. This may well apply to those small sects whose members are very poor or belong to ethnic minority groups; such sects believe that they alone will go to heaven, while the rich certainly will not. Beit-Hallahmi (1992) found that there was a sudden increase in sect membership in Israel after the Yom Kippur war in 1973, when the near-defeat of Israel caused great distress in that country.

Other theories, of Freudian inspiration, suggest that religious beliefs are solutions to internal conflicts, such as guilt over sex. Batson, Schoenrade and Ventis (1993) suggested that religious conversion is the outcome of an 'existential crisis' with intense self-dissatisfaction, leading to self-surrender, a kind of creative problem-solving in which the solution consists of a new vision of life. This is supported by studies showing that many converts had recently been through such a period of anxiety and distress.

The explanation of religious ritual calls for a different kind of theory. Rituals – religious and otherwise – are shared patterns of behaviour which are purely symbolic, but which perform 'ritual work'. For example, greetings have the effect of preparing people to talk to and engage with one another; weddings enable couples to see themselves and be seen by others as married couples, with certain commitments. The symbolism, the non-verbal communications and the music give rituals greater emotive force than words alone could convey. Religious rituals express beliefs; some say that they are prior to beliefs. They strengthen beliefs, they attempt to influence the deity, to heal members, and to deal with life's passages, of birth, marriage and death (Argyle & Beit-Hallahmi, 1975). A dramatic example was reported by Turner (1967), who described a ritual in East Africa which is reported to help barren women. It involves emotive symbolism such as red paint for menstrual blood and gourds for babies. And while rituals may play a powerful role in helping those in distress, they are also sources of enjoyment and positive moods. We saw that many more middle-class people go to church; it may be suggested that they do so to enjoy themselves, the music, the colourful display and other aspects of the ritual.

They also go to church to meet their friends. We have seen that church members report a high level of social support, and that many say their church friendships are closer than other friendships. We saw that the benefits of church for health and happiness are strongest for those who are otherwise socially isolated. It looks as if affiliative motivation is an important factor in religion. It has been particularly so at some periods, in primitive religion with its ecstatic group meetings, and in new churches and sects.

Social learning or socialization plays an important role in religion. Children accept their parents' views, but they may also be influenced later by peer groups, at college, for example. This religious socialization is like other kinds of education; acquiring understanding of religion is similar in some ways to learning about logarithms – a number of new abstract terms have to be mastered, all given meaning by their relations with each other. During adolescence a number go through a more or less sudden conversion experience, produced by evangelists, or other social influences; this is a leap of faith greatly assisted by social pressures and supports.

Research on personality differences between religious and non-religious individuals has not found very striking differences. There is no correlation with introversion and no consistent link with neuroticism, but there is some connection with suggestibility and dogmatism for some religious groups. There are greater differences between Protestants and Catholics, though these are partly, perhaps wholly, due to social class and ethnicity differences. Protestants have their work ethic, and higher achievement motivation, and do better in education and in science; there is some evidence that Protestants blame themselves and feel more guilt, (Argyle & Beit-Hallahmi, 1975).

VOLUNTARY WORK

The meaning of voluntary work

What should be included under the heading of voluntary work? In the General Household Survey for 1987 the definition used was: 'unpaid work, except for occasional out-of-pocket expenses, which is done through a group or on behalf of an organization of some kind;

247

it should be of service to other people or the community and not only to one's immediate family or personal friends'. Some of the results of this survey are given in Figure 8.5, and this shows what they included: fund-raising, running social events, visiting and counselling, et cetera. Evidently it does not include work for churches, political parties, trade unions, or helping to run sporting or other leisure groups. However, in the USA there has been a lot of research into 'voluntary organizations', and these include churches and trade unions, as well as political parties and pressure groups of various kinds, such as those pressing for civil liberties, racial equality or the welfare of the environment (Sills, 1968). They also include social-work activities and fund-raising as in the British definition, but these seem to be in a minority. Zander (1972) sampled 290 of them and only thirty-four were concerned with social welfare. Many of the findings of research in the two countries are fairly similar, but we should be careful about generalizing from American findings to the British situation.

History

In the nineteenth century in Britain most voluntary work was done by ladies of leisure, from the middle or upper classes, and voluntary work had the 'Lady Bountiful' image. When the welfare state was established in the 1950s, it was recognized, as the Beveridge Report (1942) had done already, that the official social services needed supplementing by voluntary efforts, and by the 1960s there was a boom in voluntary work. Since then there has been an increase in the amount of free time due to unemployment and shorter hours, but there has been some decline in volunteering and there is now said to be a 'crisis' due to shortage of volunteers. So there have been efforts to expand the range of people involved, to include the young, working-class, black, unemployed, and ex-mental patients, as much for the good of the volunteers as that of their clients (Hedley & Smith, 1992).

Voluntary work in the USA has been at a similar high level, but for different reasons. There was no welfare state over there, and no Labour Party, and it has been suggested that it is for this reason that voluntary organizations have flourished. It has also been suggested that the high level of religious activity there has been a factor (Lipset, 1988).

Statistics

The most extensive survey of voluntary work in Britain was by the General Household Survey for 1987, re-analysed by Matheson (1990). It was found that 15 per cent of the population had done some voluntary work during the previous four weeks, and 10 per cent did some every week. However, there have been eight surveys in Britain during the last fifteen years, and they have obtained rather varied results, presumably as a result of different definitions of voluntary work and different wording of the questions. The average of the eight is for 26 per cent of people to do some voluntary work once a month, rather than the 15 per cent found by the GHS survey. The average of weekly voluntary workers was 13.5 per cent for two surveys, and the average amount of time put in was a little under five hours a month, though some did a lot more than this (Hedley & Smith, 1992). This is fairly consistent with the time-budget analysis by Gershuny and Jones (1987), who found that women did about two hours forty minutes a week on 'civic duties', men about an hour and a half.

As Figure 8.5 shows, the most commonly reported activities in the GHS survey were, in order of frequency, raising money, committee work, collecting money, other practical help, helping at a club, helping with entertainments, administration, teaching or training, talks or canvassing, visiting institutions and giving advice.

British social workers make a lot of use of volunteers; it has been estimated that the 13,000 social workers in the country use about 40,000 volunteers, while the 4,000 probation officers use about 10,000 volunteers. They are used most when caseloads contain a large proportion of elderly or physically handicapped clients, and the jobs which volunteers are most asked to do are befriending and practical help. The advantage is that volunteers can do some of the work, but also that they offer something different and extra, such as being unofficial, committed and 'normal' (Holme & Maizels, 1978).

All these surveys report class differences; indeed this is the strongest predictor of who will or will not volunteer. It is found that

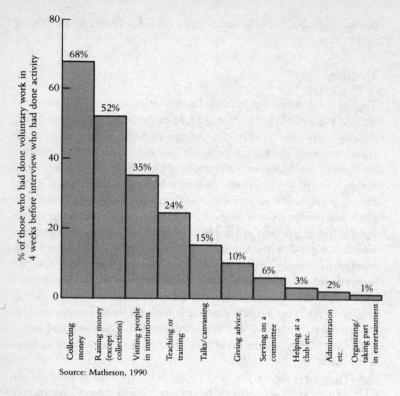

Source: Matheson, 1990

Figure 8.5: Voluntary work activities

middle-class, educated or richer people do more. In the GHS study
13 per cent of class 1 people had done some during the past four
weeks, compared with 4 per cent in class 6. Middle-class people also
do different kinds of voluntary work: they had done more committee
work (52 per cent in the last year as against 22 per cent of unskilled),
more advice giving (15 per cent as against 5 per cent), and more
talks, teaching and coaching, while manual workers did more practical things, like transport, repairs, domestic help and gardening. In
other words people use the same skills which they use at work, an
example of the 'spillover' theory of leisure. The effect of social status
on belonging to voluntary organizations is so pervasive that it has

been suggested that every conceivable aspect of status is relevant here. And it is found that more voluntary work is done not only by the middle class, but also by those who are middle-aged, married, Protestants, and live in cities (Lemon, Palisi & Jacobson, 1972). What is the explanation of this effect of social class? It could be because middle-class individuals have less pressing material needs than working-class people, or it could be because of the effect of education in creating wider concerns and sympathies (Argyle, 1994b). Or it could be an example of exchange theory – those who benefit most from the system may feel that they should give something back in exchange. Different voluntary groups, like leisure groups of all kinds, have their social niche; Wilde (1974) studied a small town in Australia and found that groups like the Red Cross and the Bushfire Brigade drew their members from a limited number of social classes. However, it should be emphasized that there is a range of social classes in any voluntary group; Wilde's Red Cross group had members from four of the six classes he distinguished, the Bushfire Brigade three classes.

In British studies it is found that women do a little more voluntary work, and men and women do different kinds. Men are more likely to do committee work and advice giving, things connected with sports or exercise; women do activities connected with children, education, health, and visiting, caring for and befriending the elderly and others.

There are some age differences. In these surveys, most voluntary work was done by those between thirty-five and forty-four, though it was done at all ages, and quite a lot is done by young people, including teenagers, and a number take it up when they retire and have more time for it. Older people do more visiting, younger people more active things, and they do things which may lead to acquiring new skills. And old people say they volunteer as part of their religious beliefs or philosophy of life.

In Britain black and Asian ethnic groups do less voluntary work – 20 per cent versus 45 per cent for whites in one survey – though this can partly be explained by class differences. Many members of such ethnic groups prefer to work within their own community, and are really engaging in mutual help.

The employment of ex-mental patients, or those who have just had a life crisis, is causing some problems. Most voluntary work needs some social skills and the capacity to handle working relations and situations; those who don't have them may be virtually unusable (Clark, 1991).

Social relationships

Voluntary work is associated with a very interesting set of relationships, firstly with the other voluntary workers. The main way in which members are recruited is by invitations from their friends, and about half join in this way (Pearce, 1993). As we shall see later, one of the main motivations of voluntary workers is through their involvement with each other. Highly cohesive groups are formed, especially among the core workers, i.e. those who put most time in and have most responsibility for running things. I have found very high levels of social support reported by members of voluntary groups, and for a third of them these friendships were closer than those with people outside the group. Perkins and Metz (1988) found that over 75 per cent of volunteer firefighters reported that most of their close friends were also firefighters.

A second interesting finding is that voluntary workers are highly egalitarian. Compared with paid employees doing similar work they are much less concerned with formal positions and do not really recognize status differences between them. We shall see below that 'leaders' have little power over their 'subordinates'. There is little seeking for promotion; this has been seen as 'member apathy', or unwillingness to take on extra work, but may really be because status carries few rewards here. Perhaps the reason that relations are different in a number of ways in this setting is that volunteers feel that they are free to construct new social relationships while being helpful to others, and have no great desire to be efficient or business-like (Pearce, 1993). Or it may be simply that many of them are women (though nearly as many are men), and they may not be accustomed to the hierarchical structure of working organizations. It has been suggested that they are caught between the two different worlds of bureaucracy with its rules and regulations, telephone rotas, insurance cover, and the world of informal, personal friendships. The TV series *Dad's Army* derived much of its comedy from the clash between these two worlds (Billis, 1989).

Supervisors or other leaders often find volunteers difficult to supervise, for several reasons. Since they are not paid and because 'volunteers depend on their organizations for very little that is truly vital to their lives', the usual incentives are lacking (Pearce, 1993). They need to be started gradually, while their involvement increases, with their work matched to their interests and skills, and they need to be appreciated. It may be difficult to meet the needs of the volunteers at the same time as getting the job done (Hedley & Smith, 1992). Volunteers are sometimes unreliable, perhaps because they are relatively untrained, and there is little personnel selection. In American studies it has often been reported that volunteers are incompetent and that little is expected of them; in British social work, 45 per cent of social workers report no problems with volunteers, though 27 per cent report unreliability or lack of skill or experience (Holme & Maizels, 1978). Other problems with volunteers are that they fail to recognize status differences, they may even be joint 'owners' of the organization, they may be of higher occupational status than their supervisor – in the case of retired people, for example – or have close links with senior members. Probably the best way in which volunteers can be controlled is by appealing to shared values (Etzioni, 1961). Pearce (1993) compared the amount of influence reported by employees and volunteers; the employees were more influenced by organizational reward and sanction power, the volunteers by social influence, both by office holders and by others. It is found that successful leaders of volunteer-staffed organizations were charismatic in the sense of having a personal vision, had great technical expertise, and were sometimes regarded as martyrs who had overcome great difficulties by very hard work. There are often problems in voluntary organizations; a common complaint is that 'things could be better organized' – about two-thirds of British volunteers agreed with this to some extent (Holme & Maizels, 1978).

Another problem is that voluntary organizations are often oligarchical rather than democratic, and are run by a small group, who are usually of higher social class than the others (Bottomore, 1954). Or they may be directed by a salaried supervisor – in the social services, for example – and here there would be little say in decisions.

There is sometimes friction with paid employees, who are usually more professionally qualified, value the hierarchy more than the volunteers do and think that they are insubordinate. There can be serious rifts between the two groups; they need careful supervision, and care by employees to give recognition to the volunteers. One supervisor said to me, 'Paid employees and volunteers don't mix.'

Volunteers have a relationship with their clients, especially those who are helped by them – the old, disabled and the rest. Since volunteers obtain so much satisfaction from their work, it looks as if they have generally positive and rewarding relations with these clients, who in many cases become dependent and very grateful for what is done.

The motivation of voluntary work

This is one of the most interesting issues about voluntary work, since it involves effort, time, often cost, with no financial or other material reward. A number of surveys have been carried out in which volunteers were asked why they volunteered. These refer primarily to why members volunteered in the first place; we shall see later that the reasons that they continue to volunteer are a little different. The results of the latest British study are shown in Table 8.2.

It can be seen that the most common reason for volunteering is because people were asked to – by a friend who was already a member. There is also an altruistic desire to help others in need: to contribute to society by making things better is a common reason given. It is found, however, that there is a decline in these motives as time passes, and a corresponding increase in the importance of social motives, such as enjoying the company of co-workers (Pearce, 1993). It has also been recognized that such altruistic motives may not be 'pure', but can be combined with maintaining a self-image as a certain kind of person. We shall discuss below the importance of empathy in motivating altruistic behaviour. It can be seen from Table 8.2 that people may volunteer because 'they had previously benefited from the activity' or they 'had someone who was involved in the activity, or would benefit from it'. These are obvious ways in which empathy might be extended: someone with a deaf child might work to help the deaf; a person who had contemplated suicide might join the Samaritans and become one of their 'clients in disguise';

Table 8.2: Reasons for volunteering for main group/organization, by sex and age

	All current volunteers	Men	Women	18–34	35–54	55 +
	%	%	%	%	%	%
Connected with my needs/interests	39	48	31	43	37	37
Connected with needs/interests of family or friends	43	43	43	45	49	31
Connected with my paid work	11	12	10	12	14	5
There was a need in the community	26	24	28	18	28	33
I wanted to improve things/help people	39	35	42	37	39	40
I wanted to meet people/make friends	25	22	28	24	22	30
Someone asked me to help	51	52	51	45	59	50
I offered to help	49	45	52	55	44	45
I started the group	5	7	3	4	5	5
I had time to spare	28	24	33	29	22	36
I'm good at it	18	21	16	21	14	18
I thought it would give me the chance to learn new skills	11	12	11	16	10	5
None of these	–	–	–	1	–	0
Base	747	298	449	262	279	205

Source: Lynn & Smith, 1991

elderly retired folk often work for Meals on Wheels, a service they may soon need themselves.

Social motives are a major source of voluntary work. Invitation from a friend is the main reason that people volunteer in the first place, there may also be social pressure from the social network to do it, and one of the main reasons they keep on working is because of links within the volunteer group. They enjoy the company of this group, they don't want to let it down, they are really working for the group. Studies of 'commitment' have found that this can be established during training by the social rewards provided by the cohesive training group (Clary & Miller, 1986). Commitment also depends on growing obligation and responsibility towards the volunteer group, and an affective attachment to the organization; it is greater the more members are able to participate in decisions (Knoke, 1986).

Voluntary work may also be motivated by more instrumental needs, the hope of gaining knowledge, skills, work experience or other benefits. Young people sometimes hope to gain new skills which will enable them to get into a new career; old volunteers are more interested in keeping up their social contacts.

There has been some speculation that volunteers may be motivated by more hidden motives, for example to reduce guilt feelings, or deal in some way with inner conflicts. This has not been found to be important, though it was found that AIDS volunteers had low self-esteem, a high need for social recognition and high death anxiety (Omoto & Snyder, 1990).

Another way of looking at the motivation issue is to find out what benefits volunteers receive from their voluntary efforts. It has been found that belonging to voluntary organizations is a source of happiness or satisfaction (for example Palisi, 1985). The Lynn and Smith (1991) study asked about the specific benefits of this kind of work, and the results are shown in Table 8.3.

The main benefit reported is that they 'really enjoy it'. The next most important is satisfaction with the results of their work. This suggests that volunteers really are motivated to do good works and to help others. Making friends is important, but so is feeling less selfish, which is a self-image motive, though it could be seen as an ego-defensive one. In my survey of the emotions generated by different kinds of leisure groups, voluntary work came highest as a source of social support, and it was quite high as a source of joy (see p. 118).

There is no great mystery about altruistic motivation. Helping behaviour has been much studied by psychologists, though we have been more concerned with informal and spontaneous forms of it. Most help is given to family, friends and members of the immediate group, and there may an evolutionary, 'selfish gene' explanation for this. According to Batson's two-stage model of helping (1991), there is first empathic concern for another in need, and this then motivates

Table 8.3: The benefits of volunteering

	Very important %	Fairly important %	Not very important %	Not important at all %	(Don't know) %
I meet people and make friends through it	48	37	11	4	0
It's the satisfaction of seeing the results	67	26	5	2	1
It gives me the chance to do things that I'm good at	33	36	24	7	–
It makes me feel less selfish as a person	29	33	24	13	2
I really enjoy it	72	21	6	2	–
It's part of my religious belief or philosophy of life to give help	44	22	9	23	2
It broadens my experience of life	39	36	15	9	1
It gives me a sense of personal achievement	47	31	16	6	–
It gives me the chance to learn new skills	25	22	29	23	1
It gives me a position in the community	12	16	33	38	1
It gets me 'out of myself'	35	30	19	15	1
It gives me the chance to get a recognized qualification	3	7	15	74	1

Source: Lynn & Smith, 1991

the helping behaviour. Voluntary work, however, is directed to people who are not family or friends, and this initially reduces the extent of such empathy. Volunteers are people who have succeeded in extending the range of their empathic concern. Altruistic behaviour can also be explained in terms of social learning: children are rewarded for it, imitate their parents, and are given explanation and other persuasion to do it. It is supported by ideologies, such as religion, which teach concern for looking after others. We saw that some people, especially old people, engage in help as part of their religious life. And many voluntary organizations in the American sense depend on concerns with civil rights, the environment or other social issues.

There have been a number of studies comparing the personalities of volunteers and non-volunteers. The main findings are exactly what might be expected. Volunteers are more sociable on a variety of measures, they have high self-confidence and self-esteem, and they are high in empathy (Pearce, 1993). A lot of this could be summarized in terms of extraversion, since extraverts are good at dealing with strangers, are confident that such encounters will go well, and they have good social skills, including assertiveness (Argyle & Lu, 1990).

HOLIDAYS AND TOURISM

Statistics

Holidays and tourism are a major leisure pursuit. We saw earlier that this is one of the main areas of leisure expenditure – about 25 per cent of the domestic leisure budget. In Britain it is a major part of the national economy – 12 per cent of GNP – and employs 3 million people; in countries like Spain and Greece it makes up a much greater part of the economy. In Britain most people who are at work have four to five weeks a year of paid holidays, and 60 per cent of them take a holiday involving travel. About 20 per cent of people in Britain take a holiday overseas, usually for one or two weeks, especially to Spain and France, but increasingly to the USA and Australia.

There has been a great increase in tourism since the Second World War, due to increased affluence, longer paid holidays and earlier retirement. It has been something of a social movement leading to and supported by mass package holidays with air travel, and a build-up of facilities like hotels in Spain, state parks in the USA, and new ones like Disneyland and Center-Parcs. Overseas holidays increased by a factor of four between 1965 and 1991, and trips to Australia and New Zealand by a factor of three in the last ten years (*Social Trends*, 1993). Worldwide there is now a tremendous amount of tourism; in 1950 there were 25 million tourist arrivals worldwide; by 1991 this had increased to 448 million, 22 per cent of them to Third World countries, though not all of them were on holiday. Visitors to Britain were one million in 1955 and 18 million by 1991. This is one of the greatest changes in leisure during recent times, with the exception of television. The Americans travel most, followed by the Japanese and Germans. The most favoured destination is Europe – where 62 per cent of overseas tourists go, especially to Spain, Greece and Italy – but they also go increasingly to remote places like Hawaii, Thailand and other exotic and Third World locations.

There are big class differences here, and these are shown in Figure 8.6. It can be seen that 80 per cent of those in classes A and B take a holiday, many of them two or more holidays, compared with 50 per cent of classes D and E. And of course they have different kinds of holidays.

Students and other young people travel a lot, so do families. Old people have the time and money to travel, but may be restrained by ill-health, and they like to be well looked after on holiday (Blazey, 1982).

History

We looked at the holidays and tourism of the Romans earlier. The Romans were able to travel long distances, by road, to seaside resorts, summer villas, religious shrines and historical sites, for their pleasure, health, education or spiritual life. Inns, spas and travel arrangements developed to meet the needs of these tourists. In the Middle Ages travel was more difficult, but there were pilgrimages, to as far away as the Holy Land, and again there were routes, inns and even guide books. The regular resting places became tourist spots, with feasting and entertainment.

From the sixteenth century Britain initiated several kinds of

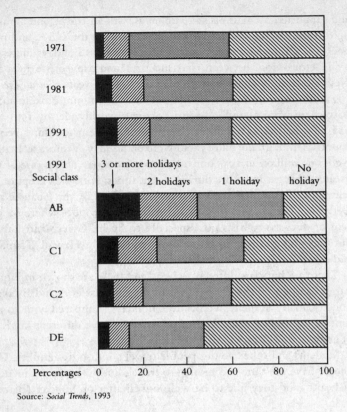

Source: *Social Trends*, 1993

Figure 8.6: Number of holidays per year by social class

ism. The grand tour became popular for aristocratic youth, with educational and cultural goals, and was on a sufficient scale to lead to hotels and regular routes. Spas appeared, for the pursuit of health, relaxation and pleasure, first of the wealthy and the middle classes; seaside resorts also appeared, but these rapidly started to cater for the working class too, though different places catered for different social groups, for example Margate and Frinton. From the 1840s travel to these places was made much easier by the railways. Working-class families would go on day trips. Thomas Cook invented the package tour, first for visits to the British seaside and Scotland, and later to Europe. After 1918 liners made foreign travel easier, more people had cars, and Butlin invented holiday camps – the first one was at Skegness in 1937 – with all-in entertainment for working-class families. Regular holidays from work became normal, and working-class holidays became longer. In the USA many people had cars, and these made trips easy, especially to the new state parks.

As we saw above, there has been a great expansion of holidays and travel since the Second World War. New kinds of holidays have been invented, especially theme parks like Disneyland, with elaborate rides, reconstructed gold mines, Indian villages and the rest. In the USA visits to the wilderness have become popular, as have reconstructed historical sites, such as that of the Battle of Gettysburg, and a number of more or less challenging and dangerous sporting activities.

However, the biggest growth area seems to be for the retired, now living longer and more prosperous than before, and with plenty of time in which to go places (Pearce, 1982).

The social behaviour of tourists

Tourists are involved in at least four sets of social relationship.

Family
Visiting family or friends is a major reason for choosing a holiday destination; it was the most common reason in a Canadian study (Canadian Government Travel Bureau, 1972). It is a major reason for British long-distance travel, for example to see family in Canada and Australia. And of course families usually go on holiday together; in American studies the hope for enjoying family closeness is given a high rating.

The tour group
Many tourists go on holiday in a group, for example on bus tours of Europe or the American West, or in groups of visitors to the Holy Land, or on other cultural or special interest tours. Gorman (1979) studied seven-day bus tours of Europe and found that strong group solidarity developed rapidly to deal with various crises and problems with what came to be seen as the 'out-group', i.e. of Belgian officials, waiters, et cetera. It is older, widowed and other isolated individuals

who choose these tours, and they do so in the hope of making friends (Quiroga, 1990). And those who do not go in a group often establish relationships, including romantic ones, with other tourists. For young people, sex is a major part of the holiday, as recognized by organizers of 'under 30s' holidays. These relationships are easy to make, since everyone is in a good mood, with nothing else to do, and a lot in common in a strange land, though holiday romances are notoriously short-lived.

Tour guides

Especially on conducted tours, but also on other holidays, tour guides are important. They provide help with travel arrangements, smooth out difficulties with the local culture, act as interpreters and provide information about local sights and facilities. They interpret the culture, and have been described as 'mediating persons', who are at home in two cultures and can explain one to another (Bochner, 1981), though they have sometimes been found to be marginal in their own culture. This is important for tourists in many parts of the world where there are serious differences between the cultures and the social rules of tourists and hosts, and great danger of culture shock for one and offence for the other. Tour guides require considerable social skills to negotiate inter-cultural contacts, and to keep parties of tourists happy and out of trouble. They are very unpopular if they give an obviously biased account of the culture, as may happen in Russia, or help in exploitation by locals at cafés and shops (Pearce, 1982).

The locals

Many holiday-makers scarcely meet the locals at all, for example those on package tours to Spain. The 'natives', especially in Third World countries, are seen as part of the scenery or as playing various servile roles; the middle-class natives are invisible (Dann, 1993). The natives have been dealing with tourists for a long time and can categorize them at a glance, and apply their own stereotypes. They may play their parts as exotic and charming natives, but they may also be sullen and resentful of the rich visitors who don't understand their culture. There are other groups of tourists who are very keen to meet the local inhabitants – students, journalists, and those who go to work abroad – partly for this reason. It has been found that the more such inter-cultural interaction there has been the more visitors say they have enjoyed their trip, and also the more their attitudes change towards the other group (Fisher & Price, 1991).

The local population gain a lot financially from tourists, but attitudes become negative when the number of tourists becomes large, as happened in a Catalan village in Spain (Pi-Sunyer, 1989). There are a number of negative consequences of tourism for the natives – the growth of prostitution, drunkenness and crime, trivializing local festivals or other aspects of the culture. Greek fishing villages, for example, may become much more prosperous as a result of tourism, but there is no more fishing; the original culture partly disappears and is replaced by a hybrid one, a kind of watered-down version of Greek food, music and other aspects of Greek culture which the tourists will like (Wickens, 1994).

Types of tourist and their motivation

Why do people go on holidays and trips? In the Roman world it is fairly obvious: they went to cooler places in summer, to the seaside, to spas for their health, and to religious and historical sites. The motivations of present-day tourists are very similar.

There have been a number of surveys in which samples of tourists were asked why they chose the holiday they did. For example Dunn, Ross and Iso-Ahola (1991) surveyed 255 bus-tour passengers and found six motivation factors: seeking knowledge, social interaction within the group, escape, impulsive decision, specialized knowledge and shopping. The Canadian Government Travel Bureau (1972) surveyed 5,000 Canadians, and found that the most common reasons given for choosing holidays were visiting friends or relatives, scenery, relaxing atmosphere, good weather, friendly people, oceans and beaches. A common theme which emerges from these surveys is escape, i.e. from boring or stressful work, an unattractive environment, to get away from it all. This may be a common motivation, but different kinds of tourists do it in very different ways. Going to another culture is important for many, but probably not for most British visitors to Spain; it is said that Spanish food is no longer served in some of the places they go to.

Psychologists have tried to systematize these motivations by use of Maslow's (1970) hierarchy of needs. The theory is that the lower needs on the list are satisfied first, and the later ones do not become activated until more basic ones are satisfied. Pearce (1982) applied this scheme to tourist motivation as follows:

1. Relaxation and satisfaction of bodily needs, for example eating and drinking, relaxing in the sun.
2. Stimulation by exciting rides (very popular with children).
3. Relationships, social needs, the search for love or for a closer, more caring community.
4. Self-esteem, and development of the self, for example the prestige and glamour of travel.
5. Self-actualization and fulfilment, finding inner peace and harmony.

However, this scheme does not mention sex, sport, good weather or fine scenery – all of which figure prominently in holiday adverts. Perhaps we can take things further forward by looking at some of the different kinds of tourists. Pearce (1982) used earlier category schemes to produce a list of twenty tourist roles, which were then rated on twenty five-point scales and subjected to multi-dimensional scaling. This produced the types shown in Figure 8.7.

Some of these types are not really on holiday, such as journalists and businessmen. However, tourist and holiday-maker are, and the latter was described as one who 'takes photos, goes to famous places, is alienated from society, buys souvenirs, contributes to the visited economy'. The most popular kind of holiday in Britain used to be going to the seaside, now it is going to a hotel in the Mediterranean, in search of sea, sun, sand and sex. Seeking good weather was important for the Romans and partly explains the exodus to the Mediterranean today.

The religious pilgrim was described as 'searches for the meaning of life, does not live a life of luxury, is not concerned with social status, does not exploit the local people, does not buy souvenirs'. It has been suggested that tourism is often a kind of 'sacred journey', like the pilgrims of former times (Allcock, 1988). Muslims and Catholics still travel to sacred places. Katz and Gurevitch (1976) found that religious

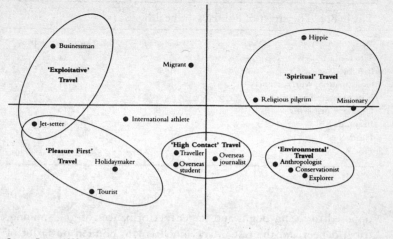

Source: Pearce, 1982

Figure 8.7: Multi-dimensional scaling and clusters of travellers

Jews in Israel went to religious shrines, but educated Jews in general went more to historical sites. In Britain many such people go on classical or other cultural tours.

Students and other young people often travel to remote places, perhaps in search of adventure, perhaps as a rite of passage to test themselves in difficult conditions or, as they say, to find themselves. They often find simply being in a strange culture very exciting. Other tourists have other fantasies: working-class people pretend they are rich as they enjoy luxurious accommodation, the rich pretend to be peasants or big-game hunters, students pretend to be poor (Pi-Sunyer, 1989). We shall have to leave these, and those on sacred journeys, to await further understanding of the psychology of self-actualization.

However, Pearce made good use of the Maslow scheme in developing the idea of the 'tourist career', in which he suggested that individuals move down the scale towards level five. He found that tourists who were at these later levels were more satisfied by more 'authentic' tourist settings, i.e. really making contact with another culture, as

Table 8.4: The effect of holidays on health

	Vacation	During past year
Tired	12	34
Irritable	8	30
Constipation, worry, anxiety	7	27
Loss of interest in sex	6	12
Digestive problems	6	16
Insomnia	4	11
Headaches	3	21

Source: Rubenstein, 1980

opposed to seeing bogus and staged performances of gold-mining, tribal dances and the rest. MacCannell (1976) pointed out a lot of 'staged authenticity' is laid on for tourists, making them the passive recipients of entertaining but bogus spectacles.

To the concept of the tourist career we could add socialization. People often go again as adults to places to which they went as adolescents, 82 per cent of them in one study (Gittelson & Kerstetter, 1982). But our main social learning probably comes from the advertising of the tourist industry, which creates glamorous and often misleading images of the heavens on earth on offer, apparently with blue skies, perfect weather, luxurious accommodation, enormous meals, friendly hosts, and so on. No mention is made of the poverty, squalor, or deaths in civil wars of the Third World countries so advertised. These images are important in choice of destination, and also build up eager anticipation of the joys of the holiday to come (Parrinello, 1993).

Holidays give several benefits. They are enjoyed at the time, they are looked forward to, as the brochures promise a paradise on earth, and they are looked back on for years afterwards when the photograph albums are taken out. While they are on holiday people are more relaxed and in better health, as Rubenstein's survey (1980) found (see Table 8.4). And relaxation is good for mental health.

Holidays also have educational benefits. Plog (1991) found that educational benefits were given the highest rating, compared with relaxation, sex, et cetera. A friend of mine, after returning from

China, said, 'Nothing will ever look the same again.' Holidays enlarge the horizon, and give a broader understanding of the world and its peoples.

CHAPTER NINE

The future of leisure

THE FUTURE OF WORK

There is now a high level of unemployment in all industrialized countries. Most labour economists doubt whether it will ever become less, and believe that it will probably become greater, as a result of the relentless increase in the use of computers and automation to do the work. It has been estimated that by early in the next century all our food and manufacturing needs could be met by 10 per cent of the population working (Stonier, 1983). It is ironic that the main sphere where jobs might increase is in leisure industries like travel and holidays, eating and drinking, sport and entertainment. There is no doubt that there will be less work to do in the future. What is not at all clear is how it will be distributed among the population. Perhaps a minority will do it all, perhaps it will be evenly shared, perhaps something in between.

Meanwhile there has been a rise in activities which are somewhere between work and leisure proper – cooking, gardening, sewing and knitting, DIY and other productive but unpaid domestic activities. Gershuny (1979) called it the 'self-service economy'; he points out that in some circles it is fashionable to be self-sufficient, able to grow your own food, make your own furniture; Handy (1985) called it the 'grey economy'. Many hours are spent in this way; middle-class women are spending more time than before, as we saw, and men are doing more as a result of female pressure. And this is one of the main areas of activity to which the unemployed and the retired turn, to replace work proper. However, many of these activities, such as gardening and sewing, are commonly regarded as 'leisure' and that is how they have been treated in this book.

There is another way in which paid work has been replaced by those who lose their jobs, and that is where people turn their hobbies into businesses, what Handy (1985) has called the 'mauve economy'. Examples are gardening, photography, carpentry, dressmaking and writing. We have looked at these as kinds of leisure, but if a living can be made out of them they become work. Those involved join the happy band of those whose work is their leisure.

There is no question that the amount of free time in Britain has increased, and the same appears to be the case in other countries. However, Schor (1991) reports that free time in the USA has actually declined since 1950. She analysed time-budget data collected by the University of Michigan Survey Research Unit in different years and found that there was an average increase of seventy-two hours of work per year for working men and twenty-four hours more for working women between 1969 and 1987. This was partly due to more hours per week, partly to more weeks per year. Many more women were working – 20 per cent of adult women in 1940, 60 per cent in 1990. More teenagers were working. She reports how ambitious lawyers and people on Wall Street work very long hours – sixty to one hundred hours a week in some cases, their offices open from 7 a.m. to 10 p.m. – and some of them are there all the time. The reason for all this extra work, she suggests, is the relentless American drive for more material possessions and a higher standard of living. The spare time of working men was also reduced by their having to do more housework – sixty-eight hours a year. The result is that most Americans are richer than they were in 1950 or 1969, but they have less time to spend it. There are groups in Britain, the famous Yuppies, who also work very long hours and are said to be burnt out by thirty. Quite apart from them, the average hours of work in manufacturing industry in Britain have increased since 1980 (see Figure 2.1a).

THE DECLINE OF WORK

Until the recent changes just described the time we spent working had been declining for a long time. In 1800 80 per cent of people in Britain worked on the land; the figure now is 3 per cent, the result of the use of agricultural machinery and more efficient farming methods. With the rise of industry many agricultural workers moved to the cities to work in factories, which became a major place of work. In the twentieth century this kind of work in turn began to disappear as automation and computerization replaced many industrial workers with machines. In some industries 40 to 50 per cent of jobs have already gone and more may go as computerization goes further. Some plants, like some oil rigs, have no workers at all. In addition whole industries, like coal-mining and steel, have all but disappeared. The result is the present high level of unemployment in all industrialized countries.

Managers prefer machines to people because they cost less, don't go on strike, and are more accurate and reliable. However, clerical workers and managers are being replaced too, by office automation and 'expert systems', for example where the client sits at a VDU and answers questions about their health, finances, et cetera. Large numbers have been replaced in banking. The increasing power of electronic systems has been dramatic: microchips can contain 100,000 components and the speed of processing by computers has increased by a factor of 10,000:1 over fifteen years (Gill, 1985).

The fall in jobs was halted for a time in the 1970s by increased employment in the service industries, that is education, health, domestic work, banking and other finance, and also in leisure. However, many of these jobs have already been automated.

It has been suggested that there might be a further wave of new jobs in connection with information technology, but this remains to be seen. Hours of work over the last 150 years have also fallen. In the early days of the Industrial Revolution workers did twelve, sometimes thirteen, hours a day, six days a week, i.e. a seventy-two-hour week or more. This fell to sixty hours by 1850, and is forty-two hours today in Britain, despite the reversal in the 1980s (Gershuny, 1992); the TUC is aiming for a thirty-five-hour week. At one time there were almost no holidays; now the average is 4.25 weeks a year, and many have six weeks.

At one time some children started work at age seven or eight, now the school leaving age is sixteen; most do further education or training until they are seventeen or eighteen or go to university for longer. The retirement age has fallen too, and many men now retire at sixty, so the working life has fallen, like hours of work, and weeks worked in the year (Veal, 1987).

THE PROBLEM OF UNEMPLOYMENT

The main reason for our increased free time is the fall in the amount of work, and the rise in unemployment is an important part of this. We saw earlier that the unemployed are often distressed, depressed, in poor health and generally demoralized. This is one of the major social problems of our time. Many politicians seem to think that this is a temporary problem caused by incompetent government and that the only solution is to create more jobs. However, most industrial economists disagree, and think that unemployment is caused by technological changes in the way work is done, that it is part of a long-term trend and that it will get worse. This is my belief too, and I think that the problem will have to be alleviated in other ways, of which I shall mention four.

Work sharing

This is happening already, since everyone is working shorter hours, for fewer years and fewer weeks in the year. Unemployment could be totally abolished by modest changes in some or all of these variables. For example, it has been calculated that simply abolishing overtime would create a quarter of a million new jobs. However, those who have jobs are reluctant to share them out, so unions are against work sharing; managers are against it too, since they would have to manage larger numbers of part-time workers.

'Workfare'

This means paying the unemployed to do socially useful jobs, and requiring them to do this in order to receive benefits. Those involved would feel useful and get the benefits of work. It was used by President Roosevelt in the depression of the 1930s. We have no experience of this scheme in Britain yet, but it is now on the political agenda.

Weaken the Protestant work ethic

The theory is that this would prevent the unemployed from feeling useless. In fact, the Protestant work ethic is probably fairly weak already; several surveys in Britain and other European countries have found that many workers see their jobs as a means to being paid and say that their free-time activity is more important than their work (Veal, 1987). They may not realize how much satisfaction their work provides until they lose it (Argyle, 1989).

Leisure which provides the satisfactions of work

Leisure which provides challenges, uses skills, and leads to a socially recognized product is like this, for example the kinds of serious leisure which Csikszentmihalyi found produced flow. These include hobbies, voluntary work, sport, music, education, religion, and other construct-ive activities which are taken fairly seriously. The trouble is that a great deal of leisure isn't like this at all, and people often prefer to relax in front of the TV or with a good book, or to have a very relaxed social life with friends. But there are also many people who do voluntary work and belong to active and often serious leisure groups.

We have looked at the ways in which people spend their new free time, when they have lost their jobs or retired, for example. A Canadian study showed how the minutes of this free time were spent (note that these are all *increased* times spent on each activity):

TV	65 minutes
reading	57
study	30
home chores	28
conversation at home and with friends	40

Source: Elliot & Elliott, 1990

British studies have found that the unemployed and the retired spend a lot of time watching TV, doing housework and sitting or hanging around doing nothing. Few make use of the opportunity to take up new kinds of leisure, or to join new leisure groups. General trends in leisure activity during the present century show that there has been a fall in church attendance and in the cinema, but more TV watching, sport and exercise, reading, trips in cars, DIY and other domestic leisure.

I conclude that there really is a problem here, in that free time has greatly increased but that those who have had the greatest increase have not been able to convert it into satisfying forms of leisure.

CHOICE OF LEISURE AND THE PURPOSE OF LIFE

From a biological point of view the purpose of life is to stay alive and to produce the next generation. The advance of civilization has been driven by other purposes – to raise the standard of living, with better houses, clothes, education and, of course, leisure. Leisure was partly to relax, to recover from work or battle, but there have always been more serious, more demanding forms of leisure as well, in the form of sport, music, social life and the rest. And we have seen the benefits that leisure can produce. For a long time leisure was mainly for the rich, while slaves or the working classes did the work. Now we can all have leisure, and we have to decide how to spend it. We have to decide on the purpose of life so that we can decide how to spend our leisure. Can psychologists contribute to solving this problem?

We looked at the effects of various kinds of leisure in Chapter 4. Some leisure has an effect on joy and happiness; exercise, music, some TV programmes and social life produce joy; more serious leisure, such as hobbies, education and voluntary work, produce satisfaction, the more reflective side of happiness; music, art, religion and education may produce experiences of a vision, glimpses of eternity, 'peak experiences'. Health is enhanced by aerobic exercise, by church because of the good health behaviour encouraged, and by close relationships because of the social support; it is damaged by drink and drugs, and by dangerous sports. Mental health is helped by close relationships and by the support of leisure groups; depression is relieved by exercise, anxiety is relieved by holidays and other forms of relaxation. Some kinds of leisure give benefits for others, such as voluntary work, church, improvement of the environment. These are all benefits from a psychological point of view. There will be some who are prepared to sacrifice their health or happiness for some higher goal, such as service to others, scientific discovery, music, or union with God. We have seen that it is, in fact, beneficial to individuals to have such purposes, apart from those who damage their health in the mission field or as subjects in their own dangerous scientific experiments.

Groups for whom leisure has failed

There are, of course, great individual differences in the leisure people pursue, as a result of their experiences in the family, contact with groups, and opportunities in the course of education. That is no problem; what is a problem is that the development of leisure interests does not always succeed. There are several groups of people who have failed to find satisfying and enriching leisure. (1) Those who have not acquired enough interests, with the result that they are bored and don't know what to do with their free time. We have seen that many of the young unemployed and the retired are in this situation. (2) Those who only have very undemanding leisure interests, such as watching TV, going to the pub or reading very light fiction. Their level of leisure satisfaction and their happiness are relatively low as a result. Some social critics, like Hoggart (1957), have been concerned that the mass media and other mass leisure have created shallow and low-grade working-class leisure and popular culture. We shall see that governments often try to combat this by supporting the arts. (3) Those whose leisure is bad for them, for example drinking, taking drugs, or gambling. Enthusiasts for certain dangerous sports, like potholing, or ice-climbing, also face some adverse consequences. (4) Those whose leisure is bad for others, by their getting aggressively drunk, making too much noise, driving dangerously or being antisocial in other ways.

Leisure needs of special populations

There are a number of special populations with problems which can be solved or alleviated by leisure, though this is not widely realized. (1) Heart disease and other patients can be greatly helped by exercise regimes, if they can be persuaded to take them up and stick to them. (2) Depression and, perhaps, anxiety can also be greatly helped by regular exercise, though for different reasons. Leisure, in the form of greatly expanded occupational therapy, might make a big contribution to the treatment of mental patients, for example by giving training in social skills, using play for social learning (Meyer, 1983). (3) The socially isolated, some of them mental patients, are often helped by social workers who organize support groups; leisure groups can produce the same benefits through the companionship in shared activities, and the self-disclosure and support in some groups. (4) Prisoners, drug addicts and others are helped in institutions by the provision of constructive leisure activities, such as hobbies, team sports, arts and crafts, which are believed to help with the process of treatment and rehabilitation (Stein & Sessoms, 1983). This is important in light of evidence that delinquents turn to crime because they can't find any sufficiently exciting and satisfying form of leisure (Roberts, 1970). Various kinds of leisure education and physical activity have been found to increase the self-esteem of young offenders (Munson, 1988).

Leisure counselling

Individuals can be helped to find satisfying leisure in various ways. In the USA leisure counselling is common as part of other counselling. There are a variety of approaches; some concentrate on education and providing information, others on counselling proper; most focus on selecting leisure activities, but some on personal growth. It usually takes from one to three sessions, or may just be a lecture to a group. A number of questionnaires have been constructed to find a client's interests (Dowd, 1984).

Some systems of counselling have made good use of leisure research. For example Witt, Ellis and Niles (1984) use the following goals: increase perceived control, for example through knowledge and decision-making; increase perceived competence; increase intrinsic motivation; increase depth of involvement; and increase playfulness. These are interesting and valuable goals, though they are difficult to achieve by counselling alone.

From a quite different tradition, of happiness research, a different method has emerged. Lewinsohn and Graf (1973) devised 'pleasant activities therapy'; clients keep a diary for a month of the pleasant things which they have done each day, and of their mood by the end of the day. Computation shows which activities have the most positive effects, and clients are persuaded to do them more often. The activities are nearly all leisure activities. This has been found to work both for normal and depressed patients.

Leisure education

We saw in Chapter 6 how often leisure interests are acquired at school or college. Much of the school curriculum is directed more to leisure than to work – sport, music, English and languages, for example. In addition there are a lot of extramural activities, such as photography, more sports and more music, acting, camping and mountaineering, which are entirely about leisure. For those who go on to college there is an amazing variety of leisure pursuits on offer. We should add that education is in itself a form of leisure for many in Britain, via evening classes, the Open University and the University of the Third Age. In order to acquire one of these leisure interests, a person needs to know about it, to have access to training and facilities in many cases, and to be in contact with individuals or groups which do it.

But all this fails with a large section of the population, partly because some reject school and all it has to offer, or the curriculum is seen as work, school sports such as team games are little practised by adults, or school leisure is different from popular culture (Veal, 1987). 'Leisure education' often means special courses for those who need to acquire some leisure interests in later life, rather like leisure counselling under another name. This may take the form of one-hour-a-week workshops, with activities, films, talks and discussion – some of it simply to provide information. Some of these schemes have been successful in modifying leisure attitudes, such as perceived leisure competence (Searle & Mahon, 1991).

Much of the research which has been presented in this book suggests that the most effective way of building up leisure interests is through membership of social groups – which is how they are usually acquired. The easiest way to find a new leisure activity is to join a group which does it. In some cases, but not all, some degree of competence must be acquired, but in these cases the group usually supplies the training.

FORCES CONTROLLING THE FUTURE OF LEISURE

Central government

Leisure is not very prominent on the national political scene; other topics, such as industry and incomes, receive much more attention. However, there are some aspects of leisure which attract the attention of governments in most countries: sport, partly for national prestige, but also to keep rebellious and unemployed youth quiet; culture and the arts; exercise and parks for health; countryside and the national heritage. In this country the Labour government of Harold Wilson from 1964 to 1970 set up the Arts Council and the Sports Council as part of the welfare state. These and similar bodies, like the Countryside Commission, are technically quangos (quasi-autonomous non-governmental organizations), which receive government funding. In the USA the National Park Service was created in 1916, and the parks thus created have played a major role in encouraging leisure in wilderness areas. Some American writing on leisure identifies it with backpacking and camping. Several countries have promoted competitive sport, mainly to enhance national prestige, though this would filter down to lower levels. This has happened in the former East Germany, China and now Australia. But Sweden and China for a time did not allow competitive sport (Bramham *et al.*, 1993).

In Britain the Arts Council spent £155 million in 1989–90, mainly to subsidize high-level performers, thus enhancing entertainment in music and the arts of a sophisticated kind. The Sports Council spent £42 million, partly to encourage and train in sport, and partly to reduce urban frustration. The Countryside Commission spent £22 million. We saw how schemes to provide sports facilities and training for unemployed youth have been very successful. Public taste and the cultural heritage are kept up by the Arts Council and also by the BBC and the Independent Broadcasting Authority.

Government has considerable powers, which it sometimes uses in this sphere. In the last century it discouraged sports like cock-fighting by law, and it still tries to discourage drinking through taxes. But there is little discussion of leisure issues at the political level, and central government is not the main provider of leisure. To more important sources we now turn.

Local government

Local government is a much more important provider than central government. It spends about £1.4 billion a year on leisure, about £24 per head, from the rates. This is spent on swimming pools, sports halls, leisure centres, indoor and outdoor sports facilities of all kinds, parks and allotments, theatres and concert halls, libraries and museums, youth clubs and adult education, and it pays for the staff for these facilities, who may act as trainers or 'animaters', and for the administration of all this.

Commerce

Business doesn't pay for leisure; it makes money from it, but in so doing it creates new leisure facilities and popularizes new leisure activities. In the last century trains made seaside holidays possible, as well as large-scale sports and other events. In this century cars have made trips to the country popular; aeroplanes have made foreign holidays possible. Above all, commercial interests have produced mass leisure, mass holidays, masses at football matches, and other passive spectators in front of the TV. The leisure industry is one of the largest now; we spend 17 per cent of our household budget on leisure, a lot more than the £24 per year which local government spends on our behalf. It is spent on hotels and travel, eating and drinking, entertainment, sports, DIY and domestic equipment, including TV and other electronic apparatus, and leisure equipment of all kinds. This included £8.2 billion on eating out in 1984, plus the same amount on holidays, and £2.2 billion on sports, a lot of this on sports equipment (Henley Centre for Forecasting, 1985).

Commerce creates new needs; we had to be persuaded that we needed ski slopes, bowling alleys, white-knuckle rides at Alton Towers and Blackpool, or that to go for a walk it is necessary to have special boots, hats and other kit.

Voluntary bodies

We have seen that leisure is dominated by small leisure groups of all kinds, run by enthusiasts, unpaid and unconnected with either government or commerce. Many of these clubs are connected to national bodies for regulating and encouraging their particular activity. There are associations for every kind of sport and hobby; for other kinds of leisure; for different kinds of voluntary work, such as those concerned with youth or the elderly; for churches and political parties; for adult education; and for pressure groups concerned with the countryside, peace or other matters.

Many of these associations are very idealistic. In the last century temperance and other middle-class reform groups did a lot to improve the leisure of the poor, to replace drinking, fighting and gambling by 'rational recreation', and they were influential in increasing literacy and in promoting parks and libraries. Some of these groups are able to exert influence in local or central government. The associations for particular sports, music or other activities play an important role in keeping up standards, awarding qualifications, providing training, and in developing the activity itself, for example the rules of rugby football (Torkildsen, 1986).

Technology

Some of the greatest changes in leisure during the last hundred years have been mainly due to inventions and technology. Such developments make predictions of the future all but impossible, since inventions can't be predicted. The invention of the train, car, aeroplane and now TV have totally changed our lives. The fastest technical changes going on now are in the fields of computing and information technology, and these are bound to affect our leisure. It is possible, for example, that we will spend more time and money on domestic electronic equipment, so that we can use remote databases, engage in interactive video and play more computer games. That is until another invention appears which will replace all this. The cinema came during this century and now few go to it, though recently it has revived. Let us hope that bear-baiting, gladiatorial shows and chariot racing don't come back.

THE ROLE OF IDEAS — THE POSSIBILITY OF A LEISURE ETHIC

Ideas play an important part in how we spend our leisure. These ideas come from individuals and groups, are spread by books and in other ways, and affect whole communities and historical periods. In Chapter 2 we looked at some of the main ideas about leisure in the past. The Greeks, that is the citizens, believed that leisure was more important than work, which could be done by slaves, and that leisure should be for self-development through education and contemplation, music, philosophy and athletics. In the Middle Ages the Church thought that leisure should be spent in worship, as it is today by monks and nuns; later the Protestant church thought that work was the main goal of life, together with good works. In the Renaissance, leisure was greatly valued, particularly creative expression in the arts, and exercise. In the early nineteenth century, the middle classes thought that leisure should be more than pleasure or rest, and advocated rational recreation, for the poor and for themselves, in the form of education, sport, parks and the open air, social clubs and Sunday tea parties.

In the USSR, before it broke up, there were other ideas about rational education, that leisure should enrich the individual and hence society, especially the cohesion of society. Some kinds of leisure were thought not to be rational and were discouraged – female wrestling, male body-building, yoga, karate, dominoes, bingo, horse racing and cards (Riordan, 1993). In Sweden, and in China for a time, competitive sport was frowned upon; indeed every culture has its own values, its own preferences for and against various kinds of leisure.

It has been suggested that we need to develop a new leisure ethic to replace the work ethic, that is a set of ideas and values to the effect that leisure is the most important goal of life, that it is leisure which can give life meaning and purpose, and give individuals a sense of identity and fulfilment. For those who have no work to provide such meaning and fulfilment, leisure can fill the gap. Work might be seen as merely the necessary means of providing food and other necessities, while leisure can provide real pleasure and satisfaction through pursuing one's real interests. Attitude scales have been constructed which measure the extent to which people hold such attitudes, with items like: I would like to lead a life of complete leisure; I admire a person who knows how to relax; leisure time activities are more interesting than work; and more leisure time is good for people. Research with scales using items like these finds that there is most agreement with them among the young, those of higher occupational status, in Americans compared with Scots, and less agreement for those with conservative beliefs, high work ethic scores and high job involvement (Furnham, 1990).

However, the items above – examples from the scales used so far – make no mention at all of the quality of leisure; they refer only to the quantity of leisure, or to pleasure and relaxation. However, social thinkers down the ages have thought that leisure was more than relaxation, pleasure or entertainment. Aristotle thought that these were not part of leisure proper, which was about such activities as sport, music and philosophy. More recent thinkers like Csikszentmihalyi have recommended serious commitment and facing challenges. We have repeatedly found in the course of this book that certain kinds of leisure produce far more benefits than others.

A second criticism of the leisure ethic doctrine described above is that it values leisure at the expense of work. Surely both are valuable: there will always be some work and some who find their purpose in life from doing it.

Lane (1978) developed a more elaborate plan for a 'leisure ideology', based on contrasting leisure with rational market behaviour. He made use of ideas about leisure from a number of sources, most of which have been discussed in this book. However, some of these ideas need to be modified in the light of empirical research into leisure. Here are some of the main components:

1. Leisure behaviour is based on intrinsic motivation, not external rewards or deficiency needs; it is motivated by the pursuit of individual pleasure and growth, free from constraints, or is individualistic and libertarian. Research which we have examined earlier shows that most leisure is done with others, and in many cases cannot be done alone. Some leisure is motivated by the desire to help others.
2. Leisure is for individual self-expression, development and fulfilment. It could be argued that it is also about the development of others and of social groups and institutions.
3. Leisure needs no external control or discipline. However, sports teams and leisure groups of all kinds need leaders, and we have found, surprisingly, that quite authoritarian leadership is often accepted in both cases.

4. Csikszentmihalyi's ideas of flow are approved. However, we have seen that facing the challenges needed to produce such intense states is a minority taste, and most people prefer challenges which are easily within their powers.
5. Huizinger's ideas about the importance of play are also approved. There has been no research on this model of leisure, perhaps because it is not readily testable. A great deal of leisure is not like play at all: even games, in the Olympic sense, are intensely serious. Nevertheless there *is* a playful side to most leisure, making it different from most work.

Other utopian thinkers have prescribed how leisure should be spent, some of their ideas being fairly wild. Thomas More, in his *Utopia*, for example, planned for several hours a day of leisure to be spent in attending lectures, music, conversation and games like chess. Aldous Huxley, in his *Brave New World*, saw various high-tech games and artistic performances, including the feelies, erotic play and country games to consume transport and sports equipment. One of the most frightening looks at the future was in the recent book by Francis Fukuyama (1992), *The End of History and the Last Man*. When all our work is done by machines, injustices overcome and wars over, he fears, all we will have to do is to lie in the sun like dogs.

The best way to avoid this terrifying scenario is through the development of leisure. From psychology we have our own ideas about how leisure should be spent, and we can lay out an entirely empirical leisure ethic – quite different from the one we started with.

1. It should contain a strong social component, providing social support, cooperation and companionship, in the pursuit of shared goals, pursuing the development and pleasure of others as well as the self.
2. Some of it should be serious and committed, where effort is put into the pursuit of these goals, and standards of performance are met. This gives some of the satisfaction formerly found in work.
3. It should enable the experience of intense satisfaction or vision, through religion or the arts, meeting challenges or close social relationships.

4. It should include exercise, because of the benefits for mind and body.
5. It can certainly include relaxation, from watching TV, holidays, or low-key social events, as long as these do not become the whole of leisure.

REFERENCES

Adorno, T. W., Frenkel-Brunswik, E., Levinson, D. J., & Sanford, R. N. (1950). *The Authoritarian Personality*. New York: Harper.

Allcock, J. B. (1988). Tourism as a sacred journey. *Society and Leisure, 11*, 33–48.

Allen, L. R., & Beattie, R. J. (1984). The role of leisure as an indicator of overall satisfaction with community life. *Journal of Leisure Research, 16*, 99–109.

Allison, M. T., & Duncan, M. C. (1988). Women, work and flow. In M. Csikszentmihalyi & I. S. Csikszentmihalyi (eds.), *Optimal Experience*. Cambridge: Cambridge University Press.

Altick, R. D. (1957). *The English Common Reader*. Chicago: University of Chicago Press.

Ames, C. (1992). Achievement goals, motivational climate, and motivational processes. In G. C. Roberts (ed.), *Motivation in Sport and Exercise*. Champaign, Ill.: Human Kinetics.

Andreason, M. (1990). Evolution in the family's use of television: normative data from industry and academe. In J. Bryant (ed.), *Television and the American Family*. Hillsdale, N.J.: Erlbaum.

Andrews, E. M., & Withey, S. B. (1976). *Social Indicators of Well-being*. New York: Plenum.

Apter, M. J. (1982). *The Experience of Motivation: The Theory of Psychological Reversal*. London: Academic Press.

Apter, M. J., Fontana, D., & Murgatroyd, S. (1985). *Reversal Theory: Applications and Developments*. Oxford: Clarendon Press.

Argyle, M. (1969). *Social Interaction*. London: Methuen.

Argyle, M. (1987). *The Psychology of Happiness*. London: Methuen.

Argyle, M. (1989). *The Social Psychology of Work* (2nd edn). Harmondsworth: Penguin Books.

Argyle, M. (1991). *Cooperation*. London: Routledge.

Argyle, M. (1992). *The Social Psychology of Everyday Life*. London: Routledge.

Argyle, M. (1994a). *Psychology and the Quality of Life*. Oxford: Oxford Brookes University.

Argyle, M. (1994b). *The Psychology of School Class*. London: Routledge.

Argyle, M. (1994c). Social skills. In A. M. Colman (ed.), *Companion Encyclopedia of Psychology* (pp. 454–81). London: Routledge.

Argyle, M. (1994d). *The Psychology of Interpersonal Behaviour* (5th edn). Harmondsworth: Penguin Books.

Argyle, M., & Beit-Hallahmi, B. (1975). *The Social Psychology of Religion*. London: Routledge and Kegan Paul.

Argyle, M., & Furnham, A. (1982). The ecology of relationships: choice of situation as a function of relationship. *British Journal of Social Psychology*, *21*, 259–62.

Argyle, M., & Furnham, A. (1983). Sources of satisfaction and conflict in long-term relationships. *Journal of Marriage and the Family*, *45*, 481–93.

Argyle, M., & Henderson, M. (1985). *The Anatomy of Relationships*. Harmondsworth: Penguin Books.

Argyle, M., & Lu, L. (1990). The happiness of extraverts. *Personality and Individual Differences*, *11*, 1011–17.

Ashford, S., & Timms, N. (1992). *What Europe Thinks*. Aldershot: Dartmouth.

Aversa, A. (1990). When blue collars and white collars meet at play. *Qualitative Sociology*, *13*, 63–83.

Bailey, P. (1978). *Leisure and Class in Victorian England*. London: Routledge and Kegan Paul.

Bakker, F. C. (1988). Personality differences between young dancers and non-dancers. *Personality and Individual Differences*, *9*, 121–31.

Bakker, F. C., Whiting, H. T. A., & van der Brug, H. (1990). *Sport Psychology*. Chichester: Wiley.

Blacking, J. (1985). Movement, dance, music, and the Venda girls' initiation cycle. In P. Spencer (ed.), *Society and the Dance*. Cambridge: Cambridge University Press.

Bandura, A. (1977). Self-efficacy: toward a unifying theory of behavioral change. *Psychological Review*, *84*, 191–215.

Barnard, P. (1994). Cheats and bounders are more fun. *The Times*, 11 February 1994.

Barnett, L. A. (1980). The social psychology of children's play: effects of extrinsic rewards on free play and intrinsic motivation. In S. E. Iso-Ahola (ed.), *Social Psychological Perspectives on Leisure and Recreation*. Springfield, Ill.: Charles C. Thomas.

Barschak, E. (1951). A study of happiness and unhappiness in childhood and adolescence of girls in different cultures. *Journal of Psychology*, *32*, 173–215.

Barwise, P., & Ehrenberg, A. (1988). *Television and its Audience*. London: Sage.

Batson, C. D. (1991). *The Altruism Question: Toward a Social–Psychological Answer*. Hillsdale, N.J.: Erlbaum.

Batson, C. D., Schoenrade, P., & Ventis, W. L. (1993). *Religion and the Individual*. New York: Oxford University Press.

Baumann, G. (1987). *National Integration and Local Integrity*. Oxford: Clarendon Press.

BBC (1989). *Annual Review of BBC Broadcasting Research Findings*. London: John Libbey.

Becker, H. (1963). *Outsiders*. New York: Free Press.

Beit-Hallahmi, B. (1992). *Despair and Deliverance*. Albany, N.Y.: State University of New York Press.

Belson, W. (1967). *The Impact of Television*. London: Cheshire.

Berger, P. L., & Luckman, T. (1967). *The Social Construction of Reality*. Harmondsworth: Penguin.

Berkman, L. F., & Syme, S. L. (1979). Social networks, host resistance, and mortality: a nine year follow-up of Alameda County residents. *American Journal of Epidemiology, 109*, 186–204.

Berkowitz, L. (1993). *Aggression: Its Causes, Consequences and Control*. New York: McGraw-Hill.

Berlyne, D. E. (1971). *Aesthetics and Psychobiology*. New York: Appleton-Century-Crofts.

Best, G. (1971). *Mid-Victorian Britain*. London: Weidenfeld & Nicolson.

Beveridge, W. E. (1968). Problems in preparing for retirement. In H. B. Wright (ed.), *Solving the Problems of Retirement* (pp. 68–73). London: Institute of Directors.

Beveridge Report (1942). *Social Insurance and Allied Services*. London: HMSO.

Biddle, S., & Mutrie, N. (1991). *Psychology of Physical Activity and Exercise*. London: Springer-Verlag.

Billis, D. (1989). *A Theory of the Voluntary Sector. Implications for Policy and Practice*. London: L.S.E., Centre for Voluntary Organizations.

Birch, P. (1979). Leisure patterns in 1973 and 1977. *Population Trends, 17*, 2–8.

Bird, A. M. (1977). Team structure and success as related to cohesiveness and leadership. *Journal of Social Psychology, 103*, 217–23.

Bishop, D. W., & Ikeda, M. (1970). Status and role factors in the leisure behavior of different occupations. *Sociology and Social Research, 54*, 190–208.

Bishop, J., & Hoggett, J. (1986). *Organising Around Enthusiasms*. London: Comedia Publishing Group.

Blacking, J. (1987). *A Commonsense View of all Music*. Cambridge: Cambridge University Press.

Blazey, M. A. (1982). Travel and retirement status. *Annals of Tourism Research*, *19*, 771–83.

Blood, R. O. (1972). *The Family*. London: Collier-Macmillan.

Blumler, J. G. (1985). The social character of media gratifications. In K. E. Rosengren, L. A. Wenner, & P. Palmgreen (eds.), *Media Gratifications Research*. Beverly Hills, Calif.: Sage.

Boardman, J., Griffin, J., & Murray, O. (1986). *The Oxford History of the Classical World*. Oxford: Oxford University Press.

Bochner, S. (1981). *The Mediating Person*. Cambridge, Mass.: Schenkman.

Bolger, N., & Eckenrode, J. (1991). Social relationships, personality, and anxiety during a major stressful event. *Journal of Personality and Social Psychology*, *61*, 440–49.

Bortz, W. M. *et al.* (1981). Catecholamines, dopamine, and endorphin levels during extreme exercise. *New England Journal of Medicine*, *305*, 466–7.

Bottomore, P. (1954). Social stratification in voluntary organizations. In D. V. Glass (ed.), *Social Mobility in Britain*. London: Routledge and Kegan Paul.

Bramham, P., Henry, I., Mommas, H., & van der Poel, H. (eds.) (1993). *Leisure Policies in Europe*. Wallingford: CAB International.

Brandenburg, J. *et al.* (1982). A conceptual model of how people adopt recreation activities. *Leisure Studies*, *1*, 263–76.

Brierley, P. (1991). *Christian Handbook*. London: Evangelical Alliance/Bible Society/MARC Europe.

British Museum (1929). *A Guide to the Exhibition Illustrating Greek and Roman Life*. London: Trustees of the British Museum.

Brook, J. A. (1993). Leisure meanings and comparisons with work. *Leisure Studies*, *12*, 149–62.

Brown, G. W. (1992). Social support: an investigator-based approach. In H. O. F. Veiel & U. Baumann (eds.), *The Meaning and Measurement of Social Support*. New York: Hemisphere.

Brown, J. D. (1991). Staying fit and staying well. *Journal of Personality and Social Psychology*, *60*, 555–61.

Bruner, J. S., Jolly, A., & Sylva, K. (eds.) (1976). *Play*. Harmondsworth: Penguin Books.

Bryant, J., Comisky, P., & Zillman, D. (1981). The appeal of rough-and-tumble play in televised professional football. *Communication Quarterly*, *29*, 256–62.

Bryant, J., & Zillman, D. (1984). Using television to relieve boredom as a function of induced excitational states. *Journal of Broadcasting*, *28*, 1–20.

Burton, T. L. (1971). *Experiments in Recreation Research*. London: Allen and Unwin.

Calhoun, D. W. (1987). *Sport, Culture and Personality*. Champaign, Ill.: Human Kinetics.

Caltabiano, M. L. (1994). Measuring the similarity among leisure activities based on a perceived stress-reduction benefit. *Leisure Studies, 13,* 17–31.

Campbell, A., Converse, P. E., & Rogers, W. L. (1976). *The Quality of American Life*. New York: Sage.

Canadian Government Travel Bureau (1972). *Motivations to Travel and Vacations Trends*. Ottawa: Canadian Government Travel Bureau.

Canter, D., Comber, M., & Uzzell, D. L. (1989). *Football in its Place*. London: Routledge.

Caplow, T. (1954). *The Sociology of Work*. Minneapolis: University of Minnesota Press.

Carli, M., Delle Fave, A., & Massimi, F. (1988). The quality of experience in the flow channels: comparison of Italian and US students. In M. Csikszentmihalyi & I. S. Csikszentmihalyi (eds.), *Optimal Experience*. Cambridge: Cambridge University Press.

Cheek, N. H., & Burch, W. R. (1976). *The Social Organization of Leisure in Human Society*. New York: Harper and Row.

Chelladurai, P. (1984). Leadership in sports. In J. M. Silva & R. S. Weinberg (eds.), *Psychological Foundations of Sport*. Champaign, Ill.: Human Kinetics.

Cherry, G. E. (1984). Leisure and the home: a review of changing relationships. *Leisure Studies, 3,* 35–52.

Clark, C. L. (1991). *Theory and Practice in Voluntary Social Action*. Aldershot: Avebury.

Clark, S. M., Harvey, A. S., & Shaw, S. M. (1990). Time use and leisure: subjective and objective aspects. *Social Indicators Research, 23,* 337–52.

Clarke, J., & Critcher, C. (1985). *The Devil Makes Work*. Basingstoke: Macmillan.

Clary, E. G., & Miller, J. (1986). Socialization and situational influences on sustained altruism. *Child Development, 57,* 1358–69.

Clary, E. G., & Snyder, M. (1991). A functional analysis of altruism and prosocial behavior: the case of volunteerism. *Review of Personality and Social Psychology, 12,* 119–48.

Clough, P. J., Shepherd, J., & Maughan, R. (1989). Motives for participation in recreational running. *Journal of Leisure Research, 21,* 297–309.

Coalter, F. (1993). Sports participation: price or priorities? *Leisure Studies, 12,* 171–82.

Cohen, S., & Wills, T. A. (1985). Stress, social support, and the buffering hypothesis. *Psychological Bulletin, 98*, 310–57.

Coleman, D., & Iso-Ahola, S. E. (1993). Leisure and health: the role of social support and self-determination. *Journal of Leisure Research, 25*, 111–28.

Collett, P. (1987). Real-life responses to TV commercials. *Proceedings of the 40th ESOMAR Marketing Research Congress, Montreux*, 713–21.

Comstock, G., Chaffee, S., Katzman, N., McCombs, M., & Roberts, D. (1978). *Television and Human Behavior*. New York: Columbia University Press.

Comstock, G. W., & Partridge, K. B. (1972). Church attendance and health. *Journal of Chronic Diseases, 25*, 665–72.

Consterdine, G. (1988). *Readership Research and the Planning of Press Schedules*. Aldershot: Gower.

Coulton, G. C. (1938). *Medieval Panorama*. Cambridge: Cambridge University Press.

Crandall, R. (1980). Motivations for leisure. *Journal of Leisure Research, 12*, 45–54.

Crews, D. J., & Landers, D. M. (1987). A meta-analytic review of aerobic fitness and reactivity to psychosocial stressors. *Medicine and Science in Sports and Exercise, 19* (5, Supplement), S114–S120.

Csikszentmihalyi, M. (1975). *Beyond Boredom and Anxiety*. San Francisco: Jossey-Bass.

Csikszentmihalyi, M., & Csikszentmihalyi, I. S. (1988). *Optimal Experience*. Cambridge: Cambridge University Press.

Csikszentmihalyi, M., & Kubey, R. (1981). Television and the rest of life. *Public Opinion Quarterly, 45*, 317–28.

Cumberbatch, G., & Howitt, D. (1989). *A Measure of Uncertainty*. London: John Libby and the Broadcasting Standards Council.

Cunningham, H. (1980). *Leisure in the Industrial Revolution*. London: Croom Helm.

Cunningham, M. R. (1988). What do you do when you're happy or blue? Mood, expectancies, and behavioral intent. *Motivation and Emotion, 12*, 309–31.

Cutler, N. E. (1976). Membership in different kinds of voluntary association and psychological well-being. *Gerontologist, 16*, 335–9.

Daniel, R. T. (1989). Music: the history of Western music. *Encyclopaedia Britannica, 24*, 551–62.

Dann, G. M. S. (1993). Limitations in the use of 'nationality' and 'country of residence' variable. In D. G. Pearce & R. W. Butler (eds.), *Tourism Research*. London: Routledge.

Davies, D. (1989). *Psychological Factors in Competitive Sport*. London: Falmer Press.

Deci, E. L., & Ryan, R. M. (1991). A motivational approach to self: integration in personality. In R. Dienstbier (ed.), *Perspectives on Motivation. Nebraska Symposium on Motivation 1990* (Vol. 38, pp. 237–88). Lincoln: University of Nebraska Press.

Deem, R. (1986). *All Work and No Play? The Sociology of Women and Leisure*. Milton Keynes: Open University Press.

Dick, F. W. (1989). *Sports Training Principles* (2nd edn). London: A. and C. Black.

DiMaggio, P., & Ostrower, F. (1990). Participation in the arts by black and white Americans. *Social Forces, 68*, 753–78.

Dixey, R. (1987). It's a great feeling when you win: women and bingo. *Leisure Studies, 6*, 199–214.

Dowd, E. T. (ed.) (1984). *Leisure Counseling*. Springfield, Ill.: Charles C. Thomas.

Dowd, R., & Innes, J. M. (1981). Sport and personality: effects of type of sport and level of competition. *Perceptual and Motor Skills, 53*, 78–89.

Driver, B. L., Brown, P. J., & Peterson, G. L. (eds.) (1991). *Benefits of Leisure*. State College, Pa: Venture Publishing Co.

Dumazadier, J. (1967). *Toward a Society of Leisure*. New York: The Free Press.

Dunn Ross, E. L., & Iso-Ahola, S. E. (1991). Sightseeing tourists' motivation and satisfaction. *Annals of Tourism Research, 18*, 226–37.

Dwyer, J. J. (1992). Internal structure of participation motivation questionnaire completed by undergraduates. *Psychological Reports, 70*, 283–90.

Dwyer, J. W., Clarke, L. L., & Miller, M. K. (1990). The effect of religious concentration and affiliation on county cancer mortality rates. *Journal of Health and Social Behavior, 31*, 185–202.

Easley, A. T. (1991). Programmed, nonclinical skill development benefits of leisure activities. In B. L. Driver, P. J. Brown, & G. L. Peterson (eds.), *Benefits of Leisure*. State College, Pa: Venture Publishing Co.

Edwards, J. (1979). The home-field advantage. In J. H. Goldstein (ed.), *Sports, Games and Play*. New York: Wiley.

Elias, N., & Dunning, E. (1986). *The Quest for Excitement*. Oxford: Blackwell.

Elliott, D. H., & Elliott, J. L. (1990). Behavior and the life cycle: a consideration of the role of longitudinal time-use studies. *Social Indicators Research, 23*, 395–414.

Ellison, C. G. (1993). Religious involvement in black Americans. *Social Forces, 71*, 1027–55.

Ellison, C. G., Gay, D. A., & Glass, T. A. (1989). Does religious commitment contribute to individual life satisfaction? *Social Forces, 68*, 100–123.

Etzioni, A. (1961). *A Comparative Analysis of Complex Organizations*. New York: Free Press.

Euromonitor (1987). *Consumer Market Surveys: Newspapers and Periodicals*. London: Euromonitor Publications Ltd.

Ewert, A., & Hollenhurst, S. (1989). Testing the adventure model: empirical support for a model of risk recreation participation. *Journal of Leisure Research, 21*, 124–9.

Eysenck, H. J. (1976). *The Measurement of Personality*. Lancaster: MTP Press.

Eysenck, H. J., Nias, D. K. B., & Cox, D. N. (1982). Sport and personality. *Advances in Behaviour Research and Therapy, 4*, 1–56.

Falkenburg, L. E. (1987). Employee fitness programs: their impact on the employee and the organization. *Academy of Management Review, 12*, 511–22.

Feist, J., & Brannon, L. (1988). *Health Psychology*. Belmont, Calif.: Wadsworth.

Feltz, D. L. (1992). Understanding motivation in sport: a self-efficacy perspective. In G. C. Roberts (ed.), *Motivation and Sport and Exercise*. Champaign, Ill.: Human Kinetics.

Fenz, W. D., & Epstein, S. (1967). Gradients of psychological arousal in parachutists as a function of an approaching jump. *Psychosomatic Medicine, 29*, 33–51.

Fife-Shaw, C. R. (1995). Prediction of sexual attitudes. *Social Psychology Section, BPS, Newsletter*, no. 33, 13–30.

Fishbein, M., & Ajzen, I. (1975). *Belief, Attitude, Intention and Behavior: An Introduction to Theory and Research*. Redding, Ma: Addison-Wesley.

Fisher, R. J., & Price, L. L. (1991). International pleasure travel motivation and satisfaction. *Journal of Leisure Research, 23*, 193–208.

Fleishman, E. A., & Quaintance, M. A. (1984). *Taxonomies of Human Performance*. New York: Academic Press.

Folkins, C. H., & Sime, W. E. (1981). Physical fitness training and mental health. *American Psychologist, 36*, 373–89.

Formanek, R. (1991). They that collect: collectors reveal their motivations. *Journal of Social Behaviour and Personality, 6*, 275–86.

Fowles, J. (1992). *Why Viewers Watch*. Newbury Park: Sage.

Fox, W., & Williams, J. (1974). Political orientation and music preferences among college students. *Public Opinion Quarterly, 38*, 352–71.

Francis, L. J. (1985). Personality and religion: theory and measurement. In L. B. Brown (ed.), *Advances in the Psychology of Religion* (pp. 171–184). Oxford: Pergamon.

Froehlicher, V. F., & Froehlicher, S. S. (1991). Cardiovascular benefits of physical activity. In B. L. Driver, P. J. Brown, & G. L. Peterson (eds.), *Benefits of Leisure*. State College, Pa: Venture Publishing Co.

Fry, L. W., Kerr, S., & Lee, C. (1986). Effects of different leader behaviors under different levels of task interdependence. *Human Relations, 39*, 1067–92.

Fryer, D., & Payne, R. (1984). Proactive behaviour in unemployment. *Leisure Studies, 3*, 273–95.

Fukuyama, F. (1992). *The End of History and the Last Man*. Harmondsworth: Penguin.

Furnham, A. (1990). Personality and demographic determinants of leisure and sports preference and performance. *International Journal of Sports Psychology, 21*, 218–36.

Furnham, A. (1990). *The Protestant Work Ethic*. London: Routledge.

Furnham, A. (1992). *Personality at Work*. London: Routledge.

Gallup, G. (1984). Religion in America. *The Gallup Report, 222*.

Geertz, C. (1973). *The Interpretation of Cultures*. New York: Basic Books.

Gerard, D. (1985). Religious attitudes and values. In M. Abrams, G. Gerard, & N. Timms (eds.), *Values and Social Change in Britain*. London: Macmillan.

Gershuny, J. (1979). *After Industrial Society: the Emerging Self-service Society*. London: Macmillan.

Gershuny, J. (1992). Are we running out of time? *Futures*, January/February, 3–18.

Gershuny, J., & Jones, S. (1987). The changing work/leisure balance in Britain. In J. Horne, D. Jary, & A. Tomlinson (eds.), *Britain, 1961–84* (Sport, Leisure and Social Relations edn, pp. 9–50). London: Routledge and Kegan Paul.

Gerstl, J. E., & Hutton, S. P. (1966). *Engineers: The Anatomy of a Profession*. London: Tavistock.

Gill, C. (1985). *Work, Unemployment and New Technology*. Cambridge: Polity Press.

Gill, D. L. (1986). *Psychological Dynamics of Sport*. Champaign, Ill.: Human Kinetics.

Gittelson, R., & Kerstetter, D. (1982). Adolescent travel experiences shaping post-adolescent travel behavior. *Annals of Tourism Research, 19*, 128–31.

Glyptis, S. (1989). *Leisure and Unemployment*. Milton Keynes: Open University Press.

Goldthorpe, J. H., Llewellyn, C., & Payne, C. (1987). *Social Mobility and Class Structure in Modern Britain*. Oxford: Clarendon Press.

Goodale, T. L., & Godbey, G. C. (1988). *The Evolution of Leisure*. State College, Pa: Venture Publishing Co.

Goodhardt, G. J., Ahrenberg, A. S. C., & Collins, M. A. (1987). *The Television Audience: Patterns of Viewing* (2nd edn). Aldershot: Gower.

Gorman, B. (1979). Seven days, five countries. *Urban Life,* 7, 469–71.

Graef, R, Csikszentmihalyi, M., & Gianinno, S. M. (1983). Measuring intrinsic motivation in daily life. *Leisure Studies,* 2, 158–68.

Gratton, C., & Tice, A. (1994). Trends in sports participation in Britain 1977–1987. *Leisure Studies, 13,* 49–66.

Green, E., Hebron, S., & Woodward, D. (1990). *Women's Leisure: What Leisure?* London: Macmillan.

Greist, J. H. (1984). *Coping with Mental Stress.* Washington, DC: National Institute of Mental Health.

Greist, J. H., Eischens, R. R., Klein, M. H., & Faris, J. W. (1979). Antidepressant running. *Psychiatric Annals,* 9, 134–40.

Griffiths, M. (1993). Are computer games bad for children? *The Psychologist,* 6, 401–7.

Griffiths, M. D. (1991). Amusement machine playing in childhood and adolescence: a comparative analysis of video games and fruit machines. *Journal of Adolescence, 14,* 53–73.

Grusky, O. (1963). The effects of formal structure on managerial recruitment: a study of baseball organisation. *Sociometry, 26,* 245–53.

Guttmann, A. (1986). *Sports Spectators.* Oxford: Blackwell.

Hackman, J. R. (1977). Work design. In J. R. Hackman & J. L. Suttle (eds.), *Improving Life at Work.* Santa Monica: Goodyear.

Hackman, J. R. (1980). *Work Redesign.* Redding, Ma: Addison-Wesley.

Hackman, J. R., & Oldham, G. R. (1976). Motivation through the design of work: test of a theory. *Organizational Behavior and Human Performance, 16,* 250–279.

Haggard, L. M., & Williams, D. R. (1992). Identity affirmation through leisure activities. *Journal of Leisure Research, 24,* 1–18.

Hamilton, M., & Stasinopoulos, M. (1987). *Literacy, Numeracy, and Adults.* Lancaster: Adult Literacy and Basic Skills Unit.

Handy, C. (1985). *The Future of Work.* Oxford: Blackwell.

Hargreaves, D. J. (1986). *The Developmental Psychology of Music.* Cambridge: Cambridge University Press.

Haworth, J. T. (1993). Skill–challenge relationships and psychological well-being in everyday life. *Society and Leisure, 16,* 115–28.

Hay, D. (1982). *Exploring Inner Space.* Harmondsworth: Pelican Books.

Hayden, B. (1987). Alliances and ritual ecstasy. *Journal for the Scientific Study of Religion, 26,* 81–91.

Headey, B., & Wearing, A. (1991). Subjective well-being: a stocks and flows framework. In F. Strack, M. Argyle, & N. Schwarz (eds.), *Subjective Well-Being* (pp. 49–73). Oxford: Pergamon.

Headey, B., & Wearing, A. (1992). *Understanding Happiness*. Melbourne: Longman Cheshire.

Hedley, R., & Smith, J. D. (1992). *Volunteering and Society*. London: NCBO Publications.

Henderson, M., & Argyle, M. (1985). Social support by four categories of work colleagues: relationships between activities, stress and satisfaction. *Journal of Occupational Behaviour, 6*, 229–39.

Hendry, L. B., Raymond, M., & Stewart, C. (1984). School and leisure: an adolescent study. *Leisure Studies, 3*, 175–87.

Hendry, L. B., Shucksmith, J., Love, J. G., & Glendinning, A. (1993). *Young People's Leisure and Lifestyles*. London: Routledge.

Henley Centre for Forecasting (1985). *Leisure Futures*. London: Quarterly.

Herzberg, F., Mauser, B., & Snyderman, B. B. (1959). *The Motivation to Work*. New York: Wiley.

Hinkle, S., & Brown, R. (1990). Intergroup comparisons and social identity: some links and lacunae. In D. Abrams & M. Hogg (eds.), *Social Identity Theory: Critical and Constructive Advances*. Hemel Hempstead: Harvester.

Hoff, A. E., & Ellis, G. D. (1992). Influence of agents of leisure socialisation on leisure self-efficacy of university students. *Journal of Leisure Research, 24*, 114–26.

Hoggart, R. (1957). *The Uses of Literacy*. London: Chatto & Windus.

Hoggett, P., & Bishop, J. (1985). *The Social Organization of Leisure*. London: Sports Council and ESRC.

Holman, T. B., & Epperson, A. (1984). Family and leisure: a review of the literature with research recommendations. *Journal of Leisure Research, 16*, 277–94.

Holme, A., & Maizels, J. (1978). *Social Workers and Volunteers*. London: Allen and Unwin.

Höltzman, J. T., & Black, D. R. (1989). Primary meta-analysis in leisure research: results from Neulinger's 'What am I doing?' instrument. *Journal of Leisure Research, 21*, 18–31.

Homans, G. C. (1951). *The Human Group*. London: Routledge and Kegan Paul.

Horna, J. L. A. (1989). The leisure component of the parental role. *Journal of Leisure Research, 21*, 228–41.

Horton, D., & Wohl, R. R. (1956). Mass communication and parasocial interaction. *Psychiatry, 19*, 215–29.

House, J., Robbins, C., & Metzner, H. L. (1982). The association of social relationships and activities with mortality: prospective evidence from the Tucumseh Community Health Survey. *American Journal of Epidemiology, 116,* 123–40.

House, J. S., Landis, K. R., & Umberson, D. (1988). Social relationships and health. *Science, 241,* 540–45.

Howard, D. R. (1976). Multivariate relationships between leisure activities and personality. *Research Quarterly, 47,* 226–37.

Howarth, E. (1969). Personality differences in serial learning under distraction. *Perceptual & Motor Skills, 28,* 377–92.

Hu, J. C. (1990). Hobbies of retired people in the People's Republic of China. *International Journal of Aging and Human Development, 31,* 31–44.

Huesmann, L. R., Lagerspetz, K., & Eron, L. D. (1984). Intervening variables in the TV violence–aggression relation: evidence from two countries. *Developmental Psychology, 20,* 746–75.

Huizinger, J. (1939). *Homo Ludens.* Boston: Beacon Press.

Hunnicutt, B. K. (1985). Economic constraints in leisure. In M. G. Wade (ed.), *Constraints on Leisure.* Springfield, Ill.: Charles C. Thomas.

Inglehart, R. (1990). *Culture Shift in Advanced Industrial Society.* Princeton, N. J.: Princeton University Press.

Iso-Ahola, S. E. (1980). *The Social Psychology of Leisure and Recreation.* Springfield, Ill.: Charles C. Thomas.

Iversen, S. D., & Iversen, L. L. (1981). *Behavioral Pharmacology.* New York: Oxford University Press.

Jackson, C., & Wilson, G. D. (1993). Mad, bad or sad? The personality of bikers. *Personality and Individual Differences, 14,* 241–2.

Jackson, E. L. (1993). Recognising patterns of leisure constraints: results from alternative analyses. *Journal of Leisure Research, 25,* 129–49.

Jarvis, G. K., & Northcott, H. C. (1987). Religion and differences in morbidity and mortality. *Social Science and Medicine, 25,* 813–24.

Jasnowski, M. L., & Holmes, D. S. (1981). Influence of initial aerobic fitness, aerobic training and change in aerobic fitness on personality functioning. *Journal of Psychosomatic Research, 25,* 553–6.

Johnson, S. (1987). Early developed sex differences in science and mathematics in the United Kingdom: sex differences in early adolescents. *Journal of Early Adolescence, 7,* 21–33.

Kabanoff, B. (1982). Occupational and sex differences in leisure needs and leisure satisfaction. *Journal of Occupational Behaviour, 3,* 233–45.

Kandel, D. B. (1986). Processes of peer influences in adolescence. In R. K. Silbereisen, K. Eyferth, & G. Rudinger (eds.), *Development as Action in Context* (pp. 203–27). Berlin: Springer-Verlag.

Karasek, R. A. (1979). Job demands, job decision latitude, and mental strain: implications for job design. *Administrative Science Quarterly*, *24*, 285–308.

Kasl, S. V. (1987). Epidemiological contributions to the study of work stress. In C. L. Cooper & R. Payne (eds.), *Current Concerns in Occupational Stress*. Chichester: Wiley.

Katz, E., & Gurevitch, M. (1976). *The Secularization of Leisure*. London: Faber and Faber.

Kay, T., & Jackson, G. (1991). Leisure despite constraint: the impact of leisure constraints on leisure participation. *Journal of Leisure Research*, *23*, 301–13.

Kelly, J. R. (1977). Leisure socialization: replication and extension. *Journal of Leisure Research*, *9*, 121–32.

Kelly, J. R. (1983). *Leisure Identities and Interactions*. London: Allen and Unwin.

Kelly, J. R., Steinkamp, M. W., & Kelly, J. R. (1987). Later life satisfaction: does leisure contribute? *Leisure Sciences*, *9*, 189–200.

Kelly, T. (1962). *A History of Adult Education in Great Britain*. Liverpool: Liverpool University Press.

Kelvin, P., Dewberry, C., & Morley-Bunker, N. (1984). *Unemployment and Leisure*. London: Sports Council and ESRC.

Kelvin, P., & Jarrett, J. E. (1985). *Unemployment*. Cambridge: Cambridge University Press.

Kennedy, S., Kiecolt-Glaser, J. K., & Glaser, R. (1990). Social support, stress, and the immune system. In B. R. Sarason, I. G. Sarason, & G. R. Pierce (eds.), *Social Support: An Interactional View*. New York: Wiley.

Kenyon, G. S., & McPherson, B. D. (1973). Becoming involved in physical activity and sport: a process of socialization. In G. L. Rarick (ed.), *Physical Activity, Human Growth and Development*. New York: Academic Press, pp. 304–33.

Khanna, S., Rajendra, P. N., & Channabasavanna, S. M. (1988). Social adjustment in obsessive compulsive disorder. *International Journal of Social Psychiatry*, *34*, 118–22.

Kippax, S., Koenig, S., & Dowsett, G. (1984). Potential arts audiences: attitudes and representations. Unpublished report, Macquarrie University.

Kirkcaldy, B. D. (1982). Personality profiles at various levels of athletic participation. *Personality and Individual Differences*, *3*, 321–26.

Kirkcaldy, B. D. (1985). The value of traits in sport. In B. D. Kirkcaldy (ed.), *Individual Differences in Movement* (pp. 257–77). Lancaster: MTP Press.

Kirkcaldy, B., & Cooper, C. L. (1992). Work attitudes and leisure preferences: sex differences. *Personality and Individual Differences*, *13*, 329–34.

Kirkcaldy, B. D., & Furnham, A. (1991) Extraversion, neuroticism, psychoticism and recreational choice. *Personality and Individual Differences*, 7, 737–45.

Kirkpatrick, L. A. (1992). An attachment-theory approach to the psychology of religion. *International Journal for the Psychology of Religion*, 2, 3–28.

Kleiber, D., Larson, R., & Csikszentmihalyi, M. (1986). The experience of leisure in adolescence. *Journal of Leisure Research*, 18, 169–76.

Klein, M. H., Greist, J. H., Gurman, A. S., *et al.* (1985). A comparative outcome study of group psychotherapy vs. exercise treatments for depression. *International Journal of Mental Health*, 13, 148–77.

Knoke, D. (1986). Associations and interest groups. *Annual Review of Sociology*, 12, 1–21.

Kobasa, S. C., Maddi, S. R., & Puccetti, M. C. (1982). Personality and exercise as buffers in the stress–illness relationship. *Journal of Behavioral Medicine*, 5, 491–504.

Kohn, M. L., & Schooler, K. A. (1983). *Work and Personality*. Norwood, N.J.: Ablex.

Komarovsky, M. (1964). *Blue Collar Marriage*. New Haven: Yale University Press.

Konecni, V. J. (1982). Social interaction and musical preference. In D. Deutsch (ed.), *The Psychology of Music*. New York: Academic Press.

Kraus, R. (1971). *Recreation and Leisure in Modern Society*. New York: Appleton-Century-Crofts.

Kraut, R. E., & Johnston, R. E. (1979). Social and emotional messages of smiling: an ethological approach. *Journal of Personality and Social Psychology*, 37, 1539–53.

Kremer, Y., & Harpaz, I. (1982). Leisure patterns among retired workers: spillover or compensatory trends. *Journal of Vocational Behavior*, 21, 183–95.

Kubey, R., & Csikszentmihalyi, M. (1990). *Television and the Quality of Life*. Hillsdale, N.J.: Erlbaum.

Kuhn, M. H., & McPartland, T. S. (1954). An empirical investigation of self-attitudes. *American Sociological Review*, 19, 68–76.

Kune, G. A., Kune, S., & Watson, L. F. (1993). Perceived religiousness is protective for colorectal cancer: data from the Melbourne colorectal cancer study. *Journal of the Royal Society of Medicine*, 86, 645–7.

Kuwahara, Y. (1992). Power to the people y'all: rap music, resistance and black college students. *Humanity and Society*, 16, 54–73.

Lamb, K. L., Dench, S., Brodie, D. A., & Roberts, K. (1988). Sports participation and health status: a preliminary analysis. *Social Science and Medicine*, 27, 1309–16.

Lane, R. E. (1978). The regulation of experience: leisure in a market economy. *Social Science Information*, *17*, 147–84.

Langer, S. K. (1942). *Philosophy in a New Key*. Cambridge, Mass.: Harvard University Press.

Larson, R., Csikszentmihalyi, M., & Freeman, M. (1984). Alcohol and marihuana use in adolescents' daily lives: a random sample of experiences. *International Journal of the Addictions*, *19*, 367–81.

Larson, R. W. (1990). The solitary side of life: an examination of the time people spend alone from childhood to old age. *Developmental Review*, *10*, 155–83.

Legge, D. (1982). *The Education of Adults in Britain*. Milton Keynes: Open University Press.

Lemon, M., Palisi, B. J., & Jacobson, P. E. (1972). Dominant statuses and involvement in formal voluntary associations. *Journal of Voluntary Action Research*, *1*, 30–42.

Levy, M. R. (1978). The audience experience with television news. *Journalism Monographs*, *55*, 1–29.

Lewinsohn, P. M., & Graf, M. (1973). Pleasant activities and depression. *Journal of Consulting and Clinical Psychology*, *41*, 261–8.

Liebes, T., & Livingstone, S. (1992). Mothers and lovers: managing women's role conflicts in American and British soap operas. In J. G. Blumler, J. M. McLeod, & K. E. Rosengren (eds.), *Comparatively Speaking: Communication and Culture across Space and Time*. Newbury Park: Sage.

Liedka, R. V. (1991). Who do you know in the group?: Location of organizations in interpersonal networks. *Social Forces*, *70*, 455–76.

Lin, N., Simeone, R. S., Ensel, W. M., & Kuo, W. (1979). Social support, stressful life events, and illness: a model and an empirical test. *Journal of Health and Social Behavior*, *20*, 108–19.

Lipset, S. M. (1988). American exceptionalism reaffirmed. *International Review of Sociology*, *3*, 25–69.

Livingstone, S. (1990). *Making Sense of Television*. Oxford: Pergamon.

Livingstone, S. (1995). On the difficulties of measuring everyday experience. *Semiotica*, *104*, 225–31.

Livingstone, S. M. (1988). Why people watch soap opera: an analysis of the explanations of British viewers. *European Journal of Communication*, *3*, 55–80.

Locke, H. J. (1951). *Predicting Adjustment in Marriage*. New York: Holt, Rinehart and Winston.

Loehlin, J. C., & Nichols, R. C. (1976). *Heredity, Environment, and Personality*. Austin: University of Texas Press.

London, M., Crandall, R., & Seals, G. W. (1977). The contribution of job and leisure satisfaction to quality of life. *Journal of Applied Psychology, 62,* 328.

Long, J. (1987). Continuity as a basis for change: leisure and male retirement. *Leisure Studies, 6,* 55–70.

Losier, G. F., Bourque, P. E., & Vallerand, R. J. (1993). A motivational model of leisure participation in the elderly. *Journal of Psychology, 127,* 153–70.

Lu, L., & Argyle, M. (1993). TV watching, soap opera and happiness. *Kaohsiung Journal of Medical Sciences, 9,* 501–7.

Lu, L., & Argyle, M. (1994). Leisure satisfaction and happiness as a function of leisure activity. *Kaohsiung Journal of Medical Sciences, 10,* 89–96.

Lull, J. (1990). *Inside Family Viewing.* London: Routledge.

Luszki, M., & Luszki, W. (1985). Advantages of growing old. *Journal of the American Geriatrics Society, 33,* 216–17.

Lynn, P., & Smith, J. D. (1991). *Voluntary Action Research.* London: The Volunteer Centre.

McAleer, J. (1992). *Popular Reading and Publishing in Britain 1914–50.* Oxford: Clarendon Press.

McAuley, E. (1992). Understanding exercise behavior: a self-efficacy perspective. In G. C. Roberts (ed.), *Motivation in Exercise and Sport.* Champaign, Ill.: Human Kinetics.

MacCannell, D. (1976). *The Tourist: A New Theory of the Leisure Class.* New York: Schocken.

McClelland, D. C. (1987). *Human Motivation.* Cambridge: Cambridge University Press.

McClelland, D. C., & Boyatzis, R. E. (1982). Leadership motive pattern and long-term success in management. *Journal of Applied Psychology, 67,* 737–43.

McDonald, B. L., & Schreyer, R. (1991). Spiritual benefits of leisure participation and settings. In B. L. Driver, L. L. Clarke, & G. L. Peterson (eds.), *Benefits of Leisure.* State College, Pa: Venture Publishing Co.

McGoldrick, A. (1982). Early retirement: a new leisure opportunity. *Work and Leisure, 15,* 73–89.

McIntosh, D. N., Silver, R. C., & Westman, C. B. (1993). Religion's role in adjustment to a negative life event: coping with loss of a child. *Journal of Personality and Social Psychology, 65,* 812–21.

McIntyre, N. (1992). Involvement in risk recreation: a comparison of objective and subjective measures of engagement. *Journal of Leisure Research, 24,* 64–71.

McPherson, B. D., Curtis, J. E., & Loy, J. W. (1989). *The Social Significance of Sport*. Champaign, Ill.: Human Kinetics.

McQuail, D., Blumler, J. G., & Brown, J. R. (1972). The television audience: a revised perspective. In D. McQuail (ed.), *Sociology of Mass Communications*. Harmondsworth: Penguin.

Malcolmson, R. W. (1973). *Popular Recreations in English Society*. Cambridge: Cambridge University Press.

Mann, L. (1979). Sports crowds viewed from the perspective of collective behavior. In J. H. Goldstein (ed.), *Sports, Games, and Play* (pp. 337–68). Hillsdale, N.J.: Erlbaum.

Mann, P. H. (1969). *The Romantic Novel*. London: Mills and Boon.

Mann, P. H. (1982). *From Author to Reader*. London: Routledge and Kegan Paul.

Mannell, R. C., Zuzanek, J., & Larson, R. (1988). Leisure states and 'flow' experiences: testing perceived freedom and intrinsic motivation hypotheses. *Journal of Leisure Research, 20*, 289–304.

Marchant-Haycox, S. E., & Wilson, G. D. (1992). Personality and stress in performing artists. *Personality and Individual Differences, 13*, 1061–8.

Markland, D., & Hardy, L. (1993). The exercise motivations inventory: preliminary development and validity of a measure of individuals' reasons for participation in regular physical exercise. *Personality and Individual Differences, 15*, 289–96.

Maroulakis, E., & Zervas, Y. (1993). Effects of aerobic exercise on mood of adult women. *Perceptual and Motor Skills, 76*, 795–801.

Marsh, P., Rosser, E., & Harré, R. (1978). *The Rules of Disorder*. London: Routledge and Kegan Paul.

Maslow, A. H. (1970). *Motivation and Personality*. New York: Harper and Row.

Massimi, F., & Carli, M. (1988). The systematic assessment of flow in daily experience. In M. Csikszentmihalyi & I. S. Csikszentmihalyi (eds.), *Optimal Experience*. Cambridge: Cambridge University Press.

Matheson, J. (1990). *Voluntary Work*. London: General Household Survey and HMSO.

Maton, K. I. (1989). The stress-buffering role of spiritual support: cross-cultural and prospective investigations. *Journal for the Scientific Study of Religion, 28*, 310–23.

Meyer, L. E. (1983). Recreation and the mentally ill. In T. A. Stein & H. D. Sessoms (eds.), *Recreation and Special Populations* (2nd edn). Boston: Allyn and Bacon.

Moberg, D. O., & Taves, M. J. (1965). Church participation and adjustment in old age. In A. M. Rose & W. A. Peterson (eds.), *Older People and their Social World*. Philadelphia: F. A. Davis.

Mobily, K. E. *et al.* (1993). Leisure repertoire in a sample of mid-Western elderly: the case for exercise. *Journal of Leisure Research, 25,* 84–96.

MORI (Market Opinion and Research International) (1982). *Neighbours and Loneliness.* London: MORI.

Morley, D. (1986). *Family Television.* London: Routledge.

Morris, D. (1981). *The Soccer Tribe.* London: Cape.

Munson, W. W. (1988). Effects of leisure education versus physical activity or informal discussion on behaviorally disordered youth offenders. *Adapted Physical Activity Quarterly, 5,* 305–17.

Murdoch, G., & Phelps, G. (1973). *Mass Media and the Secondary School.* London: Schools Council/Macmillan.

Murphy, P., Williams, J., & Dunning, E. (1990). *Football on Trial.* London: Routledge.

Murray, J. P., & Kippax, S. (1977). Television diffusion and social behaviour in three communities: a field experiment. *Australian Journal of Psychology, 29,* 31–43.

Myers, D. G. (1993). *Social Psychology* (4th edn). New York: McGraw-Hill.

National Readership Survey (1987). London: Joint Industry Committee for National Readership Surveys.

Neulinger, J. (1981). *The Psychology of Leisure* (2nd edn). Springfield, Ill.: Charles C. Thomas.

Nias, D. K. B. (1977). The structuring of recreational interests. *Social Behavior and Personality, 5,* 383–8.

Nias, D. K. B. (1985). Personality and recreational behaviour. In B. D. Kirkcaldy (ed.), *Individual Differences in Movement* (pp. 279–92). Lancaster: MTP Press.

Nolen-Hoeksema, S. (1987). Sex differences in unipolar depression: evidence and theory. *Psychological Bulletin, 101,* 259–82.

O'Brien, G. E. (1981). Leisure attributes and retirement satisfaction. *Journal of Applied Psychology, 66,* 371–84.

Olmsted, A. D. (1991). Collecting leisure, investment or obsession? *Journal of Social Behaviour and Personality, 6,* 297–306.

Omoto, A. M., & Snyder, M. N. (1990). Basic research in action: volunteerism and society's response to AIDS. *Personality and Social Psychology Bulletin, 16,* 152–66.

Orthner, D. K., & Mancini, J. A. (1991). Benefits of leisure for family bonding. In B. L. Driver, L. L. Clarke, & M. K. Miller (eds.), *Benefits of Leisure.* State College, Pa.: Venture Publishing Co.

Paffenbarger, R. S., Hyde, R. T., & Dow, A. (1991). Health benefits of physical activity. In B. L. Driver, P. J. Brown, & G. L. Peterson (eds.), *Benefits of Leisure.* State College, Pa.: Venture Publishing Co.

Paffenbarger, R. S., Wing, A. L., & Hyde, R. T. (1978). Physical activity as an index of heart attacks in college alumni. *American Journal of Epidemiology, 108,* 161–75.

Pahnke, W. H. (1966). Drugs and mysticism. *International Journal of Psychology, 8,* 295–314.

Palinkas, L. A., Wingard, D. L., & Barrett, C. E. (1990). The biocultural context of social networks and depression among the elderly. *Social Science and Medicine, 30,* 441–7.

Palisi, B. J. (1985). Voluntary associations and well-being in three metropolitan areas: cross-cultural evidence. *International Journal of Contemporary Sociology, 22,* 265–88.

Palisi, B. J. (1985). Formal and informal participation in urban areas. *Journal of Social Psychology, 125,* 429–47.

Pargament, K. I. *et al.* (1988). Religion and the problem-solving process: three styles of coping. *Journal for the Scientific Study of Religion, 27,* 90–104.

Park, C., Cohen, L. H., & Herb, L. (1990). Intrinsic religiousness and religious coping as life stress moderators for Catholics versus Protestants. *Journal of Personality and Social Psychology, 59,* 562–74.

Parker, S. (1982). *Work and Retirement.* London: Allen and Unwin.

Parker, S. (1983). *Leisure and Work.* London: Allen and Unwin.

Parrinello, G. L. (1993). Motivation and anticipation in post-industrial tourism. *Annals of Tourism Research, 20,* 233–49.

Pearce, J. L. (1993). *Volunteers.* London: Routledge.

Pearce, P. L. (1982). *The Social Psychology of Tourist Behaviour.* Oxford: Pergamon.

Pearce, P. L. (1993). Fundamentals of tourist motivation. In D. G. Pearce & R. W. Butler (eds.), *Tourism Research.* London: Routledge.

Peiper, J. (1963). *Leisure, the Basis of Culture.* New York: New American Library.

Peppers, L. F. (1976). Patterns of leisure and adjustment to retirement. *Gerontologist, 16,* 441–6.

Perkins, K. B. (1988). Note on commitment and community among volunteer firefighters. *Sociological Inquiry, 58,* 117–21.

Perris, A. (1985). *Music as Propaganda.* London: Greenwood.

Piet, S. (1987). What motivates stunt men? *Motivation and Emotion, 11,* 195–213.

Pignatiello, M. F., Camp, C. J., & Rasar, L. J. (1986). Musical mood induction: an alternative to the Velten technique. *Journal of Abnormal Psychology 95,* 295–7.

Pi-Sunyer, O. (1989). Changing perceptions of tourism and tourists in a

Catalan resort town. In V. L. Smith (ed.), *Hosts and Guests*. Philadelphia: University of Pennsylvania Press.

Plante, T. G., & Schwartz, G. E. (1990). Defensive and repressive coping styles: self-presentation, leisure activities, and assessment. *Journal of Research in Personality, 24,* 173–90.

Plog, S. C. (1991). *Leisure Travel: Making it a Growth Market*. New York: Wiley.

Pollner, M. (1989). Divine relations, social relations, and well-being. *Journal of Health and Social Behavior, 30,* 92–104.

Pope, L. (1942). *Millhands and Preachers*. New Haven, Conn.: Yale University Press.

Postman, N. (1985). *Amusing Ourselves to Death*. London: Methuen.

Preston, J. M., & Clair, S. A. (1994). Selective viewing: cognition, personality and television genres. *British Journal of Social Psychology, 33,* 273–88.

Puner, M. (1974). *To the Good Long Life*. London: Macmillan.

Quiroga, I. (1990). Characteristics of package tours in Europe. *Annals of Tourism Research, 17,* 185–207.

Rainbow, E. L. (1965). A pilot study to investigate the constructs of musical aptitude. *Journal of Research in Musical Education, 13,* 3–14.

Rapoport, R., & Rapoport, R. N. (1975). *Leisure and the Family Life-Cycle*. London: Routledge and Kegan Paul.

Rasanen, E., & Arajarvi, T. (1985). Social acceptability of child psychiatric inpatients from 15–18 years of age. *Psychiatria Fennica, 1,* 6.

Ray, S. G. (1982). *The Blyton Phenomenon*. London: Deutsch.

Raymore, L., Godbey, G., Crawford, D., & von Eye, A. (1993). Nature and process of leisure constraints: an empirical test. *Leisure Sciences, 15,* 99–113.

Rees, C. R. (1983). Instrumental and expressive leadership in team sports: a test of leadership role differentiation theory. *Journal of Sport Behavior, 6,* 17–27.

Reich, J. W., & Zautra, A. (1981). Life events and personal causation. *Journal of Personality and Social Psychology, 41,* 1002–12.

Reid, I. (1989). *Social Class Differences in Britain* (3rd edn). London: Fontana Press.

Reid, I., & Stratta, E. (1989). *Sex Differences in Britain* (2nd edn). London: Gower.

Reis, H. T., Nezlek, J., Kernis, M. H., & Spiegel, N. (1984). On specificity in the impact of social participation on physical and mental health. *Journal of Personality and Social Psychology, 48,* 456–71.

Reisman, D. (1953). *Thorstein Veblen: a Critical Interpretation*. New York: Scribners.

Riddick, C. C. (1985). Life satisfaction determinants of older males and females. *Leisure Sciences, 7,* 47–63.

Riordan, J. (1993). Leisure policies in the Soviet Union. In P. Bramham, I. Henry, H. Mommas, & H. van der Poel (eds.), *Leisure Policies in Europe.* Wallingford: CAB International.

Roberts, G. C. (1989). *Motivation in Sport and Exercise.* Champaign, Ill.: Human Kinetics.

Roberts, K. (1970). *Leisure.* London: Longman.

Roberts, K. (1978). *Contemporary Society and the Growth of Leisure.* London: Longman.

Roberts, K. (1983). *Youth and Leisure.* London: Allen and Unwin.

Roberts, K., Lamb, K. L., Dench, S., & Brodie, D. A. (1989). Leisure patterns, health status and employment status. *Leisure Studies, 8,* 229–35.

Robertson, K., *et al.* (1988). Psychological health and squash play. *Ergonomics, 31,* 1567–72.

Robins, D. (1982). Sport and youth culture. In J. Hargreaves (ed.), *Sport, Culture and Ideology.* London: Routledge and Kegan Paul.

Robinson, J. P. (1977). *How Americans Use Time.* New York: Praeger.

Robinson, J. P. (1990). Television's effects on families' use of time. In J. Bryant (ed.), *Television and the American Family.* Hillsdale, N.J.: Erlbaum.

Rook, K. S. (1987). Social support versus companionship: effects on life stress. *Journal of Personality and Social Psychology, 52,* 1132–47.

Rosenberg, E., & Chelte, A. F. (1980). Avowed happiness of members of sport and non-sport voluntary associations. *International Journal of Sport Psychology, 11,* 263–75.

Rowland, G., Franken, R., & Harrison, K. (1986). Sensation seeking and participation in sporting activity. *Journal of Sport Psychology, 8,* 212–20.

Rubenstein, C. (1980). Vacations. *Psychology Today, 13,* May, 62–76.

Rushton, J. P. (1979). Effects of prosocial television and film material on the behaviour of viewers. *Advances in Experimental Social Psychology, 12,* 321–51.

Sack, H. (1975). Cited by Eysenck *et al.* (1982).

Sagi, M., & Vitanyi, I. (1988). Experimental research into musical generative ability. In J. A. Sloboda (ed.), *Generative Processes in Music.* Oxford: Clarendon Press.

Sahlins, M. (1974). *Stone Age Economics.* London: Tavistock.

Scherer, K. R., Wallbott, H. G., & Summerfield, A. B. (1986). *Experiencing Emotion.* Cambridge: Cambridge University Press.

Scherer, K. R., & Oshinsky, J. J. (1977). Cue utilization in emotion attribution from auditory stimuli. *Motivation and Emotion, 1,* 331–46.

Schor, J. B. (1991). *The Overworked American.* New York: Basic Books.

Searle, M. S., & Mahon, M. J. (1991). Leisure education in a day hospital: the effects on selected socio-psychological variables among older adults. *Canadian Journal of Community Mental Health, 10,* 95–109.

Shamir, B. (1985). Unemploynent and 'free time' – the role of Protestant Work Ethic and work involvement. *Leisure Studies, 4,* 333–45.

Shamir, B. (1992). Some correlates of leisure identity salience: three exploratory studies. *Journal of Leisure Research, 24,* 301–23.

Shanas, P., *et al.* (1968). *Old People in Three Industrial Societies.* New York: Atherton.

Shaw, S. M., Bonen, A., & McCabe, J. F. (1991). Do more constraints mean less leisure? Examining the relationship between constraints and participation. *Journal of Leisure Research, 23,* 286–300.

Shuter, R. (1968). *The Psychology of Musical Ability.* London: Methuen.

Shuter-Dyson, R. (1982). Musical ability. In D. Deutsch (ed.), *The Psychology of Music* (pp. 391–412). New York: Harcourt Brace.

Sills, D. L. (1968). Voluntary associations: sociological aspects. In *International Encyclopedia of the Social Sciences* (Vol. 16, pp. 362–79). New York: Macmillan and Free Press.

Sloboda, J. A. (1987). Musical performance. In D. Deutsch (ed.), *The Psychology of Music* (pp. 479–516). New York: Academic Press.

Small, C. (1987). Performance as ritual: sketch for an enquiry into the true nature of a symphony concert. In A. V. White (ed.), *Lost in Music: Culture, Style and the Musical Event.* London: Routledge and Kegan Paul.

Smith, C. S. (1973). Adolescence. In M. A. Smith, S. Parker, & C. S. Smith (eds.), *Leisure and Society in Britain.* London: Allen Lane.

Smith, J. (1987). Men and women at play: gender, life-cycle and leisure. In J. Horne, D. Jary, & A. Tomlinson (eds.), *Sport, Leisure and Social Relations.* London: Routledge and Kegan Paul.

Smith, M. A. (1983). Social usages of the public drinking house: changing aspects of class and leisure. *British Journal of Sociology, 34,* 36–85.

Smith, M. D. (1979). Social determinants of violence in ice hockey: a review. *Canadian Journal of Applied Sport Sciences, 4,* 76–82.

Sneegas, J. J. (1986). Components of life satisfaction in middle and later life adults: perceived social competence, leisure participation, and leisure satisfaction. *Journal of Leisure Research, 18,* 248–58.

Solomon, R. C. (1986). Literacy and the education of the emotions. In S. de Castell, A. Luke, & K. Egan (eds.), *Literacy, Society and Schooling.* Cambridge: Cambridge University Press.

Solomon, R. L., & Corbit, J. D. (1973). An opponent-process theory of motivation: II cigarette addiction. *Journal of Applied Psychology, 81,* 158–71.

Spickard, J. V. (1991). Experiencing religious rituals: a Schutzian analysis of Navajo ceremonies. *Sociological Analysis, 52,* 191–204.

Spreitzer, E., & Snyder, E. E.(1976). Socialisation into sport: an exploratory path analysis. *Research Quarterly, 47,* 238–45.

Staines, G. L. (1980). Spillover versus compensation: a review of the literature on the relationship between work and non-work. *Human Relations, 33,* 111–29.

Stebbins, R. A. (1979). *Amateurs.* Beverly Hills: Sage.

Stebbins, R. A. (1992). Costs and rewards in barbershop singing. *Leisure Studies, 11,* 123–33.

Stein, T. A., & Sessoms, H. D. (eds) (1983). *Recreation and Special Populations* (2nd edn). Boston: Allyn and Bacon.

Steinberg, H., & Sykes, E. A. (1985). Introduction to symposium on endorphins and behavioural processes; review of literature on endorphins and exercise. *Pharmacology, Biochemistry and Behavior, 23,* 857–62.

Steptoe, A., & Bolton, J. (1988). The short-term influence of high and low intensity physical exercise on mood. *Health and Psychology, 2,* 91–106.

Steptoe, A., Moses, J., Edwards, S., & Matthews, A. (1988). Effects of aerobic conditioning on mental well-being and reactivity to stress. In *Sport, Health Psychology and Exercise Symposium Proceedings.* London: Sports Council/Health Education Authority.

Stockdale, J. E. (1987). *Methodological Techniques in Leisure Research.* London: ESRC and Sports Council.

Stonier, T. (1983). *The Wealth of Information.* London: Methuen.

Storr, A. (1992). *Music and the Mind.* London: HarperCollins.

Sveback, S., & Kerr, J. H. (1989). The role of impulsivity in preference for sports. *Personality and Individual Differences, 10,* 51–8.

Swenson, W. M. (1961). Attitudes towards death in an aged population. *Journal of Gerontology, 16,* 49–52.

Syme, S. L. (1984). Sociocultural factors and disease etiology. In W. G. Gentry (ed.), *Handbook of Behavioral Medicine.* New York: Guilford.

Tajfel, H. (1978). *Differentiation Between Social Groups.* London: Academic Press.

Tanner, J. M. (1964). *The Physique of the Olympic Athlete.* London: Allen and Unwin.

Teiremaa, E. (1981). Psychosomatic aspects of asthma. *Psychiatria Fennica, Supp.,* 75–7.

Thaut, M. H. (1989). The influence of music therapy interventions on self-rated changes in relaxation, affect, and thought in psychiatric prisoner-patients. *Journal of Music Therapy, 26,* 155–66.

Thayer, R. E. (1989). *The Biopsychology of Mood and Emotion*. New York: Oxford University Press.

Thoits, P. A. (1985). Social support and psychological well-being: theoretical possibilities. In I. G. Sarason & B. R. Sarason (eds.), *Social Support: Theory, Research and Applications*. Dordrecht: Nijkhoff.

Thompson, F. M. L. (1988). *The Rise of Respectable Society*. London: Fontana.

Tiger, L. (1970). *Men in Groups*. New York: Vintage.

Torkildsen, G. (1986). *Leisure and Recreation Management* (2nd edn). London: E. & F. N. Spon.

Tucker, L. A. (1990). Physical fitness and psychological distress. *International Journal of Sport Psychology, 21,* 185–201.

Tunstall, J. (1962). *The Fishermen*. London: MacGibbon and Kee.

Turner, V. W. (1967). *The Forest of Symbols*. London: Cornell University Press.

Ulrich, R. S., Dimberg, U., & Driver, B. L. (1991). Psychophysiological indicators of leisure benefits. In B. L. Driver, P. J. Brown, & G. L. Peterson (eds.), *Benefits of Leisure*. State College, Pa: Venture Publishing Co.

Valentine, C. W. (1962). *The Experimental Psychology of Beauty*. London: Methuen.

Van Loon, F., & Dooghe, G. (1978). Social participation and life satisfaction of aged people. *Tijdschrift voor Sociale Weterschappen, 28,* 285–93.

Veal, A. J. (1987). *Leisure and the Future*. London: Unwin Hyman.

Veblen, T. (1899). *The Theory of the Leisure Class*. New York: Viking.

Veiel, H. O. F., & Baumann, U. (eds.) (1992). *The Meaning and Measurement of Social Support*. New York: Hemisphere.

Veroff, J., Douvan, E., & Kulka, R. A. (1981). *The Inner American*. New York: Basic Books.

Vijhalmsson, R., & Thorlindsson, T. (1992). The integrative and physiological effects of sport participation: a study of adolescents. *Sociological Quarterly, 33,* 637–47.

Walker, M. B. (1992). *The Psychology of Gambling*. Oxford: Pergamon.

Waller, N. G., Kojetin, B. A., Bouchard, T. J., & Lykken, D. T. (1990). Genetic and environmental influences on religious interests, attitudes and values: a study of twins reared apart and together. *Psychological Science, 1,* 138–42.

Walvin, J. (1978). *Leisure and Society 1830–1950*. Harmondsworth: Longman.

Wankel, L. M., & Berger, B. G. (1991). The personal and social benefits of sport and physical activity. In B. L. Driver, P. J. Brown, & G. L.

Peterson (eds.), *Benefits of Leisure*. State College, Pa.: Venture Publishing Co.

Wannamethee, G., Shaper, A. G., & Macfarlane, P. W. (1993). Heart rate, physical activity, and mortality from cancer and other noncardiovascular diseases. *American Journal of Epidemiology, 137,* 735–48.

Warner, W. L. (1963). *Yankee City*. New Haven, Conn.: Yale University Press.

Waser, A. M. (1989). A study of three tennis clubs; Le Marche des partenaires. Etude de trois clubs de tennis. *Actes de la Recherche en Sciences Sociales, 80,* 2–21.

Watson, D., & Pennebaker, J. W. (1989). Health complaints, stress, and disease: exploring the role of negative affectivity. *Journal of Personality and Social Psychology, 96,* 234–54.

Weidenfeld, S. A., *et al.* (1990). Impact of perceived self-efficacy in coping with stressors on components of the immune system. *Journal of Personality and Social Psychology, 59,* 1082–90.

Wheeler, R. J., & Frank, M. A. (1988). Identification of stress buffers. *Psychological Medicine, 14,* 78–89.

White, A. V. (1987). A professional jazz group. In A. V. White (ed.), *Lost in Music: Culture, Style and the Musical Event*. London: Routledge and Kegan Paul.

Whiting, H. T. A. (1970). *Teaching the Persistent Non-Swimmer*. London: Bell.

Wickens, E. (1994). The effect of tourism on a Greek village. Seminar at Oxford Brookes University.

Widmeyer, W. N., Brawley, L. R., & Carron, A. V. (1992). Group dynamics in sport. In T. S. Horn (ed.), *Advances in Sport Psychology* (pp. 163–80). Champaign, Ill.: Human Kinetics.

Wilde, R. A. (1974). *Bradstow: A Study of Status, Class and Power in a Small Australian Town*. Sydney: Angus and Robertson.

Wilensky, H. (1969). Work, careers and social integration. *International Social Science Journal, 12,* 543–60.

Williams, A. W., Ware, J. E., & Donal, C. A. (1981). A model of mental health, life events, and social supports applicable to general populations. *Journal of Health and Social Behavior, 22,* 324–36.

Williams, D. R., Larson, D. B., & Buckler, R. E. (1991). Religion and psychological distress in a community sample. *Social Science and Medicine, 32,* 1257–62.

Williams, J. M., & Getty, D. (1986). Effect of levels of exercise on psychological mood states, physical fitness, and plasma beta-endorphin. *Perceptual and Motor Skills, 63,* 1099–1105.

Willits, F. K., & Crider, D. M. (1988). Health rating and life satisfaction in the later middle years. *Journal of Gerontology, 43,* S.172–6.

Willmott, P. (1987). *Friendship Networks and Social Support.* London: Policy Studies Institute.

Wilson, E. O. (1975). *Sociobiology.* Cambridge, Mass.: Harvard University Press.

Winefield, A. H., Tiggemann M., & Winefield, H. R. (1992). Spare time use and psychological well-being in employed and unemployed young people. *Journal of Occupational and Ozganizational Psychology, 65,* 307–13.

Winefield, A. H., Tiggemann, M., Winefield, H. R., & Goldney, R. D. (1993). *Growing up with Unemployment.* London: Routledge.

Winnifrith, T. (1989). Playing the game: morality versus leisure. In T. Winnifrith & C. Barrett (eds.), *The Philosophy of Leisure.* London: Macmillan.

Winton, M., Heather, N., & Robertson, I. (1986). Effects of unemployment on drinking behavior: a review of the relevant evidence. *International Journal of the Addictions, 21,* 1261–83.

Witt, P. A., Ellis, G., & Niles, S. H. (1984). Leisure counseling with special populations. In E. T. Dowd (ed.), *Leisure Counseling.* Springfield, Ill.: Charles C. Thomas.

Witt, P. A., & Goodale, T. L. (1985). Barriers to leisure across family stages. In M. G. Wade (ed.), *Constraints on Leisure.* Springfield, Ill.: Charles C. Thomas.

Wittig, A. F., & Schurr, K. T. (1994). Psychological characteristics of women volleyball players: relationships with injuries, rehabilitation, and team. *Personality and Social Psychology Bulletin, 20,* 322–30.

Woodley, A., Wagner, L., Slowey, M., Hamilton, M., & Fulton, O. (1987). *Choosing to Learn.* Milton Keynes: Society for Research into Higher Education and Open University Press.

Wrightson, K. (1981). Alehouses, order and Reformation in rural England 1590–1660. In E. Yeo & S. Yeo (eds.), *Popular Culture and Class 1560–1914.* Sussex: Harvester.

Wulff, D. (1991). *Psychology of Religion.* Chichester: Wiley.

Yair, G. (1992). What keeps them running? The 'circle of commitment' of long distance runners. *Leisure Studies, 11,* 257–70.

Young, M., & Willmott, P. (1973). *The Symmetrical Family.* London: Routledge and Kegan Paul.

Zander, A. (1972). The purposes of voluntary associations. *Journal of Voluntary Action Research, 1,* 20–29.

Zehner, R. B. (1976). *Indicators of the Quality of Life.* Cambridge, Mass.: Ballinger.

Zillman, D. (1985). The experimental exploration of gratifications from media entertainment. In K. E. Rosengren, L. A. Wenner, & P. Palmgreen (eds.), *Media Gratifications Research*. Beverly Hills, Calif.: Sage.

Zillman, D., Sapolsky, B. S., & Bryant, J. (1979). The enjoyment of watching sport contests. In J. H. Goldstein (ed.), *Sports, Games, and Play* (pp. 297–335). Hillsdale, N.J.: Erlbaum.

Zuckernan, M. (1979). *Sensation Seeking*. Hillsdale, N.J.: Erlbaum.

Zuckerman, M. (1983). Sensation seeking and sports. *Personality and Individual Differences, 4*, 285–93.